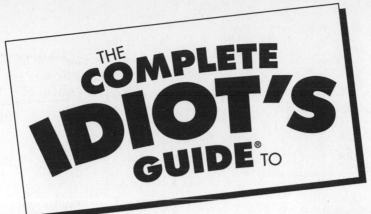

THE COMPLETE IDIOT'S GUIDE® TO

Wine Basics

Second Edition

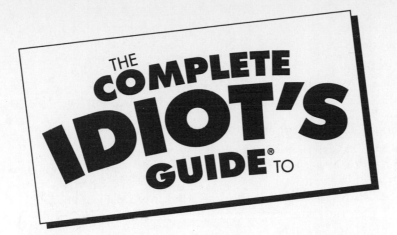

Wine Basics

Second Edition

by Tara Q. Thomas

ALPHA

A member of Penguin Group (USA) Inc.

ALPHA BOOKS

Published by the Penguin Group

Penguin Group (USA) Inc., 375 Hudson Street, New York, New York 10014, USA

Penguin Group (Canada), 90 Eglinton Avenue East, Suite 700, Toronto, Ontario M4P 2Y3, Canada (a division of Pearson Penguin Canada Inc.)

Penguin Books Ltd., 80 Strand, London WC2R 0RL, England

Penguin Ireland, 25 St. Stephen's Green, Dublin 2, Ireland (a division of Penguin Books Ltd.)

Penguin Group (Australia), 250 Camberwell Road, Camberwell, Victoria 3124, Australia (a division of Pearson Australia Group Pty. Ltd.)

Penguin Books India Pvt. Ltd., 11 Community Centre, Panchsheel Park, New Delhi—110 017, India

Penguin Group (NZ), 67 Apollo Drive, Rosedale, North Shore, Auckland 1311, New Zealand (a division of Pearson New Zealand Ltd.)

Penguin Books (South Africa) (Pty.) Ltd., 24 Sturdee Avenue, Rosebank, Johannesburg 2196, South Africa

Penguin Books Ltd., Registered Offices: 80 Strand, London WC2R 0RL, England

Copyright © 2008 by Tara Q. Thomas

International Standard Book Number: 978-1-59257-786-6
Library of Congress Catalog Card Number: 2008927327

10 09   8 7 6 5 4 3 2

Interpretation of the printing code: The rightmost number of the first series of numbers is the year of the book's printing; the rightmost number of the second series of numbers is the number of the book's printing. For example, a printing code of 08-1 shows that the first printing occurred in 2008.

Printed in the United States of America

Note: This publication contains the opinions and ideas of its author. It is intended to provide helpful and informative material on the subject matter covered. It is sold with the understanding that the author and publisher are not engaged in rendering professional services in the book. If the reader requires personal assistance or advice, a competent professional should be consulted.

The author and publisher specifically disclaim any responsibility for any liability, loss, or risk, personal or otherwise, which is incurred as a consequence, directly or indirectly, of the use and application of any of the contents of this book.

Most Alpha books are available at special quantity discounts for bulk purchases for sales promotions, premiums, fund-raising, or educational use. Special books, or book excerpts, can also be created to fit specific needs.

For details, write: Special Markets, Alpha Books, 375 Hudson Street, New York, NY 10014.

Publisher: *Marie Butler-Knight*
Editorial Director: *Mike Sanders*
Senior Managing Editor: *Billy Fields*
Acquisitions Editor: *Michele Wells*
Development Editor: *Jennifer Moore*
Production Editor: *Megan Douglass*
Copy Editor: *Nancy Wagner*

Cartoonist: *Steve Barr*
Cover Designer: *Bill Thomas*
Book Designer: *Trina Wurst*
Indexer: *Brad Herriman*
Layout: *Brian Massey*
Proofreader: *John Etchison*

Contents at a Glance

Contents

Foreword

Tara is my friend. Though I haven't seen her lately because our insanely crazy schedules of wine researching, vineyard globetrotting, and business-as-usual projects have kept us our calendars solidly booked, Tara remains close to my heart because she understands how to bring wine to the masses. Almost an anomaly in the sometimes elite world of wine, she delivers winespeak in a way that engages the public-at-large yet never insults her audience with patronizing wine "baby talk."

In my role as Cellarmaster for BevMo, a retail chain with more than 80 stores, I face the daily challenge of wine communication with an audience ranging from youthful neophytes to seasoned wine geeks. As an overtrained wine professional, I must guard myself from forgetting that I came from exactly the same place nearly four decades ago: a young adult without a clue about the subject of wine.

Wine education, unlike mandatory formal or informal schooling, is an elective. One chooses to learn about wine because of desire, not because of basic necessities of survival in the modern world. Even the most experienced wine person, less a few wine brats born into wine families, starts out with some kind of desire or even (in my case) an epiphany. When I started managing my family's beverage department in 1968 at the Ashbury Market in San Francisco's Haight Ashbury, we had very little premium wine to sell. By the time I revamped it, a decade later, we offered hundreds of fascinating wines from all over the globe. How did this happen?

I had literally stumbled into a cellar of a family friend in 1973 and a pour of the 1968 Beaulieu Vineyard Special Bottling Burgundy found itself in my glass. Immediately bitten by the incurable wine bug, I could not stop thinking for weeks, "There must something to this wine stuff." From that point, I became so mesmerized with the subject that I became a hopeless wine romantic.

The relentless journey had begun, researching like crazy—I even resorted to searching the back stacks at the main branch of the San Francisco Public Library. Great wine information was hard to find in those days, and nothing as comprehensive and delightful as Tara's book, *The Complete Idiot's Guide to Wine Basics, Second Edition*. Where was Tara, one of the top wine educators for the people, when I really needed her? I am not sure if she was even born yet.

Over the years, Tara has been one of those special people in my life, to whom I would always try to sit close at a formal wine dinner. Why? Because, I always enjoy her company and would always get honest comments. Fun and exciting, we would often share stories, ideas, and antidotes about wine, food, and life without one-upmanship that is too often rule and not the exception. I would always learn something new without pretension, and that is always refreshing amongst wine pros.

The Complete Idiot's Guide to Wine Basics, Second Edition, is a complete wine education for not just the novice but for everyone. While my research is pretty good, I will never get to the point where I have stopped learning. While some professionals will pooh-pooh such a seemingly "Wine 101" kind of a book, I challenge even the super pros in the wine world to say that they can't learn from this book. Covering the subject matter, *The Complete Idiot's Guide to Wine Basics, Second Edition*, could easily become everyone's bible of wines. At the very least, this book is an indispensable reference guide. In my recent reading of the first edition, I learned stuff that was so stunningly simple yet put in such a logical, commonsense way making her explanation incredibly obvious.

In my 35 years of service in the wine industry, I have met more people than I even care to admit. Tara Thomas stands out because she cares about her subject and presents it authoritatively without the overuse of jargon. Never pandering nor over-intellectualizing, Tara brings herself into your living room as if you have invited her over as a friend to enjoy a glass of wine. You ask her a question; she listens and answers without lecturing. Everyone in the living room is simply having a good time and learning, too. My hope is that you will enjoy *The Complete Idiot's Guide to Wine Basics, Second Edition*, as if Tara personally wrote if for you so that you can genuinely enjoy wine just as she does.

Wilfred Wong
Cellarmaster, Beverages, more!

Introduction

Let's get this straight right off the bat: you're not an idiot. If you were you wouldn't have picked up this book, because the only idiots out there when it comes to wine are those who think they know it all.

The world of wine is a huge and exciting one. There are as many types of wine as there are grapes, places, and people making them—in other words, there are more wines than any one of us could get through in our lifetime. Add to this the fact that wines change with every year, and it's an endless array.

That may sound depressing—I mean, how can you even begin to learn about something that has so many permutations and variables? But it's actually not that hard. All it takes is an open mind and an open mouth.

I started in the wine business with little but the desire to know more about wine—much like many of you. I didn't plan to study wine for a living, which is essentially what I do. But after so many delicious bottles, after so many bad bottles that made me want the delicious bottles more, and after meeting so many interesting, kind people, I was hooked and decided to work on sharing the excitement with others.

I hope you'll find that excitement in this book. If you haven't spent a lot of time tasting different wines, you might find it a bit slow going in the beginning. But stick with it: learning about wine is all about paying attention to what you're tasting. This book is just here to help you along and encourage you in helpful directions. At the very least, by the end you should have drunk a lot of great wine.

How to Use This Book

Wine isn't so hard to learn about if you just break it down into small steps.

Part 1, "Grape Expectations: Laying Down the Basics," covers exactly that: what wine is, how it's made, and why there's such endless, wonderful variation from grape to grape and place to place. You also learn how to parse any wine label you come across and how to get the most out of every glass of wine.

Part 2, "What to Taste: The Big Nine," tackles the most popular wine grapes in the world: Chardonnay, Sauvignon Blanc, Riesling, Pinot Grigio, Cabernet Sauvignon, Merlot, Pinot Noir, Syrah, and Zinfandel.

Part 3, "Regional Specialties," covers wines made from grapes that excel only in certain places and blends unique to different parts of the world.

Part 4, "Special Styles," is where you find out what makes sparkling wine sparkle, dessert wines sweet, and fortified wines strong, with details on where to look for the best examples.

Part 5, "Shopping Time," helps you find good deals on wine, as well as offers tips on where to put it all.

Part 6, "Now You Have the Wine List ...," offers pointers on how to navigate any restaurant wine list like a pro. You find out what's the deal behind the tasting ceremony, too, and how (and when) to send back wine gracefully. And speaking of restaurants, this section also gets to the heart of why we study wine: to be able to drink better with dinner or any meal. You find tips on pairing wine and food whether you're dining out or in.

Although I endeavor not to use much jargon in this book, if you find an unfamiliar term or hear one while you're out on the town, check in the glossary for an explanation. If you're hungry to read more about wine, you can also find a select list of outstanding books and websites.

Extras

Though I try to help myself, I am in the end a wine geek who desperately wants to share my knowledge and enthusiasm with anyone who wants to listen. So I've sprinkled in some extras in each chapter, which you'll find under these headings:

Off the Vine

This space is for little bits of interesting extra information that will help further your understanding of the topic in the chapter—or might just be funny stories I want to share.

Quick Sips

These short blurbs give you the very least you need to know in a nutshell and highlight important points you might miss in the text if you're quickly flipping through.

Sour Grapes

These are warnings about challenging or confusing details in the wine world, with tips on how to spot the issue and avoid or understand it.

Winespeak

Here I define words that might be unfamiliar but are frequently used in the wine world.

Acknowledgments

A huge thanks to Joshua Greene and everyone else at *Wine & Spirits* magazine, where I've learned more than is good for anyone on the topic of wine and have had a great time doing so. I'm extremely grateful to all the sommeliers, wine store owners, vintners, and wine writers who have taught me enormous amounts over the years; thanks especially to Patrick Comiskey, Randall Grahm, Peter Liem, David Lynch, Patricio Tapia, and Wolfgang Weber for help way beyond the call of duty. Thanks also to Marilyn Allen, who approached me to write this book, and to editor Michele Wells, who suggested the second edition. This book would be a lesser product without Siobhán Thomas's map skills as well as moral support, and this edition wouldn't even exist without Jeanie Simeon: a giant thank you. Most of all, thanks to Robert Pincus for being extraordinarily patient, supportive, and tolerant of my obsession, and to Laila Rose, without whom this book wouldn't matter a whit.

Special Thanks to the Technical Reviewer

The Complete Idiot's Guide to Wine Basics, Second Edition, was reviewed by an expert who double-checked the accuracy of what you learn here, to help us ensure that this book gives you everything you need to know about wine. A huge thanks to Mollie Battenhouse, D.W.S.

Trademarks

All terms mentioned in this book that are known to be or are suspected of being trademarks or service marks have been appropriately capitalized. Alpha Books and Penguin Group (USA) Inc. cannot attest to the accuracy of this information. Use of a term in this book should not be regarded as affecting the validity of any trademark or service mark.

Part  1

Grape Expectations: Laying Down the Basics

Wouldn't it be nice if all you had to do to learn about wine was to drink it? Then you wouldn't need this book, and you could chalk up every glass to research and development.

In fact, drinking wine is part of learning about it—reading about it won't help much if you never taste it. But without a little background, learning about wine is like learning to swim without having been in the water before: there's a lot of unnecessary flailing around.

In this part, you get a firm grounding in the basics: what wine is, where it comes from, and what makes it so interesting. You also get some most important information, like how to decipher a wine label and how to taste. Armed with this knowledge, you'll be well prepared to get the most out of the rest of the book—and every bottle of wine thereafter.

What Is Wine, Anyway?

In This Chapter

- A simple definition of wine
- The magic of fermentation
- Growing great wine
- Making great wine

What is wine? Wine is fermented fruit juice. It can be made from any fruit, from pineapples to peaches and pears, though over time, grapes have been singled out as the most successful primary ingredient.

Sounds pretty simple, doesn't it? Obviously, there's a little more to it, or we'd all have a crock of fruit fermenting away in our basement. Only our basement crocks would probably do more festering than fermenting, which makes all the difference in the end.

Fabulous Fermentation

Wine owes its greatness to fermentation: without fermentation, it's just fruit juice. Once fermented, this formerly staid and simple juice becomes complex with different flavors as time, yeast, and chemistry work their transformational magic.

Most strikingly, fermentation makes fruit juice alcoholic—not so much to make one's head spin after just a few sips but about 8 to 14 percent alcohol on average, enough to lubricate the tongue and provoke an appetite for food and socializing alike.

Off the Vine

If wine averages 8 to 14 percent alcohol, where does that put it in regard to other alcoholic beverages? In the middle but toward the lower end. Beer averages 3 to 6 percent alcohol; fortified wines, like Port, run 18 to 21 percent; most hard liquors reach 40 to 50 percent (which is equivalent to 80 to 100 proof). Another way to think about it is that a 5-ounce glass of wine, a 12-ounce beer, and a 1.5-ounce shot of 80-proof vodka or other spirit all contain the same amount of alcohol.

How does fermentation happen? The short answer is this: a grape is a grape until yeast gets into it. Yeasts are single-celled fungi, essentially sugar junkies found on grape skins, in vineyards, in wineries, and in the air everywhere. When they get into a grape, they begin to devour its sugar. As they eat, they give off alcohol, carbon dioxide, and a certain amount of water vapor. When the yeasts have eaten all the sugar or when they've produced so much alcohol it kills them, fermentation stops.

Broken down into its simplest steps, fermentation looks like this:

sugar + yeast = ethanol (alcohol) + carbon dioxide

or more technically:

$$C_6H_{12}O_6 + yeast = 2(CH_3CH_2OH) + 2(CO_2)$$

How anyone figured out that this process is a good thing when applied to grapes is a mystery historians, archaeologists, and scientists have researched for ages and still continue to study today.

Buzzed Birds and Tipsy Princesses

The exact where, when, and why of wine's discovery is lost to history, but it happened early on and probably entirely naturally because grapes contain everything they need to become wine.

Early Accidents

Various musings suggest that birds could have discovered the magic of fermented fruit when they became tipsy after sucking at fruits fermented on the plant or on the ground. A Greek myth credits a king named Oenos, who one day noticed a very happy goat frolicking among the grapevines. (*Oenos*, the root of the word *enology*, means "wine" in Greek.) More romantic is the tale of the Persian princess who became so stressed out that she tried to kill herself by eating some rotting grapes; instead of dying, she forgot all her worries, and soon wine became the Persian Prozac.

Quick Sips _____

For more information on the history of wine, check out www.museum.upenn.edu/ new/exhibits/online_exhibits/wine/wineintro.html, compiled by Dr. Patrick McGovern, author of *The Origins and Ancient History of Wine*, as well as www.wine-maker.net, a fascinating collection of ancient texts compiled by California vintner Sean Thackrey.

The last tale is probably closest to the truth; after all, while it's possible for grapes to ferment on the vine, one would have to eat a lot of them to get tipsy. More likely, given the lack of refrigeration in ancient times, crocks of grapes or grape juice simply went "bad" in storage, and people drank the foaming, bubbling fruit juice anyway. It wouldn't have been long before these people recognized wine's inebriating effects. Shards of wine-stained pottery found in Iran suggest that people were trying to capture and control fermenting fruit as early as 6000 or 5000 B.C.E.

Off the Vine _____

The oldest bottle of wine ever found dates to 325 B.C.E. Discovered in a Roman sarcophagus in Speyer, Germany, it now rests in the *Historisches Museum der Pfalz* in Germany.

Culture and Connoisseurship

Although alcohol is frowned upon in some circles—and almost everywhere when it's indulged in to extremes—the time and energy we've spent on perfecting alcoholic beverages over the centuries points to the important position they hold in society. More so than any other drink, wine has played, and still plays, an important part in rituals, religion, trade, war, and the economy, as well as in personal quality of life. It's become something we not only drink but also treasure, study, and collect. And as such, people have gone to great lengths to discover how to make it well.

Growing Good Wine

Wine is much more than a bunch of fermented grapes, and the process starts in the vineyard. Good wine must have the following conditions:

- Good grapes
- A hospitable location
- Farming finesse
- Decent weather

Let's look more closely at each condition in turn.

Good Grapes

Every fall, my friend's dad would pick big, beautiful purple grapes and make wine in his basement. He knew a bit about making wine, and the grapes were always delicious eaten out of hand. The wine, though, didn't taste very good—not to him nor to me. So what went wrong?

The main problem was the type of grapes he chose. Not every grape is created equal. He used our local Concords, better known for their role in Welch's grape juice than in wine. He would have gotten a better wine if he had selected a *Vitis vinifera* grape.

Vitis Vinifera Rules

Remember high school biology and learning the classification of the world into kingdom, phylum, class, order, family, genus, and species? Well, all grapes fall under the genus *Vitis*, from which comes *viticulture*, the study of grape growing.

However, there are about 60 different grape *species*, such as *Vitis labrusca* (think of the grapey Concords that go into Welch's grape juice) to *Vitis rotundifola* (think of Scuppernong wine made from sprawling Muscadine vines in the American Southeast). Both can be made into wine, but once fermented, these grapes tend to take on a character commonly described as "musky" or "foxy." Who knows what exactly a fox smells like, but you get the point: they aren't the highest-class wines available.

Great wines come instead from the European species, *Vitis vinifera*. This species is so revered for the comparatively fine, delicate wines it makes that its vines have been shipped all over the world, and it now accounts for all the world's best wines. *Vitis vinifera* includes hundreds of different grape *varieties*, including all the big-name grapes you've probably heard of, like Chardonnay, Merlot, and Zinfandel.

Winespeak _____

Variety is a noun, as in "a grape variety." **Varietal** is an adjective often used incorrectly as a noun and refers to a wine made from a certain type of grape, such as Merlot or Chardonnay—for example, "a varietal wine."

Quality Counts

An old adage in the wine business states, "You can make bad wine from good grapes, but you can't make good wine from bad grapes." There's a lot of truth in that; just as in food, the ingredients are of utmost importance. So even if you have *Vitis vinifera* grapes, they must be in good shape.

And what's a grape in good shape look like? Like any fruit, really: ripe and clean, free of blemishes like holes pecked by birds or tears made by hail, and free of molds that would give it an off flavor.

It should taste pretty good, too, though most ripe wine grapes are far sweeter and more acidic than the table grapes we buy in the store, making them, shall we say, very intense. If grapes, however, are too ripe, they'll have lots of sweetness (and potential alcohol) but they'll have lost the *acidity* that balances it, making the resultant wine taste dull, too sweet, or too high in alcohol. Unripe grapes are no better; without time to develop sweetness and complete flavors, they are puckery, bland, and often vegetal. For instance, wines made from unripe Cabernet Sauvignon grapes often taste more like bell peppers than sweet, juicy fruit.

Winespeak _____

Acidity is what makes wine taste bright and fresh; a wine that lacks acidity is often described as flabby. Different varieties of grapes have different amounts of acidity; Riesling, for instance, is naturally more acidic than Chardonnay. Ripeness also affects acidity: the riper the grape, the less acid. Growing conditions, such as soil and climate, also play in; generally, the cooler the climate, the higher the acidity.

So how does one grow good-quality grapes? As with any sort of farming (for that's what winegrowing is), it takes a lot of work and begins with finding a suitable place to grow the vines.

> ### Off the Vine
>
> Viticulture, the study of grapevines, and viniculture, the study of winemaking, fit together naturally, yet not every viniculturalist is a viticulturist. The study of grapevines is a consuming profession in itself. Viticulturalists study for years which grape varieties are most suitable for a given place and how to raise them to make the best wines. Many wineries have both a viticulturalist to take care of the vineyards and a winemaker to make the wines.

Location, Location, Location

Place matters so much in winegrowing that some countries refer to their wines by the name of the place in which they are grown rather than by the variety of grape. The French, for instance, refer to red wines from the Burgundy region simply as Burgundy, instead of labeling them as Pinot Noir, the grape from which they are made. It's not that the grape variety doesn't matter, because it determines the primary character of the wine. Rather, it's that the grape is such an integral part of the culture of the region that it's understood as part of the definition of the place.

Place includes many different factors, including ...

- Climate.
- Sun.
- Exposition.
- Water.
- Wind.
- Soil.
- Ambient vegetation.

Every one of these factors—and probably others that are more subtle—affect the character of a wine, give it what wine geeks might call a sense of *terroir*, a feeling that it belongs to a certain place. So let's look at each of them.

Winespeak _____

Terroir (tare-wahr) is a French term derived from the Latin *terra*, earth. It refers to the qualities in a wine that derive from the physical characteristics of the place it was grown, from climate through soil, angle of slope, native vegetation, even the quality of the air itself. When people speak of a wine having a sense of *terroir*, they mean it tastes as if it came from a particular place as opposed to "international" wines, which taste like they could come from anywhere.

Climate

What matters most about the place grapes grow is the climate. Merlot won't grow any better in Jakarta than bananas do in Minnesota. Climate is the long-term weather pattern of a place, and in general, grapes don't like extreme weather. Some grapes like it colder than others—for instance, Riesling can thrive in Germany's chilly Mosel, the most northerly major winegrowing region. Others, such as Grenache, prefer the languorous climes of the Mediterranean.

Quick Sips _____

As a general guideline, the warmer the region, the richer and more powerful its wines. Wines from colder climates tend to have higher acidity and lower alcohol, which makes them feel lighter and leaner.

Sun and Exposition

Grapes also need a certain amount of sun, but not too much; in some places where the sun is very strong, winemakers will practice "canopy management," meaning they'll use the vine's own leaves to shade its fruit.

The best situation for most grapes is to have gentle sun all day long. That's why, in the Northern Hemisphere, winemakers often talk covetously about south-facing slopes, especially for red grapes. In the Southern Hemisphere, they want north-facing slopes. This positioning is referred to as *exposition*.

Winespeak _____

Exposition is the position of a vineyard in relation to the sun, including the angle of the slope and the direction it faces.

In areas that get a lot of rain, slopes are also favored, as they drain water away from the vine's roots. Most grapevines don't like to have wet feet, at least during the growing season.

Water and Wind

With too little water, grapes won't be able to photosynthesize properly; with too much, they won't ripen well or will become diluted. Most European countries ban the irrigation of wine vineyards for fear that doing so would create huge crops of low-quality grapes and dilute the wine's regional characteristics. Therefore, the vineyards need to be located where they'll naturally receive enough moisture, whether from rain, fog, or water seeping up from the water table.

In the United States and other New World countries, like Argentina and Australia, irrigation is permitted for grapevines, allowing them to be grown in areas they wouldn't naturally. Even so, most vintners take great care to limit the amount of water they use so as not to encourage excessive growth or waterlogged grapes. Many also irrigate only when the vines are young and sensitive or when a severe drought puts the vines in peril. Either way, it helps to have a natural source of moisture.

> **Off the Vine**
>
> Not all moldy grapes are bad. Vintners around the world actually court *Botrytis cinerea* so they can make heavenly sweet wines, like Sauternes. When this mold attacks, it sucks the water out of the berries, leaving behind shriveled grapes filled with sweet, concentrated juice. It also adds its own particular sultry, smoky, honeyed scent and flavor to the wine.

Of course, wet or humid conditions can make the vines a prime place for mold and fungus to set up shop. However, a nice breeze moving through the vines will dry the grapes before disease sets in. A cool breeze on a hot day also helps the vines maintain equilibrium in the heat.

Ideally, grapevines want a wet winter so that the ground can soak up enough moisture to hold them through some of the dry spells in summer. They also appreciate spring showers, which help them gear up to send out buds and new shoots, though it's better if it doesn't rain while they are flowering. Once the vines produce grapes, they'd prefer to soak in sunny warmth and work on getting the grapes ripe. A few summer showers can provide welcome rehydration, but too much water isn't good. Once the grapes are nearly ripe, winemakers pray for no significant rainfall because it might dilute the grape's sweet, concentrated fruit flavors.

Of course, the type of soil in which the grapevines grow also affects their water requirements, among other things.

The Dirt on Dirt, and the Plants It Supports

In Germany's Mosel region, it's sometimes difficult to tell how the vines have attached themselves to the ground because the vineyards sit at a precipitous angle to the river below, and the soil appears to be sheer, crumbling slate.

In Châteauneuf-du-Pape in France's Rhône Valley, the slopes aren't that steep, but the ground looks to be made up entirely of round stones the size of racquetballs or larger.

In both places, there is dirt—you just have to dig down deep enough to find it. Vines tend to like this challenge. The stony layers help water drain away from the trunks and channel the moisture deep into the earth, where the roots are. The deeper the roots, the sturdier the vine. Some think that deeply rooted vines—essentially old vines—produce wines of exceptional depth and complexity.

Different grapes like different soils; Chardonnay, for instance, prefers chalky soils. The particular soils in a vineyard can also affect the flavor of the wine. For example, the Chardonnay-based wines of Chablis, France, are often said to have a chalky, oyster-shell flavor. As it turns out, Chablis sits on an ancient seabed, and its soils are chock-full of decayed oyster shells. While there's no scientific proof that the vines absorb the particular elements of the shells, the wines taste noticeably different from Chardonnays grown in, say, California.

Plants that grow around vineyards also factor into the life of the grapevine. Not only do they provide a more complex ecology— beneficial insects eat the insects that damage the vines, for instance—but sometimes they may lend flavor to a wine as well. Some Australian reds, for example, often have a minty flavor that some attribute to the local eucalyptus trees. Some wines from Southern France are said to smell of *garrigue*, the fragrant mix of wild thyme, juniper, and other plants that grow on the warm hillsides.

Winespeak

Garrigue (gare-eeg) is a French term to describe the mix of fragrant wild herbs and brush common to the Mediterranean countryside. It also is used to describe wine. When a wine from Southern France has scents and flavors that recall the countryside, it's often said to taste of *garrigue*.

So if you have *Vitis vinifera* vines growing in a comfortably temperate climate on a stony, sun-catching slope where there's enough water to support their life, will you have great wine? Well, chances are better than if you were using Concords grown in a frigid clime, but to bring out their best, you need to treat the vines right.

Farming Finesse

Growing good grapes is tough work. Vines by nature want to take over the world. They want to travel, tangle their tendrils around anything they can reach, climb on it, strangle it, make the space their own, drop their fruits far away, and continue the quest for world domination.

In nature, other plants put up resistance against infringing grapevines. In the vineyard, however, grapevines are the main event, and humans need to expend near-constant effort to control them. The vines must be pruned and trellised to keep them concentrated on their task, which is to grow great fruit, not leaves or tendrils.

The way the vines are trained to grow affects the quality of their grapes. In Santorini, Greece, where the hot sun beats down on the sandy soil, vines are traditionally nestled into the sand in a basketlike coil, so the leaves form a protective parasol over the grapes. In some vineyards of Argentina, vines are trellised to grow far enough off the ground that vineyard workers can stroll under them and plenty of air can circulate through the warm canopy. Other places, grapevines may trail along wires, twisting their tendrils around one another, or they might stand alone, not touching. The rows might head down the slope or follow its contours. The options are endless and depend on the vine's preferences, the physical requirements of the vineyard, the position of the sun, and the degree of slope, to name just a few factors.

Winespeak

Vintners will often perform a **green harvest** or "cluster thinning"—that is, they will cut off unripe grapes in hopes that the vines will concentrate their energy on ripening the remaining bunches.

And trellising isn't all that the grower needs to do. Most grapevines, if left to their own devices, would produce as many grapes as possible in the hopes of increasing their chance of genetic immortality. Often, however, the more fruit on a single vine, the less concentrated the flavor in each grape, so vineyard workers often thin the grapes, performing what they call a *green harvest*. They harvest excess bunches in the hope that the vines will expend more energy to ripen the remaining grapes.

Vintners also need to keep the vineyards free from destruction by pests and disease. A vineyard has its own ecosystem of plants, animals, insects, fungi, and bacteria, and when everything is in balance, they generally keep each other in check. However, maintaining equilibrium in a monoculture like a vineyard isn't easy, and often a pest will get out of hand and become dangerously destructive.

The most dramatic example of the destruction a pest can wreak is the story of phylloxera, a tiny aphid that sucks the life out of a grapevine through the roots. Native to North America, phylloxera lives in harmony with American grapevines, which have a natural resistance to the pest. Phylloxera didn't become a problem until it was accidentally transported to Europe in the mid-1800s. There, the native *Vitis vinifera* vines were highly susceptible to its attack. The aphid ravished the vineyards, nearly destroying entire winegrowing regions like Bordeaux.

It wasn't until the discovery that *Vitis vinifera* vines could be *grafted* onto phylloxera-resistant American *rootstock* that the vineyards could be re-established. Today, we still have no cure for phylloxera; the only known solution is to graft vines onto resistant rootstock.

Winespeak

Grafting is attaching the scion (or fruiting variety—in the case of grapevines, a selection of *Vitis vinifera*) of one plant on top of another—the **rootstock**—so that they will grow into a single plant.

Pesticides and herbicides can control other pests, but many of these treatments require chemical applications that also kill beneficial flora and fauna, such as spiders that eat destructive aphids as well as some of the unseen beneficial microflora of the soil. They also aren't very good for the health of people who work in and around the vineyards, and they can contaminate nearby water supplies. Today, more vintners are turning to natural methods of control, sometimes called "integrated" or "biobased pest management," in which predators are encouraged in order to control the pests. Either way, managing vineyard pests from birds to bacteria requires an enormous amount of time, energy, and money.

And the work doesn't end when the grapes are harvested. Pest management is a year-round occupation. Plus, more pruning must be done in preparation for the next season, and some vines will need to be replanted, whether from sickness or age. As a vine gets older, it produces fewer and fewer grapes, until it's not worth its upkeep. Rarely do we find vines that are 80 years old or more, although some very old vines are prized for the intense fruit they give.

But no matter how hard the vintner works in the vineyards, no vineyard is immune from the challenges of bad weather.

Weathering Weather

Climate is the long-term weather pattern; weather is what we actually get from day to day. And weather can be cruel. Rain at the wrong time can be disastrous; untimely rain at harvest, for example, can leave vine growers with grapes fat with water instead of flavorful juice. Torrential rains can cause landslides, and a five-minute hailstorm can take out an entire vineyard, not only destroying that year's grapes, but also damaging the vines so that they will have trouble producing good grapes the next year, too. Any sort of extreme tends to be damaging: a spring cold snap can kill; a summer heat wave can halt growth as the grapevine shuts down to conserve energy and save itself.

Working and worrying all the time in an effort to control a plant that really would love to return to the wild sounds like quite a life, no?

The real kicker is that no matter how great the vine's location, how perfect the weather, and how excellent the grape grower's work, good wine doesn't make itself. Growing great grapes is only half the battle. The winemaker still needs to take those grapes and make them into wine.

Turning Grapes into Wine

So now you know how to get great grapes—sweet and fully ripe, ready to be picked. And what's next? About two months of fast and furious work, followed by a few months to a few years more waiting, working, and worrying before the wine is bottled and sent off to stores to be sold.

Quick Sips

Winemaking in a nutshell: harvest, crush, ferment, and bottle.

The intricate details of the winemaking process fill books and require many years of study and experience—far more information than we can cover here. But we can get an idea of what's involved by breaking winemaking down into its basic processes.

1. Harvest 'Em

At harvest time, the anxiety is palpable. Once the grapes are ripe and ready, there's no waiting; for some varieties the sugar-acid balance in a grape can change within hours. There are different ways to harvest the grapes. Some people use harvesting machines, but many find that practiced people are more effective at picking the grapes without damage and culling out bad bunches. Some vintners will even send grape pickers into the same vineyard several times over the course of a week or two, each time picking only the perfectly ripe grapes.

As the harvesters pick the grapes, they put them into small lugs or half-ton bins and stack them on a truck to go to the winery. Some wineries have the harvesters just dump the grapes into a truck bed, but since a truck load of grapes weighs a lot, the grapes on the bottom tend to get smashed, so this isn't the preferred technique.

However the grapes are picked, they are rushed to the winery because every minute between coming off the vine and being made into wine increases the chances that the juice will begin to oxidize or spontaneously ferment. At the winery, many vintners empty the crates onto a sorting table, where a team of eagle-eyed winery workers weeds out any bad berries, bugs, weeds, leaves, or anything else that might leave a bad taste in the wine.

2. Crush 'Em

After sorting, the grapes typically get dumped into a crusher-destemmer, which—get this—crushes the grapes and gets rid of the stems, which can contribute a bitter or stemmy flavor to the wine.

Now things get tricky; what happens next depends on the sort of grapes and the wine desired. If the grapes are what we call white grapes—a pale shade of yellow, gold, green, or pink—they'll make white wine. If they are red grapes—dark-skinned, purple-hued—they can make white, pink, or red wine, depending on how they're treated. In most grapes, pigments—the components responsible for giving the grape color—are in the grape's skin, not the pulp. If you peel and squeeze most red grapes, the juice will be white.

So now that the grapes are crushed and the juices are mingling with the skins, the next step differs depending on whether the vintner wants a white or red wine.

Off the Vine

Have you ever seen a white grape? Me neither. "White" grapes aren't actually white; they just make white wines, which are actually somewhere between colorless and green-yellow or gold. Most white grapes are pale shades of yellow, green, gold, or pink, depending on the variety. And it's the same with red grapes: most are more purple than red, but they typically make red wines.

White Wine

If a vintner is making white wine, he's got to work cold and quick. If the grapes get too warm, they'll loose acidity and their fresh flavors. If they are exposed too long to air, they'll oxidize, just as a sliced apple does when left out on a plate; they turn brownish and develop nutty, aged flavors.

Winespeak

Tannins are both color-contributing pigments and compounds that create a drying, astringent feel in the mouth, like that of oversteeped tea. These compounds occur naturally in many plants, such as grape skins, walnut skins, tea leaves, unripe fruits, and oak.

So to make white wine from white grapes, a vintner might let the crushed grapes mingle with their juice in a cold container, like a chilled, stainless-steel tank, for a few hours to extract more aroma and flavor, or he might simply elect to press the grapes straightaway with no skin contact at all. Skins and seeds contain *tannins*, elements that can give wines a dry, astringent feel. Although tannins can be desirable in red wines, they don't feel too good in a nice, light white wine. So soon after crushing and maybe a quick cold soak, the winemaker lightly presses the juice out of the grapes and into a tank, leaving behind the grape skins and seeds.

Red Wines

Grape skins are essential for making red wine as they contain most of the color pigments, so the skins remain with the grape pulp and juice for as long as it takes to extract the desired color, tannin, and flavor. This can be anywhere from a few days to several weeks.

Whether white, pink, or red, after crushing the grapes, it's time for fermentation.

Off the Vine

Pink wines acquire their pale red hue in one of two ways. One is to let the juice of red wine grapes sit with the grape skins just long enough to extract a little bit of color, then strain it off. In the trade, this is referred to as *Saignée*, to bleed pink juice off the grape skins. The other technique is to add a little red wine to a white wine to pink it up, a common practice in Champagne.

3. Ferment 'Em

If the wine is white, the juice pressed from the crushed grapes is quickly pumped into some sort of sealed container where it is typically settled for a day or two and then *racked*, or transferred, to another tank to ferment. These days, that's typically a stainless-steel tank, which can be kept both scrupulously clean and cold. Cement tanks sealed with epoxy and wooden barrels are also possibilities.

Winespeak _____

To **rack** wine is to move it from one container to another (for instance, from tank to barrel), leaving behind any sediment.

In red wines, the crushed grapes are pumped into a container, skins, seeds, and all. Sometimes this is a sealed container, but often it's open-topped.

Then the juice is ready for fermentation. The winemaker might opt to let the indigenous yeasts, those that occur naturally on the grape skins, ferment the wine, or he can inoculate the wine with cultured yeasts, strains of natural yeasts, isolated for their particular traits and raised in a controlled environment like a laboratory.

Off the Vine _____

Some winemakers feel wild yeasts give the wine a truer expression of the place where it was grown, but most vintners find they are too slow and unpredictable. Some ambient yeasts can spoil the wine; some may peter out early or even never take hold, leaving the vintner with a tank of partially fermented grape juice, a "stuck fermentation."

Cultured yeasts, on the other hand, are chosen for particular traits, such as the ability to withstand low temperatures or high alcohol. Some cultured yeasts can be used to emphasize a particular character in a wine, for instance, to bring out a variety's floral character.

Once the wine begins to ferment, it can take anywhere from a few days to many weeks to reach its point of completion, depending on the type of grape, quantity, strain of yeast, and temperature. As anyone who's made yeasted bread knows, the colder the temperature, the slower the yeasts work. Since fermentation also produces heat, winemakers often chill the containers in which the grapes ferment to control the temperature of the fermentation and lengthen its duration.

Getting Maximum Flavor

When fermenting is done, the juice is called wine, but vintners can do more to extract additional flavor. In red wines, the longer the skins, seeds, pulp, and juice sits together, the more pigment, flavor, and tannin is extracted, and so winemakers will often let the mass macerate in the juice.

It's not so easy, though, because the CO_2 produced during fermentation pushes the solids to the top of the tank, forming a thick cap on the juice. To get the most flavor out of the skins, this cap needs to be punched down or broken up. This typically requires climbing on top of the tank every so often with a large paddle to press the cap down and break it up, all the while trying not to get woozy from the carbon dioxide rising from the warm mass. Mixing the cap with the rest of the tank's contents is also crucial to keep the tank from overheating, as the cap will typically be 10 to 15°F. warmer than the juice itself.

Alternatively, the vintner can use a hose to take the wine from the bottom of the tank and spray it over the cap so it will percolate through the cap, a process called pumping over. Either way, once the juice has extracted enough tannin and textural mass from the cap, the skins and seeds must be removed by draining the juice into another container and shoveling the heavy mass of spent skins out of the tank. Sounds like fun, no?

Winespeak

The **lees** are dead yeast cells, miniscule particles of grape skins, and other detritus that precipitates out of a wine during and after fermentation.

Malolactic fermentation is a secondary fermentation that converts hard malic acid (think unripe apples) to softer lactic acid (think milk). Malo or ML in wine slang is common to most all red wines and a stylistic option for whites.

White wines don't have skins from which to take flavor, but they do have the *lees*. The lees are the miniscule particles of grape skins, dead yeast, and the like, that fall to the bottom of the tank. Winemakers will often stir up the lees in wines, which gives them a creamier texture.

Wines can also take on extra flavor complexity by going through *malolactic fermentation*. In this secondary fermentation, hard malic acid is converted to softer lactic acid, giving the wine a softer, smoother texture. Nearly all red wines undergo malolactic fermentation (malo or ML in wine lingo); otherwise, they'd be too harsh for pleasant drinking. In white wines, malolactic fermentation is optional; some winemakers choose to let only part or none of the juice go through malo. Malo will often give a white wine a buttery or milky flavor.

4. Bottle 'Em

If all the winemaker wants is a simple, fresh, drink-now type of wine, he's just going to rack the juice into another tank, leaving any sediment behind. From there, it is nearly ready to bottle.

Before bottling, however, some winemakers fine and/or filter the wine. To fine is to remove the fine particles by adding a fining agent, which can be a compound with a positive or negative charge, such as bentonite, or a proteinaceous material such as skim milk, which will bind to the particles and fall to the bottom of the solution. In red wines, fining is typically done to remove excess tannins; white wines are typically fined to remove any particles that might cloud the wine or make it unstable, giving it off tastes or odors. After fining, the wine is racked to another container, leaving the sediment behind. To filter is to pass the wine through a fine filter that will catch any tiny particles. Some vintners eschew one or both steps, claiming they take away flavor as well as particles; that's why some bottles have "Unfined and Unfiltered" printed on the label. However, unfined and unfiltered wines run a slight risk of eventually spoiling due to remaining bacteria or yeasts.

For a richer, more complex wine—red or white—the winemaker might rack the wine into oak barrels either during fermentation or immediately thereafter for aging for some period of time before bottling it. Over time, the wine will develop more complex flavors and, in general, become smoother. Depending on the type of oak used, the barrels may also contribute tannin and flavors like vanilla, spice, or caramel to the wine.

When the winemaker decides the wine has aged long enough, he racks it into a large container, where it is blended since every barrel of wine tastes slightly different from the next. Then the wine is bottled and set aside to rest for days, months, or years, depending on space, money, and the desired effect. The longer a wine ages in the bottle, the more mature the flavors will taste; that is, they'll taste mellower and less fresh but generally more complex—unless it ages too long and loses its fruit and vitality.

Endless Variation, Endless Exploration

So now you have an idea of the endless work it takes to produce a bottle of wine—not to mention a hint of the myriad permutations of flavor possible, even from the very same grape. Grape, region, climate, weather, farming, picking, and techniques of making all contribute to the final flavor of the wine in your glass.

It's these permutations that make wine so interesting. It's not like soda pop, which tastes pretty much the same wherever it's sold. Wine comes in so many types, styles, and flavors it's impossible to know it all. Lucky for us, all we need to do is drink it—but this background information will help highlight what you're looking for and enable you to find the wines you like best.

The Least You Need to Know

♦ Wine is fermented fruit juice—from any sort of fruit.

♦ Most wine—and all the wine discussed in this book—is made from grapes.

♦ Grapes from the *Vitis vinifera* species, like Chardonnay, Merlot, and Zinfandel, make the world's best wines.

♦ Every element of nature affects a grape's flavor, which in turn affects the wine's flavor.

♦ Great wines have a sense of terroir, a flavor that is particular to the place they were raised, as opposed to an international-style wine, which may be technically correct but could come from anywhere.

♦ Winemaking in a nutshell is harvest, crush, ferment, and bottle.

♦ White wine can be made from white grapes or skinless purple grapes; for most grapes, color comes from the skins. Red wines need red wine skins.

Chapter 2

Parsing the Label

In This Chapter

◆ Decoding a wine label

◆ Why place matters

◆ What's so "special" (or not) about "special reserves"

◆ What vintage has to do with it

◆ Sustainable farming methods and natural wines

Faced with a row of bottles you've never seen before, how do you choose your wine? By the label, of course—we all do, even if we don't admit it. Why else would wineries spend so much time and money on eye-catching graphics?

The design is the most noticeable element, but it's the least helpful. To figure out what's inside the bottle, you must read the fine print, the gothic script, the Braille bumps, or whatever the winery uses to get across the essential information. After all, the purpose of the label is to tell you what's inside.

The thing is, you need to know what to look for and what to ignore. Just as you can't judge a book by its cover, you can't judge a wine by its label. But you can up your chances of finding the kind of wine you're looking for. This chapter explains what label information is important and what's just gloss.

The Lay of the Label

Wine labels have all sorts of different styles; some are minimalist, some are crowded with information; some sport the name of a grape variety, some don't. Every wine bottle sold commercially in the United States, however, bears two labels: the front label (the flashier one, with the name of the wine) and the back label (where the fine print and government warning resides).

Off the Vine

Some wine bottles may sport a nutritional label, too; the Alcohol and Tobacco Tax and Trade Bureau (TTB) declared it legal to include calorie, carbohydrate, and nutrition content on alcoholic beverages in April 2004. What's it likely to tell you? Wine isn't where you're going to get your vitamins and minerals. The average 5-ounce serving has only trace amounts of niacin, riboflavin, sodium, and thiamine. Calorie-wise, most dry wines run 20 to 30 calories an ounce; dessert wines can pack in as many as 50.

The front label is your main concern. Although front labels vary widely, somewhere on every bottle of wine that comes into the United States you'll find several things. (When in the country of origin, all bets are off.) They are …

- Whose wine it is.
- Where it's grown.
- What sort of wine it is (e.g., "Sparkling," "Red Table Wine," etc.).
- How much wine is in the bottle.
- The percent of alcohol.

That's all that's strictly necessary. In addition, the label might offer such helpful information as …

- The grape variety or varieties.
- The vintage year.
- The bottling site.
- A designation of quality.
- The name of a vineyard.

- A designation of style.

- A designation of ripeness.

- An indication of how it was farmed.

Wine labels that include the name of the grape or grapes contained within the bottle are called varietal labels; regional labels leave off the grape variety and rely instead on the name of the place the wine was grown to identify the sort of wine in the bottle. Here is an example of each:

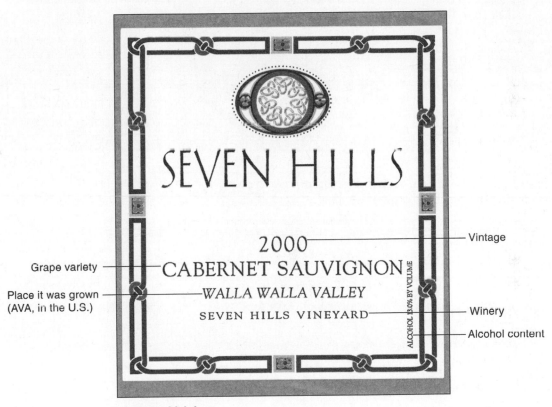

A varietal label.

Name of wine

Vintage

Place it was grown (DOC, in Italy)

Winery

Alcohol content

Volume in bottle

A regional label.

Who Made It

The most obvious element of a wine label beyond the design is typically the name of the winery from which it comes. Often, on European labels this is the name preceded by words like Château (French) or Bodega (Spanish); in English-speaking countries, the name may or may not include the term *winery*.

The winery name gives you news you can truly use only after you've become familiar with that producer's style. This is one place note-taking comes in very handy; jot down a list of producers whose wines you've liked, and you have the start of your own personal crib sheet.

Sometimes the winery name is not so obvious. The label may sport in prominent letters a proprietary name, like Sunrise. The winery responsible for Sunrise is Concha y Toro, but, in the interest of keeping things simple and memorable, they've chosen to call the wine most prominently by this short, catchy name. You have to look at the small print to find out it's made by Concha y Toro—a helpful detail if you know of that winery and trust its wines.

When none of the names are familiar—a frequent occurrence even for professionals, as so many wines crowd the wine shelves—look at where it comes from. This is the next most important clue to what you'll find inside.

Quick Sips

Some common terms which indicate a winery:

> Abbazia
> Adega
> Bodega
> Cantina
> Casa (often abbreviated Ca')
> Castello
> Caves
> Cellars
> Château
> Domaine
> Quinta
> Tenuta
> Villa
> Weingut
> Weinkeller

Where It's From

In the United States, we're used to buying wine according to the grape that went into it. It's not, however, necessary to list it on the label. Most of the wine world, in fact, doesn't. The grape variety is critical, of course, but because many places have been growing a certain grape or variety of grapes for decades, the variety is considered part of the definition of the wine from that place; it's not necessary to list both. Every wine, labeled by grape or not, indicates the place where its grapes were grown.

The origin of the grapes is so important because grapes grown in certain areas will have a flavor particular to that exact place—its terroir. For instance, Pinot Noir grown in Burgundy, France, will taste different from Pinot Noir grown in Sancerre, France.

Quick Sips

Where the grapes were grown is more important than where the wine was made; for instance, if a California winery makes wine with grape juice imported from Italy, it cannot say the resulting wine is from California. It must label the wine with the place the grapes were grown.

This idea of terroir is so strong in the Old World—places like France and Spain that have honed the fine details of their vineyards over hundreds of years—that winemakers don't even bother putting the name of the grape that made the wine on the label. To them, it's somewhere between obvious and beside the point.

But even in the New World—countries such as the United States, South America, Australia, New Zealand, and South Africa, that have had a major commercial wine industry for only a century or less—where producers typically label their wines by grape, it's important to know where the grapes grew. A Chardonnay grown in California's hot Central Valley, for instance, is going to taste much different than one grown on the cool Sonoma Coast, which in turn will taste different than a Chardonnay from Chalk Hill farther inland in Sonoma.

Of course, some places are more revered for grape growing than others. California's Napa Valley wines, for instance, are more sought after than Central Valley wines. To avoid the risk of dishonest wine bottlers misrepresenting wines, most winemaking regions have drawn up laws that define the places that can be listed on wine labels. These place names are referred to as *appellations*, after the French, *appellation d'origine contrôlée*, or controlled name of origin.

Appellations: What's in a Name?

Appellations are areas with legally defined boundaries, typically drawn up on the supposition that the land inside that boundary gives the wines grown within a particular character. The land inside the boundary may share a certain type of soil or a microclimate that sets its wines apart from wines grown outside the boundaries.

Most countries have their own system of regulating appellations. The big ones are:

- France: Appellation d'Origine Contrôlée (AOC)
- Germany: Qualitätswein bestimmter Anbaugebeite (QbA)
- Italy: Denominazione della Origine Controllata (DOC)
- Spain: Denominacion de Origen (DO)
- United States: American Viticultural Area (AVA)

All appellations guarantee that the wine comes from within a defined region. Many Old World appellations also specify what grapes go into it, how they are grown, and how the wine is made. That way, the thinking goes, the buyer is assured of getting the wine one would expect from that region, and the region's wines will retain a clear identity. For example, wines labeled Sancerre, which are from an AOC in France's Loire Valley, should always taste like Sancerre.

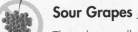

Sour Grapes

Though appellations are supposed to highlight areas that grow particularly outstanding grapes, a little skepticism can be healthy, as political concerns sometimes define boundaries more than the physical factors that actually affect the grapes.

A list of all the appellations in the world would take up its own book, but you really don't need to know all of them. What's important to know is that there are tiers of specificity in appellation systems, and knowing where the appellation falls offers another clue as to the kind of wine in the bottle.

Tiers of Specificity

The more specific the place name, the smaller the area from which it was drawn. For example, if a vintner makes wine from grapes he's bought from all over the United States, he can only label the wine as "American Table Wine." If all the grapes come from within the state of California, he can label it "California." If 85 percent of the grapes come from Napa Valley (the legal minimum for a region designation in the United States), he can label it as such.

Typically, the hierarchy looks like this:

- Table wine/vin de table/vino da tavola/vino de mesa/tafelwein: wines that do not meet the rules of even the most basic appellations; the grapes could have come from anywhere.

- Regional wine/vin de pays/indicazione geografica tipica/vino de la tierra/landwein: wines from within a particular, legally defined part of the country.

- Controlled appellation wines/Appellation d'Origine Contrôlée/Denominazione de Origine Controllata/Denominacion de Origen/Qualitatswein: wines from within a particular, legally defined part of a region.

Off the Vine

Table wines used to be associated with cheap plonk, but that's changing. Many European vintners, frustrated by appellation laws that limit their ability to experiment with grapes and techniques, are choosing to work outside the appellation systems and bottle wines with the lowly "table wine" moniker regardless how good or expensive the wine. In some areas, the quality of wines made outside the appellation regulations has led to a change in law to accommodate the wines.

Controlled appellations may be broken down into even more specific areas. The label may specify any of the following:

♦ District or county

♦ Village

♦ Vineyard

What do these degrees of specification mean? That the named area produces wines that stand out from those in the surrounding vineyards for one reason or another. The grapes may or may not be better; they might just be different. And keep in mind that even in the most specific appellations, not every vintner is as talented as the next. An appellation is not necessarily a promise of quality.

Reservations About "Reserve" and Other Terms

Many wines sport sexy-sounding terms like "Reserve," "Grand *Cru*," or "Old Vines," to name just a few. When these terms are regulated by law, they can indicate real differences in the quality of the wine. Unfortunately, a great many of these terms have no legal meaning at all.

Winespeak

Cru means growth or by extension, level or rank, but as it's used so often in reference to wines, it's also come to mean vineyard.

Here's the lowdown on those that do:

France: In Bordeaux, wines are classified in ascending order of quality as Bordeaux, Bordeaux Supérieur, Bordeaux Cru Bourgeois, Grand Cru Classé, Premier Grand Cru Classé. Alsace also calls wines from select, top vineyards Grand Cru.

Confusingly, in Burgundy, Grand Cru wines are ranked more highly than Premier Cru wines.

Italy: Classico denotes a more specific wine region; i.e., Chianti Classico is an area in Chianti, the region. Superiore and Riserva denote wines that have met more stringent quality and age requirements. The qualifications for Riserva and Superiore wines are different from one region to another, but the tiers always remain the same.

Spain: Joven (young), Crianza, Reserva, and Gran Reserva indicate, in that order, increasing levels of quality and age. As in Italy, the exact definitions of each may differ from region to region, but the hierarchy remains the same.

Some wines might also include a designation that indicates that they were made using a special method. Some of these terms are …

- *Amarone:* made from semi-dried grapes, unique to the Valpolicella region of Italy.

- *Ripasso:* literally means repassed; ripasso wines are traditionally made by adding the leftover grape skins from Amarone production to a young wine for a second fermentation in the hopes of extracting extra flavor. Today, many producers opt to add slightly dried grapes that haven't already been fermented to the young wine—a surer way of intensifying flavor.

- *Icewine/Eiswein*: made with naturally frozen grapes.

In Germany, higher-quality wines carry a designation that reflects the ripeness level of the grapes at harvest (See Chapter 6).

So a label might tell you something about how the wine inside was made. It might also tell you how the wine was grown.

Sour Grapes

Old Vines, Ancient Vines, Special Reserve, Vintners Reserve, Special Cuvée, and Select, in any language, all might sound promising, but none carries legal meaning.

Conventional vs. "Natural" Wines

Just a decade ago, organic wines were derided by the hoi polloi as being the exclusive domain of long-haired, granola-crunching hippies. Few people asked how the grapes that went into wines were grown. Farming with a reliance on industrially-produced fertilizers, pesticides, and herbicides was a given—thus the term conventional farming.

Today, strictly organic wines are still hard to come by, but reports of contaminated water supplies, infertile soil, and worker health issues, to name a few side effects of conventional farming, have made sustainable farming a hot topic. The rise of international-style wines—those that taste like they could have come from anywhere, even a factory, as opposed to those with individual character—has also inspired increased interest in natural or minimal-intervention winemaking. The wine industry has responded with a range of terms to indicate wines farmed in environmentally sensitive ways and/or made in a hands-off style. So let's go through the major variations.

Organic Wine

You may have noticed organic wines aren't very common. That's not because organic wine must be grown without any industrially processed fertilizers, herbicides, fungicides, or pesticides. It's because USDA regulations also forbid the addition of sulfites to any wine with the organic label.

The former is challenging but doable; the latter is so fraught with danger that most winemakers are not willing to take the risk. Sulfites are preservatives that occur naturally in all sorts of fermented foods, including wine, and they are regularly added to packaged foods to retain freshness. They are found in everything from prepackaged salad greens to bread, shrimp, dried fruits, and juices. Vintners typically use sulfur dioxide, a sulfite, during winemaking to protect the grapes from oxidizing (reacting with air) and to kill bad bacteria. Wines made without the addition of sulfur tend to spoil very easily. So most vintners—even those who endeavor to make their wines as naturally as possible, opt to add a discreet amount of sulfites and label their wines "made with organically grown grapes."

Sour Grapes _____

Some people are sensitive to sulfites (the FDA estimates 1 in 100, and a smaller percentage seriously allergic to them), but no evidence supports the popular opinion that sulfites give wine drinkers headaches. _Histamines_ (natural nitrogen-based compounds found in plants and animals) and phenolics (compounds responsible for color and texture, like tannin) are the likely culprits—but, as these occur naturally in wines, it's hard to avoid them.

Organically Grown Wines

A wine labeled "made from organically grown grapes" means that it comes from vineyards that are certified organic—that is, they've been farmed without synthetic fertilizers or pesticides. Vintners can add enough sulfites to keep the wine safe from spoilage.

In addition to eschewing chemicals, vintners who farm organically make efforts to strengthen the ecosystems within their vineyards. They may install birdhouses and plant a variety of flowers and plants other than grapevines to encourage a diversity of animal life; they may allow sheep, goats, or chickens into the vineyards to "mow" the cover crops planted between rows (and naturally fertilize them), and they may dry farm, or forgo any irrigation, among other techniques, to bring the vineyard in closer harmony with its environment.

In France, organic farming is known as agriculture biologique or bio for short. Bio can also refer to biodynamically-grown wines.

Biodynamic Wines

Biodynamics is a method of farming that stems from the "Agriculture" lectures (c. 1924) of Rudolph Steiner, an Austrian philosopher/scientist/mystic, in which the forces of the entire cosmos are considered in every agricultural activity taken. It might sound a little eccentric, but, for instance, biodynamic farmers follow a biodynamic calendar that suggests peak periods to plant, prune, or otherwise tend the vines, reflecting the belief that plants are sensitive to lunar, solar, and planetary cycles.

Like vintners who farm organically, biodynamicists eschew chemical fertilizers, herbicides, and pesticides, but they take it a step further, employing homemade preparations such as stinging nettle tea or aged cow manure. These solutions are meant to stimulate a more dynamic interaction between the earth and the vines.

Because of the care taken in the vineyard, certified biodynamic wines are certifiably organic, if not formally such, as the rigor in farming them is more stringent than that demanded by organic regulators.

In the effort to keep biodynamic wines as true to nature as possible, biodynamic guidelines also address winemaking issues, discouraging many common additions such as cultured yeast and acids.

Quick Sips

For a terrific layperson's explanation of biodynamics and list of practicing wineries, check out www.wineanorak.com, or go straight to the certifying agency Demeter, www.demeter-usa.org. For information on an extensive annual tasting of biodynamic wines (as well as practical information), go to www.biodynamy.com, run by Nicolas Joly, one of the most outspoken proponents of biodynamics.

Even though this may sound like hocus-pocus, biodynamically produced wines count as some of the world's best. Consider Lafon, Leflaive, Morey, and Romanée-Conti in Burgundy; Araujo and Sinskey in California; Fleury and Selosse in Champagne; Pingus in Spain; and Cayuse in Washington, among many, many others. To find certified biodynamic wines, look for the logo of Demeter or Biodyvin, two chief certifying bodies.

Sustainable Farming

Getting certified by a government agency takes time, money, and paperwork. Many wineries farm organically or biodynamically but have not yet achieved certification (a process that takes years), or have decided they do not want to bother with the paperwork, which is admittedly onerous and expensive for a small winery. To find these wines, you'll have to talk to importers and wineries and more or less take their word for it.

Many other vintners have made a conscious decision not to farm organically or biodynamically, yet want to be environmentally conscious. These vintners often claim their wines are *sustainably farmed*. Unlike organic, sustainable farming has no legal definition, but the inspiration is similar: to farm the fields with concern for and respect for the soil and the organisms that live in and around it. Farmers who farm sustainably eschew chemicals except when they feel their usage is crucial to the survival of their plants; for instance, they may not use any chemical fungicides for years, until a moist, cool spell threatens their vineyards with a fungus that might destroy the crop. They might also look for alternative energy sources (solar panels, for example) or work to reestablish the native flora and fauna near their vineyards for the general health of the ecosystem.

Off the Vine _____

Many vintners employ animal products in the making of their wines. Isinglass (derived from sturgeon bladders), gelatin (derived primarily from pig or cow skins and bones), egg whites, and caseins (derived from skim milk) are all commonly used to fine wine—that is, to either remove harsh, astringent flavors or to remove any small particles from the wine that might make it look cloudy.

These products are removed from the wine along with the particulate matter, but some vegetarians prefer to drink wines that are made without the use of any animal products. Wines can also be fined with minerals such as bentonite. There is no official vegan certification, so concerned vegans should check with the winery directly or consult a source such as vegans.frommars.org/wine.

Winemakers may also use an array of more localized terms that indicate a respect for the environment. For instance, the discovery that runoff from chemically farmed vineyards near watersheds was killing fish inspired a number of movements designed to restore fish and wildlife habitats and to improve water quality. In California, wineries may enroll in Fish-Friendly Farming; Napa wineries that are enrolled and employ water- and energy-saving methods in the winery can be certified Napa Green. In California, Idaho, Oregon, and Washington, wineries may apply for Salmon-Safe status or LIVE (Low Input Viticulture and Enology, Inc.) status, granted according to the tenets set forth by the International Organization for Biological and Integrated Control of Noxious Animals and Plants. These are just a few of the organizations that have cropped up in recent years; rising energy prices and water scarcity are encouraging more wineries around the world to invest in similar programs.

Off the Vine

Environmental concerns have also inspired winemakers to lighten up their wine packaging. Some are trading out the heavy bottles once associated with fancy wines for lighter ones; others are looking to boxes, like the light, sturdy Tetra Paks used for Three Thieves wines. Bag-in-box wines can be particularly good deals for everyday drinking: the bag inside the box protects the wine from oxygen, allowing it to stay fresh for weeks after tapping it. Check out Banrock Station, Black Box, DTour, La Petite Frog, and La Vieille Ferme for starters.

Natural Wines

Organic certification tells us a lot about how the grapes are grown but little about what happens once the grapes are in the winery (save for the lack of added sulfur). Vintners may manipulate their organic or organically grown wines in any number of ways, from using flavor-modifying yeasts to adding sugar, tannin, acid, and extra grape-based color. These interventions are completely legal but stray from what's sometimes called natural winemaking, in which vintners try to manipulate the juice as little as possible in an attempt to turn out a wine that's representative of its type and its terroir.

While there is no clear definition of "natural wine," many vintners have formed independent associations in which they pledge to make wines in certain ways; for instance, to use only indigenous yeasts; to eschew sugar, acid, or tannin additions;

or to avoid fining and filtration. It's not easy to identify these wines on the wine shelf, as they won't bear any special seals, but more wine stores are now devoting sections to these wines. Some stores and wine bars even specialize in natural wines and can help direct you to those that are made with minimal intervention.

Which Grapes?

In the United States, we're accustomed to seeing wines that trumpet the grape variety front-and-center on the label. These are often referred to as varietal wines; that is to say, wines made in large part from a single grape variety, which is listed on its label.

These varietal labels are common to all New World wine countries. American growers are still experimenting to figure out which grapes grow best where, and they are allowed to grow whatever grapes they want—unlike winemakers in some other countries.

You're most likely to find varietally labeled wines in:

- ◆ Australia and New Zealand

- ◆ North and South America

- ◆ South Africa

Quick Sips

Many famous European wines are made with grape varieties familiar to us; they just don't list them on the label. A few examples:

Burgundy: Pinot Noir (red) and Chardonnay (white)

Champagne: Chardonnay or Pinot Noir

Chianti: Sangiovese

Barolo: Nebbiolo

A few Old World winegrowing regions label most of their wines by grape variety, too. They are …

- ◆ Austria

- ◆ Germany

- ◆ Alsace and Languedoc, France

- ◆ Northeastern Italy

Varietal labels make wine buying pretty simple once you've become acquainted with a few different grape varieties. If you decide you like Chardonnay, it's easy to find a bottle as so many advertise the grape on the label.

Keep in mind, though, that varietal labels aren't always as straightforward as they seem. One Chardonnay may taste very different from the next. Its flavor will depend on where the grapes were grown and how the wine was made.

Most countries also allow a small percentage of other grapes into varietally labeled wines; in California, a wine labeled Chardonnay might contain up to 25 percent Sauvignon Blanc or any other grape. The difference is typically so slight that the wine will still taste mainly of the grape listed on the label.

When There Isn't a Grape Listed

However, many wines don't list grapes on the label. To most of Europe, knowing which region the wine comes from is more important than knowing the grape from which it was made, so European wineries will label the wine with the name of the place. To find out which wines those are, you need to do a little research and memorization (and read Part 2). Or simply do as the Europeans do: stop worrying about it and get to know wines by place.

Brave New Blends (And Ancient Ones, Too)

If a California wine contains less than 75 percent of any variety, it cannot be varietally labeled, so many vintners will give the wine a fantasy name, such as Tablas Creek's Côtes de Tablas. Why blend grapes? Because sometimes two grapes (or three or thirteen) are better than one. Say you have a grape that has wonderful flavor but lacks acidity. Then you have another grape that has great acidity but lacks great flavor. If the two have complementary flavors, when you put them together, you could have a whole greater than either one of the parts.

Off the Vine

> Prior to the acceptance of Meritage, a term coined in 1988 by the American Meritage Society, wine that contained less than 75 percent of a single grape variety had to be labeled with the unflattering minimalist moniker Red Table Wine, even if it was styled after the famous wines of Bordeaux, France. Today, vintners who make wines based on traditional Bordeaux blends may label their wine Meritage (which rhymes with heritage) instead.

European vintners have been blending wine for centuries. In part, the array of grape varieties ensured a decent harvest. If one grape variety didn't perform well, some other one may have thrived. Some grapes just seem to have a sympathetic relationship, too; they grow well in the same place and taste best when blended together.

When Vintage Matters

Almost every wine made from one single year's harvest announces the year of the harvest on its label, and that's referred to as the wine's vintage. For some wines, and in some years, it pays to pay attention to this date.

The most obvious reason to look at the vintage is to see how old the wine is. A wine's flavor changes as it ages, trading fresh, vibrant fruit flavors for softer, subtler flavors that often recall dried fruit, earth, and spice. If you prefer wines with bright, fresh flavors, you generally want to stick with wines less than five years old.

You might also have had the experience of loving a wine one year and not being so thrilled about it the next. What happened? Weather happened, most likely, or the winemaker changed, or the marketing folks insisted on a style revision. Every vintage of every wine is a little bit different from the last. When there's a particularly great or terrible vintage, sometimes it pays to know about it.

And When It Doesn't

In most cases, you don't need to worry about vintage too much. If you develop a passion (and pocketbook) for Bordeaux, Barolo, Tokaji, or other wine from an area where the weather is often iffy, you might want to invest some time in keeping up on the quality of the vintages since these wines are typically saved for many years, and wimpy wines don't age very well.

Otherwise, in wines for everyday drinking, the differences between vintages will probably be difficult to detect unless tasted side-by-side (and even then it can be really tough). Plus, these days, winemakers have plenty of tricks that allow them to make at least decent wine even in difficult vintages. It might be more appropriate to think of vintages in terms of the challenge they pose to winemakers. A gorgeous year might be easy, and a rainy year might be very challenging, but in the end, if the winemaker does his job well, both wines could turn out excellent.

It's important to remember, though, that no conscientious winemaker would release a truly bad wine. A wine from a lesser vintage may mature faster than one from a fabulous vintage, but hey, you need to have something to drink while that great vintage wine ages, right? Think of a wine from a lesser vintage as a wine to drink earlier, and it'll taste just fine.

Sour Grapes _____

Many wine critics rank vintages and publish the results in a chart so that it's easy to compare one vintage to another. These vintage charts might be handy, but they aren't necessarily accurate when it comes to individual wines. A vintage chart can only make a general statement about the quality of a vintage, but because weather affects different areas of a region to different degrees, some wines in a bad vintage might be great. You'll also find critics have different opinions, which may also differ from your own.

Back Label Details

The back label is usually pretty much ignored. The dull government warnings and those tasting notes some wineries include tend to be too general to be of much use.

But one line can be tremendously useful: the importer line. Every bottle imported into the United States bears the name of the importer on it someplace, typically the back label.

It pays to get to know which importers have portfolios that appeal to your taste. Most importers tend to specialize in a place: Spain, perhaps, or the south of France. The best importers tend to have a passion for a particular type of wine, and the collection of wines they import reflects it. For instance, Marco de Grazia and Vias are both companies that specialize in Italian wines. However, their collections differ not only in their exact wines but also in the style of those wines. De Grazia's selections tend more to the fruitier, flashier, more modern wines; Vias tends to champion the more traditional wines. If you like a wine from one of these companies, you may well like the others in its portfolio.

So when you have a wine you like, note the importer. You may find that you like that importer's taste. Then you'll have one more tool for finding wines you'll like.

Off the Vine _____

Every bottle of wine in the United States must, by law, bear a government statement warning consumers that drinking may be harmful to the drinker's health. While there is no doubt drinking impairs your ability to drive and operate heavy machinery (even if you don't notice it), and neither should happen under any circumstance, a wealth of studies show that drinking in moderation might have some positive benefits. Every person is different, however, so consult your doctor if you're concerned about wine's effects on your health.

The Least You Need to Know

♦ The place name on a wine label indicates where the grapes were grown, not where the wine was made.

♦ Wines labeled by grape (varietal wines) are made with a majority of the named grape.

♦ If no grape is named on the label, the name of the place will give a hint as to what grapes went into it.

♦ In general, the more specific the place listed on the label, the higher status the wine has in its country of origin.

♦ Old Vines and Special have no legal definition anywhere. Reserve, Grand(e), and Premier are legal definitions only in some places in the Old World and are undefined in the New World.

♦ Don't worry about the sulfites in a wine unless you're one of the few people sensitive to them.

How to Get the Most Out of Your Glass

In This Chapter

- ◆ Setting the scene
- ◆ Popping the corks—gracefully
- ◆ Tasting, one step at a time
- ◆ Talking about taste

The good news is that learning about wine requires tasting it—and how hard is that? The bad news is that it takes a little work, in the form of concentration. Most of us aren't used to concentrating on our drinks as we gulp down a soda or steal sips of coffee on the rush to work.

It's only natural to approach wine in the same way at first. Problem is, when you knock back a glass of red over dinner, it feels good, but it's hard to recall much about it later—unless you've paid it some attention. (I've usually forgotten about it by the next day, if not by the end of dinner.) If you want to learn something about wine, take time to taste it. A tasting doesn't have to be a formal affair. Just invite some friends over and crack open some wines. Talk about them; savor them; enjoy them. Here's an array of ideas on how to go about it.

Setting Up a Tasting

So you've decided you want to figure out the difference between Merlot and Cabernet Sauvignon. Or maybe you'd like to get a better grip on Chianti. Perhaps you just want to have several wine-loving friends over and taste a whole bunch of stuff. To get the most out of it, you don't have to expend a lot of energy, but these tips can help you maximize the experience.

Choose a Theme

First, what are you going to taste? A single wine is sufficient, but it's easier, more enlightening, and more fun to have a few wines to compare and contrast. The more the wines have in common, the more the comparison will illuminate. The difference between a white and a red is pretty obvious, but how about two Merlots from the same place?

Therefore, pick a theme in order to learn the most from a tasting. Choose a country or a grape, for instance, and taste only wines that fit the category. Wine geeks would call this a *horizontal tasting*. The more specific the category, the more specific the information you can glean from the flavors of the different wines.

Winespeak

A **horizontal tasting** is a lineup of wines made from the same grape or from the same place—for instance, a horizontal tasting of Merlots. A **vertical tasting** compares different vintages of the same wine.

If you choose wines from the same vintage, you won't have to worry about the difference in age and year making the flavor difference, rather than grape or place. But if you'd like to learn more about the effect of vintage, assemble different vintages of a specific wine. This is called *vertical tasting*. These tastings are often difficult for an individual to put together, as stores usually sell only the most recent vintages. Sometimes, though, older vintages do come on the market or pop up in auctions (see Chapter 22).

How Much to Buy

How many bottles of wine you need for a tasting depends on how many tasters attend and whether the wines will double as dinner wines afterwards. Figure on about 13 two-ounce servings (a generous pour for a taste, but a paltry glass for dinner) for each 750-ml (average-size) bottle.

You don't need to buy all the wine yourself; ask everyone to bring a bottle that fits the theme. When you're just starting out, keep the number of different wines to a small handful, three or four; any more can be confusing as they begin to all taste the same. With practice, you can work up to more.

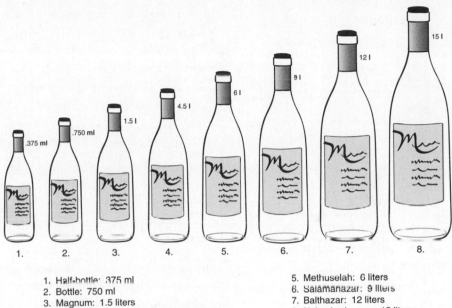

1. Half-bottle: 375 ml
2. Bottle: 750 ml
3. Magnum: 1.5 liters
3. Jeroboam: 4.5 liters (except in Champagne and Burgundy, where a Jeroboam measures 3 liters)
5. Methuselah: 6 liters
6. Salamanazar: 9 liters
7. Balthazar: 12 liters
8. Nebuchadnezzar: 15 liters

When size matters …

Get Organized

An array of open bottles on a table presents a generous invitation to a tasting. People can taste what they like in any order, and the ease of the setup makes for good conversation. This is as organized as you need to be.

If you want to get a little fancier, try to order the wines so they move from lightest to heaviest. This lessens the risk of obliterating the flavors of a light, delicate wine with those of a big, brawny one tasted just before it. It's impossible to know exactly which wines will be lighter than others, but in general, move …

♦ From white to rosé to red.

♦ From cheapest to most expensive.

- From basic to reserve.

- From youngest to oldest.

- From dry to sweet.

Winespeak

A **blind tasting** involves tasting wine without knowing its identity.

To avoid any risk of preconceived notions, hold a *blind tasting*. Tasters know what sort of wine they are tasting but do not know the exact identity of the bottles until the end of the tasting. The bottles can be put in paper bags secured by a rubber band around the neck (no peeking!), wrapped in aluminum foil, or otherwise disguised. Number the bottles so tasters can keep track of the wines they've tasted and can match their tasting notes to the revealed wine at the end of the tasting.

Blind tastings help save us from ourselves. Despite our best intentions, we all tend to judge a wine by its label. (Why else would wineries expend so much effort making them attractive?) And once we've preconceived a notion about how a wine is supposed to taste, it's often hard to taste anything but what we think we're supposed to taste.

Off the Vine

Under For Ultra Wine Geeks Only is a *double blind* tasting, where tasters aren't told anything about the wines. You could take it one step further (if you're really mean) and blindfold the tasters, so they can't even see the colors of the wines. Depending on the wine, it can be tough to tell if it's white, pink, or red by taste alone.

If you're super-organized, you can pour the wine into glasses before the guests arrive and then hide the bottles from sight. Many tastings are done this way in the wine industry. In this case, number both the bottles and the glasses. The glasses can be numbered with a wax pencil or dry-erase pen; alternatively, set each taster's place with a large sheet of white paper, and mark the number of the wine on the paper where you've set the glass. It's important to set the glasses down in the same space while tasting, or it will be impossible at the end to know which wine is which.

A Suitable Space

Now that you have chosen your wines, where are you going to taste them? You can taste wine anywhere, but it helps to find a space where it's going to be easy to concentrate. It should be …

◆ Comfortable. A room with white rugs is just going to make everyone worry about spilling red wine rather than tasting it. Find a comfy space big enough for everyone to have a place to set a glass and a notebook.

◆ Fragrance-free. Loud scents of perfume, cleansers, dogs, dinner, and the like compete with the comparatively quiet scents in a wine glass. And since taste is about 99 percent smell, if you want to taste the wine, find someplace you'll be able to smell it.

◆ Well-lighted. Leave romance for later. Right now you want to see what's in your glass.

◆ Distraction-free. Music is one thing; jackhammers are another. Wine tasting by nature is a fairly quiet, introspective adventure; jarring action and noise can be distracting.

The Right Tools

You'll need a few accoutrements to prepare for a tasting. Nothing too fancy, just …

◆ Corkscrew.

◆ Glasses (one water glass and one to five wine glasses per person).

◆ Napkins.

◆ Paper and pens.

◆ Spit buckets/cups (one per person) or dump buckets (one or two).

◆ Plain bread or crackers.

◆ Water.

A Note About Glassware

Lack of glassware shouldn't keep you from starting your study. Use what you have; a tumbler will do if that's all there is in the cabinet. As you become more experienced, you'll find that some glasses are easier to taste out of than others. In general, the perfect tasting glass has …

◆ A stem by which it can be held, so your view of the lovely-hued juice isn't marred by greasy fingerprints.

◆ A bowl large enough to fill with an ounce of wine and swirl it without spilling (at least a 6-ounce glass). The bowl should also narrow toward the top to help keep the swirling wine in the glass and better capture its aroma.

◆ A thin lip, so the feel of the glass doesn't distract from the wine in it.

◆ A price that doesn't make you scared to touch it.

Find a glass that feels good and fits your budget, and buy several. Since glass shape and size can change the perception of a wine, you'll want to taste each wine from the same kind of glass. Likewise, when many people are tasting the same wine, it's better to use the same glasses, or the differences people perceive may be more due to the glass than the wine itself.

Extra-credit experiment: take a wine, any wine, and pour it into several different glasses—a coffee cup, a tumbler, a small wine glass, a large wine glass, a Dixie cup, whatever you've got. Smell the wines. Do they smell different? Taste the wines. Do you feel the difference a glass can make?

Pop the Corks

Until the screw top becomes more popular, you'll have to learn how to remove a cork with ease. It's not hard—though you might get that impression from the number of tools developed expressly for the purpose—but it does take practice to do it quickly and gracefully.

There are many different types of openers from which to choose, but any good corkscrew should have a worm (the spiral part) about two inches long and a sharp tip.

Off the Vine

While some people still associate screw caps with wino wines, more high-end wineries are switching to them after tests have shown that high-tech screw-cap closures keep wines fresher longer and prevent the risk corks pose of infecting the wine with TCA (see Sour Grapes box later in this chapter). Besides, the vast majority of wines are opened within a few hours of purchase, making the cork little more than a showpiece.

Screw Like a Pro

To use any of these tools, first remove the foil capsule. There are special foil cutters for this job, but the knife on your basic waiter's friend, the folding corkscrews used in restaurants, or the tip of the corkscrew works fine. If you're going to show off the bottles, run the cutter under the lip of the bottle and remove just the top of the capsule. If you don't care how it looks or speed is a priority, take the whole capsule off.

Then place the tip of the worm just off-center on the cork. Twist clockwise, applying a little downward pressure. Keep screwing it in until only one spiral of the worm is showing. If you're using a winged corkscrew, push down on the wings. With a waiter's friend, position the jack firmly on the edge of the bottle, and pull up, using it as leverage.

If the cork begins to bend sideways or break, stop pulling and screw the worm down a few more turns. Gently pull the cork out; a loud pop might sound cool, but it's not polite.

Quick Sips

When the cork crumbles, don't panic; it happens to everyone. Remove the corkscrew, and using a waiter's friend, go at it, gently, from a different angle, trying to find a firmer place to sink it in. If you have an Ah-so, a double-pronged cork puller, it's great for easing out a crumbling cork. If nothing works, just push the cork into the bottle, and pour the wine through a strainer. It may not look good, but it won't hurt the wine.

Special Case: Sparkling Wine

Sparkling wine doesn't require a corkscrew, but it does require caution. Chill the bottle well; warm bubbly is more likely to foam all over the place when opened. Hold the bottle at a 45° angle, pointing away from people, including yourself. Remove the foil, and then carefully remove the metal cage that holds the cork in place—all the while, holding the cork down. If the cork is ready to blow, hold it back and let it out gently; a loud pop is not only tacky but wastes good

Off the Vine

Under "Stupid Wine Tricks," put *sabering*, a swaggering method of opening a bottle of Champagne. Here, the opener slashes the entire top off the bottle with a sharp saber. The number of bottles that become bloody puddles filled with glass shards make this a dubious achievement.

wine and dispels the bubbles faster. If the cork is firmly lodged in the bottle, hold it firmly and turn the bottle until you feel the cork move. Then, resisting the pressure, slowly ease the cork out. You've now opened a bottle of sparkling wine perfectly.

The Five Ss

When you have the wines, the glasses, and everything else assembled, you're ready to dive in. But hold on; take it slow. There's a difference between drinking and tasting wine. Drinking is done almost reflexively, unconsciously; tasting requires the attention of every one of the senses. You'll learn some things from drinking, but you'll learn far more from tasting.

Tasting isn't hard, but it does take a concerted effort. So let's break the steps into the five Ss: See, Swirl, Smell, Sip, and Spit (or Swallow).

See

A person can deduce all sorts of things from the look of a wine, but the most important question here is: is it free of foreign objects you wouldn't want to drink? Does it appear healthy, or is it bubbling like it's alive when it's supposed to be still?

Beyond that, the color can give you hints as to the kind of wine in the glass. In general, the darker the wine, the richer the flavor. For instance, a very light white typically has almost no color, while a richer white has a golden hue. Color is also an indication of age: white wines turn darker with age; red wines lighten. And different grapes have slightly different colors: Nebbiolo can have a brownish cast, for example, while Shiraz is often deep, dark purple.

Winespeak

Legs are the viscous trails that wine makes on a glass after it has been swirled. The thicker or longer the legs, the stronger in alcohol and/or sugar the wine tends to be. These are also called **tears**.

You can also swirl the wine in the glass, and watch how long it clings to the sides: generally, the longer the *legs*, or trails of wine down the glass, the richer the wine, due to higher levels of sugar or alcohol. Or you could leave all that to the hard-core wine dorks and just take in the wine's beauty for a little while.

Swirl

You can always tell the wine dork in a crowd of wine drinkers because she's the one swirling the wine in her glass. It's not an affectation; it's a way of getting more aroma out of the wine by exposing more of it to the air. Try it; smell the wine without moving the glass. Now place the glass on a flat surface, and move the base in circles to create a mini-whirlpool in the wine. Stop and smell it. There's more to smell, right? After you get the hang of it, you'll soon find yourself swirling your morning orange juice (which, by the way, looks pretty silly).

Smell

Taste is mostly smell, so this is the most important step. You can stop here, in fact, if you want. Right after swirling the wine, put the glass up to your nose and inhale deeply. Notice how the wine smells. Does it smell good? Does it make you want to take a sip? Swirl and sniff it again, and again. Try to put words to the smells. Does it smell like fruits or vegetables? Flowers or herbs? Green or red? Vivacious or wan? Whatever descriptions you can come up with will help you remember the wine.

Winespeak _____

Bouquet is a crusty old wine term for all the various scents a wine gives off—for example, "This wine has a stupendous bouquet." It's more properly used to describe the aromas a wine develops as it ages; old wines can have a bouquet, but young wines have straightforward aromas.

Sour Grapes _____

If the wine smells like wet cardboard or like your grandparents' attic, it's most likely corked. That means it's infected by TCA (trichloroanisole), a compound that enters the wine through the cork. It's harmless to people but gives wines a musty flavor. While a corked wine won't hurt you, it doesn't taste as good as an uninfected bottle, so return it to the people from whom you bought it.

Sip

From the color and smell, you have an idea of what the wine's going to taste like. Now put it to the test. Take a sip, but don't swallow it immediately. Hold the liquid in your mouth; chew on it; extract all the flavor you can from it. Act like a pro and open your mouth slightly, sucking air in over the wine in your mouth. (Try this in the comfort of your home before taking it into public, until you can do it with no fear of dribbling.) This aerates the wine as the swirling did, so more aroma will fill your head.

While the wine is in your mouth, think about how it feels. Is it silky or prickly? Juicy or drying? Mouth-coating or refreshing? Wine contains *acidity*, which acts like a dash of vinegar on a salad: it brightens, enlivens, provides a fresh taste. Some wines—mostly reds—also contain tannin. If your mouth begins to feel a little like it's been swabbed with cotton balls, that's tannin. It feels a little bit like a sip of oversteeped tea does.

Wine also develops an array of flavors. What flavors can you pick out? Fruit? What kind? Spice? Chocolate? Earth? Most importantly, do you like it? This is not a trick question: there is no wrong answer. Your taste is yours alone, and don't let anyone tell you otherwise.

Spit (or Swallow)

Finally, spit or swallow the wine. If you taste more than a few wines at a sitting, spitting is a really good idea; those little pours hold enough alcohol to dull the palate. If you're embarrassed to spit in public, practice in the shower until you've developed good form. It's less embarrassing to dribble, though, than to get drunk.

Winespeak

Finish is the lasting flavor of a wine after a sip.

The tasting still isn't done yet. Even without wine left in your mouth, flavor lingers on. How long good flavors linger is a sign of quality; you'll often hear wine tasters say a wine has a good or a long *finish*.

Reviving a Flagging Tongue

If you follow these steps for every wine, you'll get far more out of each of them than you would were you to just casually drink them. When you begin to think that every wine tastes the same, though, take a break. Drink some water, and eat some bread. Don't have anything very flavorful, like stinky blue cheese, because those flavors will linger in your mouth, making it hard to taste the rest of the wines.

Putting Wine into Words

Some people complain they can't distinguish many flavors in a glass of wine, or they can but can't put a name to them. It takes practice, and you can practice all the time. Begin to compile an internal library of scent. Smell everything you can, and try to imprint it in your mind. Smell flowers, dirt, stones, water, fruit, vegetables, candy, car seats, lead pencils, grass, farm animals, and your gym clothes. Go to a spice store and smell all the canisters. Inhale deeply at the gas station. Smell anything and everything. You'd be amazed at what smells you can find in a glass of wine.

If you have trouble getting started, check out the aroma wheel included here. Designed by Professor Anne C. Noble at the University of California at Davis, a school that has an extensive winemaking program, the aroma wheel breaks flavors into broad categories. Within those categories, it gives more exact flavor descriptors common to different wines. It can be an excellent tool to get you thinking of different ways to describe wines. Just remember that you're not limited to the words on the wheel. Whatever words help you describe the wine to yourself and others are fair game.

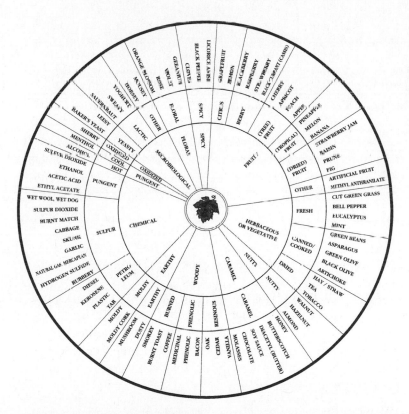

An aroma wheel.

(Copyright 1990 A. C. Noble. Colored laminated plastic copies of the wine aroma wheel may be obtained from www. winearomawheel.com or A. C. Noble, Box 72239, Davis, CA 95616, USA)

Metaphorically Speaking

Like is the key word in describing wines. Few people can say, "It tastes like Merlot," and even then, there are so many different types of Merlot, that description doesn't tell us very much. Wine also exhibits more flavors in one sip than almost anything else we ever put into our mouths. We need all the help we can get to describe what wine tastes like, and metaphors are excellent tools for this purpose. Wine can taste like specific fruits or vegetables or herbs. It can recall the scent of leather or spice, or taste like vanilla or chocolate. It can have a savory taste like meat or an earthy taste.

Some wines might recall a place: a pine forest, the seashore, a new car, a gas station. Some people like to think of wines in terms of personality: bright and bouncy, dour and mean, sophisticated, or glamorous, to name a few. It's not very PC, but there are those who divide wines into masculine and feminine or compare them to pop stars.

Whatever works for you is fine; the important thing is to make the effort to describe the wine or you'll have a hard time remembering it.

Write It Down

Whatever you do, write down your impressions. If you don't, you're likely to forget them by the next week, if not the next day. You might even want to make up a sheet that lists each of the tasting steps and gives room to make notes on each one, so you won't forget any steps. Having an empty sheet in front of you will also force you to come up with meaningful words with which to describe the wines. If you're tasting five reds and each wine "tastes like cherries," you'll quickly realize you need to search harder for words to differentiate one from the next.

Quick Sips

Check out the Complete Idiot's Guide Tasting Sheet we've provided for you in Appendix C.

Scores

Scores can be useful as long as you don't take them too seriously. They offer a way to rank wines, and thereby make sense of the wines tasted. But scores are also limiting. A score is just a snapshot of a wine, taken from a very personal point of view. It takes into account how the wine tasted at a particular moment in time to a particular person. Without a tasting note that describes why the scorer liked the wine as much as her score indicates, the score is just about useless.

It's also important to remember that wines are alive, always changing—this is one reason that people collect wine instead of, say, soda. Savor a glass of wine over the course of an hour, and chances are you'll find flavors in it by the end of the hour that weren't there when it was first poured. Some wines need time in the glass or in the bottle to show their best—and they may not have received that time when the scorer first tasted them. Food can also dramatically alter the impression a wine gives; a wine that tastes sour and puckery may taste refreshingly delicious when it's tasted with chicken in a rich cream sauce (see Chapter 25).

Quick Sips

If you begin to take yourself too seriously as a wine critic, it's time to play with Greg Sumner's Silly Tasting Notes Generator at www.gmon.com/tech/stng.shtml.

Feel free to develop a scoring system that works for you, but write notes, too, so you'll have a clue what the 85 meant when you wrote it six months ago.

The Least You Need to Know

- A clean, well-lit, scent-free space is the easiest place to taste wine.

- Glasses with a stem and a clear bowl work best, but even a tumbler will do in a pinch.

- The more specific the theme for a wine tasting, the easier it is to understand the differences between the wines.

- To get the most out of your glass, use the five steps of see, swirl, sniff, sip, and swallow (or spit, if it's not dinnertime).

- Take notes: you'll remember the wines better, even if you never look at the notes again.

- Above all else, *pay attention* to what's in your glass.

Part 2

What to Taste: The Big Nine

I hope you've been sipping something delicious all along as you've read this book, but if you haven't, now is the time to start.

Now you know the different factors that go into shaping a wine: the type of grapes, the location, the care taken both before and after picking, and Mother Nature's treatment. We've figured out how to parse a wine label, too, in hopes of getting an idea of what's behind the glass. It's all super-helpful information, but a little too broad to answer the question, "What wine will fit my mood, pocketbook, and palate tonight?"

So here, it's time to whip out the glasses and put your tongue to work. We'll go through every major grape variety and explore it in all its most popular guises, from simple, affordable bottlings to expense-account-only reserves, to get a taste of the huge array of options out there and a better idea of what works for you.

4

Chardonnay

In This Chapter

- ◆ Chardonnay is everywhere
- ◆ The taste of Chardonnay
- ◆ The best places to grow Chardonnay
- ◆ Chardonnay's myriad styles

You've undoubtedly heard of this white wine grape. It's on most every wine list, and it fills the wine store shelves; it's so popular that some wine lovers have rebelled, joining the ABC club, or Anything But Chardonnay.

Yet there's a reason for Chardonnay's fame; it makes some of the world's finest white wines and a whole lot of tasty, affordable juice, as well. Winemakers love it because it's relatively easy to grow, and the grape is easily malleable when it comes to turning it into wine. Chardonnay can be blended with other grapes, but it usually appears solo. It doesn't need any help from other varieties to be at its best.

It's also as easy to drink as it is to pronounce and comes in myriad styles. Most Chardonnays are also labeled by their grape, making them easy to identify; the few places that label Chardonnay by place instead of grape are easy to memorize. So let's talk about the range of flavors common to Chardonnay and how to find the kind you prefer.

What It Tastes Like

One of Chardonnay's greatest assets is its range of flavor; it can be light and lemony or rich as pineapple upside-down cake. The style depends both on where it's grown and how it's made.

> **Quick Sips** _____
>
> Chardonnay at a glance: its citrus and apple-like flavors can range from light, lean, and crisp to rich and ripe as a pineapple. It's frequently oaked, which can add sweet notes of vanilla, caramel, and toast.

Chardonnay's Light, Crisp Side

At its lightest, Chardonnay can be very refreshing, with lots of bracing acidity and flavors that recall lemon, lime, and green apple. These Chardonnays tend to come from cool areas, where the grapes don't get super-ripe and retain strong acidity, and they are usually made in stainless-steel tanks instead of oak barrels. To find this style, look for …

> **Quick Sips** _____
>
> The cooler the region, the crisper the fruit. This holds for most fruits in general; think of apples and pears (which prefer it chilly) as opposed to pineapple and mango (tropical fruits).

- Wines labeled *unoaked:* these will be free of the vanilla, spice, and caramel flavors that oak can give a wine.

- Wines from cooler climates: California's Green Valley or Sonoma Coast; New York State; Canada; Casablanca, Chile; Burgundy, France; Western Australia; and New Zealand, to name a few.

Big and Buttery Alternatives

At the opposite end of the Chardonnay spectrum are wines as ripe and golden as pineapple. To get such rich, sweet fruit (whether a pineapple or a grape) takes warmth; these Chardonnays are usually found in sunnier, warmer regions than those from which the crisp ones hail.

Oak also helps build body. If you put Chardonnay into oak barrels, it soaks up the vanillin and other flavor components in the wood, lending the wine vanilla and sweet spice notes.

Another method to add richness to Chardonnay is to age it on its lees—the dead yeast cells and other miniscule matter that settle out of the wine as it ferments. Then it picks up a creamy, yeasty tone, like the scent of rising bread, especially if the lees are frequently stirred up (a process you might hear referred to as *bâtonage*, the fancier-sounding French). Put Chardonnay through a second, malolactic fermentation, and it takes on a thicker, silkier texture, sometimes with a slight milky flavor.

Where Chardonnay Grows

Just about every winegrowing region in the world boasts a few acres, if not a few thousand acres, of Chardonnay. It's grown from Texas to Japan, thriving in chilly and warm areas alike and in all types of soils.

The grape reaches its most esteemed expressions in cooler regions, like the northern reaches of France (for instance, Chablis) and the breezy, foggy coastal edge of Sonoma, California. Many of the most popular Chardonnays grow in warmer areas, though, like California's Central Valley and Southeastern Australia, where the vines don't struggle so much to ripen their fruit and so can produce more grapes. Not only do the wines tend to be more affordable, but also they tend to soak up sun and warmth like a sponge to create some lip-smackingly rich, hedonistic pours.

As far as dirt goes, Chardonnay vines prefer stony, calcium-rich soil, but its wild popularity means it's grown all sorts of places, for better or worse.

To get to know Chardonnay, it's best, perhaps, to start at the original source, which is often regarded as its apex: Burgundy, in France.

France: Chardonnay's Hallowed Grounds

If you live in the United States, you're likely most familiar with California Chardonnay because California wines tend to announce the grape on the label. However, the place that's been making top-notch Chardonnay for far longer doesn't even list the grape on the label: Burgundy.

Chardonnay is so prevalent in Burgundy that it's considered unnecessary to mention the grape in a white wine unless it's not Chardonnay. So if a white wine from Burgundy doesn't list a grape on the label, you can be sure it's made from Chardonnay. Burgundy's Chardonnay wines, with their layered, complex flavors and their ability to get more complex and delicious with age, provide a model to which many compare other Chardonnays, so we'll start here on our exploration of the grape.

Sour Grapes

If a wine says Chablis or Hearty White Burgundy and it's not from France, avoid it: it's not the real thing. In the 1960s and 1970s it was common to imitate France's wines (at least in name, if nothing else) but non-French wines are no longer allowed to bear the names of French appellations like Chablis, Burgundy, and Champagne.

Burgundy—a long, thin strip of land that starts north of Lyon and stretches up to Dijon, then jumps northwest toward Paris to include Chablis—has a cool climate that keeps the growing season long and the grapes taut with crisp, acidic flavor. The wines often have a chalky, mouthwatering mineral character that may be attributed to the land as it's filled with calcium and decayed seashells from a previous life as an ocean bed.

The problem with Burgundy is that it's confusing. The region is fractured into 100 appellations, and each wine is called by the name of its appellation, rather than Burgundy. To know that a wine labeled Corton-Charlemagne comes from Burgundy, one has to know the appellations.

Compound the hundred appellations with several hundred wineries, some of whom have only an acre or two of vineyards from which they make wine and each of which has its own style, and it's exasperatingly difficult to get a grip on the place and its wines. Burgundy experts spend their lives trying to parse the different character of Chardonnay each vineyard gives and getting to know the style of each producer.

Off the Vine

Most all white wines from Burgundy are made entirely from Chardonnay, but it's worth seeking out the very few made from Aligoté, a grape known for its tart, mouthwatering qualities. Any white Burgundy wine made from Aligoté will say so prominently on the label; if the label lists no grape, it's a Chardonnay.

For those of us who don't have a lifetime, though, an overview will do. We can break the region down geographically into three major parts, each of which has a slightly different style:

◆ Chablis

◆ Côte d'Or

◆ Mâconnais

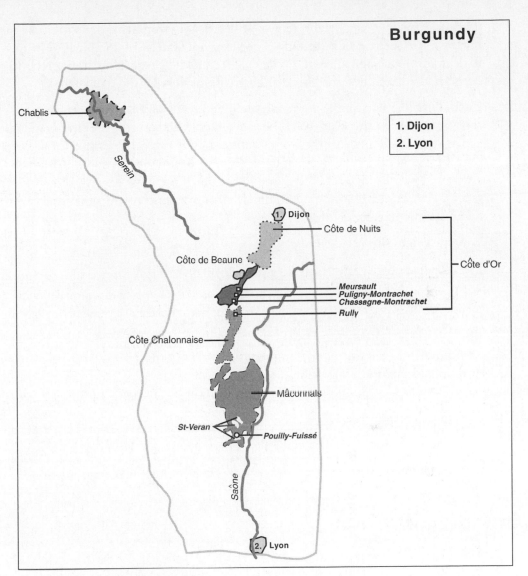

Burgundy's major Chardonnay areas.

Chablis is not a style of wine; it's a place, and the wines that come from that place are 100 percent Chardonnay and are also called Chablis. Its wines are so revered that winemakers all over the world have borrowed the name for their own white wines, though none comes close to the real article.

Chablis earns its crisp, bright, mineral-filled flavors from its unique position, far northwest of the rest of Burgundy. The very cool climate in combination with a soil high in limestone and ancient oyster shells (no joking) makes for lean, green Chardonnays that seem designed for drinking with oysters on the half shell.

Côte d'Or (Golden Slope) is a name you'll never see on a label, but if you get to know the regions inside this area, you'll be acquainted with some of the finest (and most expensive) Chardonnay in the world. This region is typically divided into two parts: the Côte de Nuits in the north and the Côte de Beaune in the south. Although Chardonnay grows throughout both parts, in the north it competes with Pinot Noir for space (see Chapter 10); most Chardonnay vines are clustered in the southern part. Some appellations to look for include …

- St-Aubin: simple, earthy.

- Meursault: rich, mineral-filled, even pleasantly funky.

- Puligny-Montrachet: cool, steely.

- Chassagne-Montrachet: opulent, citrus-tinged.

Mâconnais lies farthest south, and tends to offer the most affordable wines in white Burgundy. Look for wines from these appellations:

- Mâcon: mostly simple, medium-bodied Chardonnay (and a few outstanding, more complex examples)

- Pouilly-Fuissé: rich, mineral-laden Chardonnays

- St-Veran: between Mâcon and Pouilly-Fuissé in richness and minerality

Burgundy, in More Detail

There's one more thing to know about Burgundy: the vineyards are ranked by quality, as determined by the local authorities. Theoretically, the divisions are made on geographical differences that affect quality, though sometimes politics factor in. The ranks, in ascending order of greatness, are as follows:

- Region: Basic Bourgogne (Burgundy in French) can come from anywhere within Burgundy's boundaries. Most are everyday wines; some are surprisingly good for the $10 to $20 price.

- District wines come from within more specific areas of Burgundy, like the Côte de Beaune. Some of these wines append "-Villages" to their name, indicating that they are made from grapes grown in a more specific area of the district.

- Village wines, also called commune wines, are made from grapes from within a specific village that's been officially recognized: Chassagne-Montrachet, for instance.

- Premier Cru wines come from grapes grown in one or more of 561 vineyards deemed premier.

Quick Sips

Burgundy's White Wine Grand Crus

   Bâtard-Montrachet

   Bienvenues-Bâtard-Montrachet

   Bonnes-Mares

   Chablis Grand Cru

   Charlemagne

   Chevalier-Montrachet

   Corton-Charlemagne

   Criots-Bâtard-Montrachet

   Montrachet

- Grand Cru wines are the most esteemed in Burgundy. Made from grapes grown in one of the 33 vineyards designated as such, these vineyards are so highly regarded that the bottles bear only the name of the vineyard with no mention of Grand Cru. But don't worry; the price is usually a dead giveaway, starting at about $50 and soaring into the triple digits.

The Rest of France

Chardonnay also grows throughout the rest of France, most notably in Champagne, where it's turned into sparkling wines (see Chapter 18). The tiny, overlooked region of Limoux in the western Languedoc makes some waxy, spicy Chardonnay on its own and in combination with Pinot Blanc, but with few exceptions, the rest of the south of France puts out gallons of simple, juicy Chardonnay most notable for its low prices.

Quick Sips

Burgundy lovers will want to take advantage of the fanatical coverage of the region available on www.burgundy-report.com (free) and www.burghound.com (subscription).

California Gold

California's Chardonnay has become a serious challenge to that of France, at least in popularity. The state grows more of it than any other wine grape variety—nearly 97,000 acres in 2005, compared to runner-up Cabernet Sauvignon at almost 75,000—growing it from as far south as Temecula up to Mendocino, the state's most northern AVA, or wine-growing region. Much of the state's production comes from the hot Central Valley, where the grapes grow fast and heavy with sun-soaked sweetness. Far more interesting Chardonnay comes from cooler places, though that doesn't necessarily mean more northerly; altitude, wind, and fog can also provide buffers from heat. Here's a short list of top AVAs for Chardonnay:

♦ Sonoma County sprawls from the mountains out to the ocean, and so it's tough to generalize, but the subregions of Sonoma Coast, Russian River Valley, and Chalk Hill stand out for Chardonnay.

♦ Carneros straddles both Napa and Sonoma counties. It's defined by its position at the northern tip of San Francisco Bay, which ensures cool breezes and fog that make for a long, even growing season and allow Chardonnay to retain its acidity even as it gets sweetly ripe.

♦ Edna Valley makes the best of the cool winds off Morro Bay and abundant sun to produce Chardonnay that's luscious with lemon curd flavors.

Prices for California Chardonnay run the gamut. Expect to pay $10 to $16 for simple versions and $20 to $40 or more for significantly more complex wines.

Sour Grapes

Oak barrels were originally intended for maturing wines, not adding flavor, but people have come to love oak's vanillin flavors so much that it's often used just for flavor these days. Oak barrels are expensive, though, so many bargain-priced wines get their oaky flavor from oak chips, dust, or planks that are stirred in rather than from time spent in oak barrels. The result is akin to artificial vanilla flavor, okay, but not the same as real vanilla extract. It won't hurt you, but it may well taste a little fake, a little too obvious. Unfortunately, there's no way to tell from the wine label if oak chips were used, but if a wine seems too inexpensive to be true, it probably is.

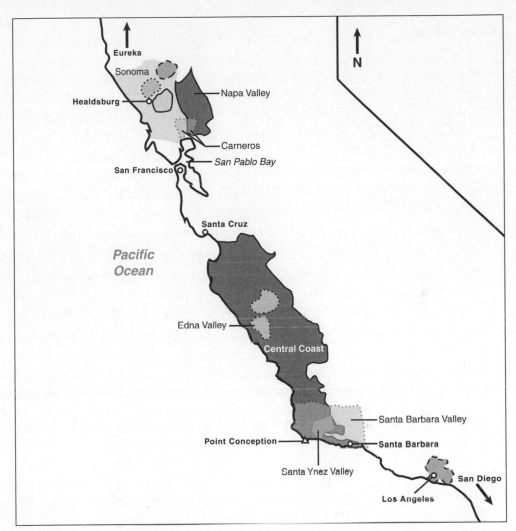

California's wine-growing regions.

Other Standouts

In North America, New York State is putting out some good Chardonnays from the chilly climes of Long Island. Across the northern border, Ontario holds promise; studies that showed climate similarities with Burgundy resulted in thousands of acres of Chardonnay plantings recently.

Quick Sips

When you want fresh, light, bright-tasting wine, look for the term *unoaked* on the label, especially in Australian Chardonnay, since the Aussies pioneered the style. This means that instead of fermenting or maturing the wine in oak barrels, it was kept in nonreactive containers like stainless-steel tanks.

On the other side of North America, the cool climes of British Columbia make for some good, nervy Chardonnay. Warmer Washington State puts out a host of examples, some as crisp as its apples, others as rich as *tarte tatin*, though they remain overshadowed by the state's excellent reds. Most run less than $25.

In the opposite hemisphere, South America turns most of its Chardonnay into cheap, everyday white wine, though a few exceptional wines come out of higher altitudes in Argentina, like Tupungato, and from Chile's ocean-cooled Casablanca Valley. The best examples are worth the $20 they might ask.

New Zealand makes some minerally, apple-crisp Chardonnay, though few reach the heights of its Sauvignon Blanc (see Chapter 5), even though there's more Chardonnay than Sauvignon planted. The best tend to come from the warmer North Island, grown in regions like Gisborne. Prices start at $10 but quickly rise beyond $20.

South Africa also makes some good Chardonnay, but the leader in quality in the Southern Hemisphere is Australia, where Chardonnay competes only with Shiraz for most-planted grape. The most elegant come from the ocean-cooled vineyards of Western Australia and the higher elevation of Adelaide Hills in South Australia. In these areas, Chardonnay retains a graceful structure of firm, ripe fruit supported with vibrant acidity. The majority, however, come from Riverland, a huge, generally warm region that covers many acres of high-production flatlands. The wines from this area are typically labeled Southeastern Australia, for the large area that encompasses Riverland, and they are mostly everyday quaffs with fruit cocktail flavors and, frequently, a generous dollop of vanilla from oak. These can be found for $10 or less; spend another $5 to $10 for significantly more elegant wines, and upward of $60 for very special bottlings.

France isn't the only European country with acres of Chardonnay. Italy has grown the grape for decades, with varying success, from light, crisp quaffers from the north to torridly rich, oaky monsters from Sicily. (Prices range as widely.) Most of Austria's Chardonnay comes from Styria, south of Vienna, where the sunny-but-cool climate makes for some mouthwatering guava-flavored beauties. They tend to run $20 to $40.

Tastings: What's Your Style?

It's one thing to read about these different styles of Chardonnay—the light, green apple style, for instance, or the bigger, richer, butter-bomb kind—and another to taste them. Tasting is the only way you'll really know what appeals to you. One taste may not be enough, either; that crisp, bright Chardonnay that feels so refreshing in midsummer could taste thin and mean when it's 10 below outside. These tastings will illuminate all the styles outlined previously. The wines suggested in these tastings, and all the tastings that follow in upcoming chapters, are just suggestions of a style; they are not necessarily the best examples, nor are they the only possibilities. Use them simply as a guideline for style; if you can't find/don't like/can't afford a listed wine, ask a salesperson to suggest something like it. You don't even need to buy the wines if you imagine well as you read. Keep in mind that your taste is your taste; there are no rights and wrongs.

Plain, or à la Mode?

Any unoaked Chardonnay: Trevor Jones Virgin Chardonnay or Mad Fish Unoaked from Australia; Four Vines Naked, Iron Horse Unoaked, or Domaine Chandon Unoaked from California, for example

An oaked Chardonnay from Australia or California such as Fetzer Barrel Select, Kendall-Jackson Vintner's Reserve, or R.H. Phillips Toasted Head from California or Grant Burge, Jacob's Creek, or Wolf Blass Yellow Label

In this tasting the differences are night and day. Take two wines, one oaked and the other not, from the list above or your own choice. Pour them side by side. Compare the colors: oaked whites usually have a deeper color. Now smell each: unadorned with oak's toasty scents, unoaked Chardonnay tends to smell bright, snappy, refreshing. Does one smell warmer, richer, toastier? Taste the unoaked Chardonnay and then the oaked one. They taste like they smell, right? Which one do you prefer? Which would you rather drink with a raw oyster? With creamy clam chowder?

Northern Reserve vs. Southern Hospitality

A Chardonnay from a cold climate like Pouilly-Fuissé or Mâcon in Burgundy, France, or Mendocino in California

A Chardonnay from a warm climate like Languedoc, France; Southeastern Australia; or Paso Robles, California

The cooler the climate, the longer it takes for a grape to ripen, and the more acidity it retains. For Chardonnay, that means the grape gets fully ripe and yet tastes cool and crisp like a Granny Smith apple. Grown in a warmer place, Chardonnay can become as luscious as flambéed pineapple. Often, the difference is visible: warmer-climate wines tend to be more golden as if the grapes got a suntan. Those warmer wines also tend to smell more effusively fruity, whereas the cold-climate Chardonnays smell more of cold, hard earth (a positive aspect, really!). Taste the wines, and see if you can tell which is which. In most cases, the cooler-climate wines feel crisper, fresher, brighter; in comparison, the wines from warmer places recall apple pie in soft, generous, baked-fruit flavor. The former would be excellent with a simple piece of poached fish; the latter is full-bodied enough to match something steakier, like salmon or swordfish.

Vineyard Matters

A Sonoma Coast Chardonnay like Flowers, Hartford Court, La Crema Sonoma Coast, or Peay

A Russian River Chardonnay like Fritz, Gallo of Sonoma Laguna, Marimar Estate, or Rochioli

A Dry Creek Valley Chardonnay such as one from Alderbrook, Ferrari-Carano, or Handley

Off the Vine

For a dramatic example of the power of terroir, save your pennies for a white Burgundy tasting. Find a producer who makes white wines from several different vineyards within an appellation—say, Chassagne-Montrachet—and taste the wines side by side. The differences you taste will be mainly due to differences in the vineyard plots, even if the vineyards are side by side.

A matter of a few feet can make a big difference in the world of wine, if those few feet mark a change in temperature, soil content, sunshine, wind, or whatever. Here, all these wines are from Sonoma County; each grouping, however, is from a different part of the county.

As we know from earlier reading, the cooler the region, the more acidity Chardonnay retains and the crisper it feels. Sonoma Coast takes advantage of the cool, salty breezes off the Pacific to keep its vineyards cool all summer long, giving them a long, slow growing season. The Russian River Valley follows the river inland where it's warmer, but it pulls cool sea air down its length, creating cool morning fog that slows ripening of the grapes. Dry Creek Valley, on the other hand, might be farther north, but it's so warm in this valley that red grapes like Zinfandel thrive. Chardonnay ripens deeper and faster here than in cooler areas toward the sea.

With all that in mind, line up a Chardonnay from each place. Look at the colors. Is one a deeper gold than the other two? Smell them. Can you smell the one that baked longest in the sun? Is there one that smells so crisp in comparison that you can imagine a chilly sea breeze? Taste them, and see if the crispness of the fruit and the richness of the fruit flavors reflect the relative warmth of the place from which it came.

The Least You Need to Know

- All white wines from Burgundy are made from Chardonnay unless otherwise clearly specified on the label.

- The cooler the climate, the crisper the Chardonnay.

- The warmer the place, the richer the Chardonnay.

- Oak can bulk up Chardonnay's flavor with sweet vanilla, spice, and toasty notes.

- If you prefer light, crisp wines, look for Chardonnays that are free of oak.

- When bigger and richer is better, look for bottlings that have spent time in oak barrels.

Sauvignon Blanc

In This Chapter

- ◆ Recognizing Sauvignon Blanc
- ◆ Places to find the best Sauvignon Blanc
- ◆ A definition for Fumé Blanc?
- ◆ Sauvignons for different situations

Sauvignon Blanc: there's no mistaking this one. It's the one that screams *green* from first whiff, the one that seems to urge, "Over here! Over here!" with its pungent scent. Even its almost colorless juice can have a slightly green cast. Sauvignon's singular scent has even gained it one of the most memorable descriptors of any grape: cat pee—although, of course, the best taste far better than that description suggests.

Sauvignon Blanc's bracing green fruit and herbal flavors have gained popularity over the years, especially in the wake of the heavy, buttery Chardonnays of the 1990s that left people's palates piqued. If you haven't discovered Sauvignon's refreshing joys, it's time. Read on.

The Smell of Sauvignon

"Cat's Pee on a Gooseberry Bush" is the name of one New Zealand Sauvignon Blanc, and, though I've never smelled a gooseberry bush that's been peed on by a cat, the name pretty much sums up the wine's scent at its extreme. It's green: green as a tart green gooseberry or a barely ripe green grape.

> **Quick Sips**
>
> Sauvignon at a glance: high acid, bright green flavors, from vegetation, like grass, herbs, peppers; fruit like green grapes, limes, melons, figs, passion fruit, or guavas; and mineral, like chalk and seashells.

Like any grape, Sauvignon Blanc tastes a little different from place to place. Sometimes—especially in warmer regions or warm vintages—the grape's green flavors might reach a rounder, richer ripeness, recalling fig, melon, or even guava, but it's still undeniably green.

More usually, the grape's scents recall grass, herbs, and vegetables more than any fruit. Add to this a snappy, lively high acidity, and you've got a head-turner of a wine.

Some vintners mature Sauvignon Blanc in oak to tame the grape's lean greenness, but rarely does oak play a large part in its flavors. If anything, it's used to give the wine a rounder texture and a slight toasty note. Most vintners, in fact, opt to keep the wine in nonreactive vessels like stainless-steel tanks to preserve its bright, crisp flavors.

Many vintners also employ battonage—that is, they let the wine rest on its lees and stir them up occasionally. This gives the wine a creamy feel that helps balance its acidity.

> **Sour Grapes**
>
> There is such a thing as too green in Sauvignon Blanc; when a Sauvignon smells like jalapeño peppers or pungent cat pee, chances are the grapes weren't ripe enough when they were picked.

So why might you want to drink Sauvignon Blanc? For the same reasons you'd sprinkle parsley over a bowl of bland buttered pasta: it provides a shock of freshness, a splash of color, a lively flavor that brightens everything up. Sauvignon Blanc at any time of the year is a liquid taste of spring: cool, quenching, and—yes—green. Plus, Sauvignon's flavors are often so light, bright, and free of oak that mineral notes shine through, adding complexity.

The Taste of Minerality

If there's anything besides fruit, grass, and herbs a vintner wants to capture in a Sauvignon Blanc, it's minerals. Because the grape's flavors are powerful without being heavy, Sauvignon Blanc is a terrific vehicle for terroir, that flavor particular to a place and its soils. For instance, in the wines from Pouilly in France's Loire, which are made from 100 percent Sauvignon Blanc, the best wines exhibit such a distinct smoky character from the region's particular mix of minerals in the soil that the wines are called Pouilly-Fumé (poo-*eee* foo-*may*), "smoked Pouilly" in translation. Steely is another description associated with Sauvignon Blanc: there is, of course, no steel in the soil, but the wine's clean, cold, hard flavors can recall the cool, metallic smoothness of steel. In France, this minerality is a defining element of Sauvignon Blanc.

Quick Sips _____

Are you confused by the idea of minerality in wines? Buy some mineral waters and taste them side by side; smell a wet blackboard to get an idea of slate; crumble some limestone in your hand; run your hand along a rusty cast-iron fence (carefully) and then smell it; go outside after a rain and try to describe the scent. You may or may not find these same scents in wines, but they'll get you thinking in a mineral direction.

Where Sauvignon Shines

As Sauvignon Blanc becomes more popular, its domain widens, following Chardonnay from one end of the earth to the other. However, whereas Chardonnay thrives just about anywhere, Sauvignon Blanc's most stellar examples belong firmly to the cooler climates of the world.

Some places that particularly stand out for their pure Sauvignon Blancs are …

- ◆ France's Loire
- ◆ New Zealand
- ◆ South Africa
- ◆ Chile's Casablanca Valley
- ◆ California's Napa and Sonoma Valleys

Sauvignon Blanc is also frequently used in blends, particularly with the Semillon grape, which is popular in Australia and Bordeaux, France.

Lovin' the Loire

To taste definitive Sauvignon Blanc, go to the historical source, France's Loire, where it's made some of the region's best wines for hundreds of years.

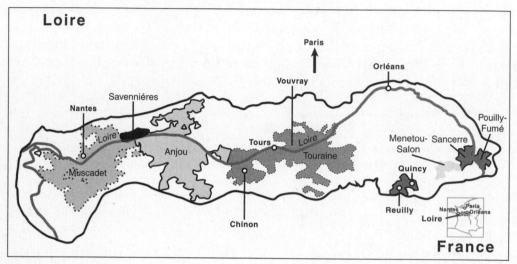

France's Loire region.

As with most French wines, Loire wines don't list the grape on the label but are labeled instead by place. The names that Sauvignon Blanc seekers need to know, in order of relative importance, are ...

- ◆ Sancerre.
- ◆ Pouilly-Fumé.
- ◆ Menetou-Salon.
- ◆ Quincy.
- ◆ Reuilly.

Now, a few different grapes grow along the 250 miles of the Loire Valley, where the Loire River pulls the cold winds of the Atlantic down its length. Sauvignon Blanc likes to grow on the eastern end, out of the reach of the ocean's influences and nearly smack-dab in the middle of the country.

In the central Loire, the weather is more dramatic than it is at the Atlantic's edge, with colder winters and warmer summers. Still, warmer is relative; little is balmy about the Loire, and in cooler summers, the grapes struggle to ripen. This coolness helps Sauvignon Blanc retain its bright, fresh acidity, and keeps its flavors lean.

Off the Vine

Many wine regions are along bodies of water—lakes, rivers, and oceans. Why? Besides the fact that these geographical features tend to offer slopes, which vines love to climb, and provide needed water and humidity, large bodies of water also tend to moderate the climate because they take a longer time to heat up and cool down than the land around them. This means the plants around them have a buffer against very hot and very cold days year-round.

There's also a lot of limestone in the Loire's soils, which gives Sauvignon Blanc a mineral note that recalls chalk or the smoky scent of struck flint.

In Sancerre, the calcium content is particularly high, and its Sauvignon wines taste like it; a good Sancerre tastes almost like chalk, dry and mineral, with just a hint of fruit. Sancerre is a large region, some 3,458 acres, so not all its wines show this mineral character to the same degree, but even a simple Sancerre will taste more mineral and herbal than overtly fruity.

The Sauvignon Blanc of Pouilly-Fumé, a 692-acre area just east of Sancerre, is quite similar to Sancerre's—most people would be hard-pressed to taste the difference, actually—but the soils of Pouilly are said to give the region's wines a smoked note; thus the *fumé* ("smoked" in French) of Pouilly-Fumé.

Quick Sips

Don't confuse Pouilly-Fumé with Pouilly-Fuissé, a wine made of Chardonnay from the appellation of the same name in Burgundy, France.

Menetou-Salon, Quincy, and Reuilly are not as large or well known as either Sancerre and Pouilly-Fumé, but they offer great value. Their simplest wines offer crisp Sauvignon Blanc flavors; their best can be every bit as good as Sancerre sans the hype and high price.

As the oldest, most famous appellations for Sauvignon Blanc, Sancerre and Pouilly-Fumé can command high prices, ranging upward of $50, though most hover between $16 and $30. When the wines are good, they earn their price, offering the sort of minerality that only these regions offer. Any cheaper than that here, and you have reason to be suspicious.

However, wines from Menetou-Salon, Quincy, and Reuilly will often give the same bang for less buck—more like $11 to $20.

New Zealand: Extreme Kiwi

Though France's Loire boasts what's often pointed to as archetypical Sauvignon Blanc, the best-known example these days is often New Zealand's.

New Zealand has only been making wine in significant commercial quantities for a little over 30 years, yet its Sauvignon Blanc quickly put it on the wine map. This is the sort of Sauvignon you can recognize from across the room with no name tag needed, though the label will always say what grape is in the bottle. It announces itself with a pungent, bright green note, somewhere between the rich, acidic green flesh of a kiwi and all the greenness of a freshly mowed golf course. It is, after all, the Sauvignon Blanc that gave rise to a wine named Cat's Pee on a Gooseberry Bush ....

Quick Sips

Some of New Zealand's best Sauvignon Blanc comes from the appellations Marlborough, at the northern end of the South Island, and Martinborough, at the southern end of the North Island.

The thing is, almost everyone loves New Zealand Sauvignon Blanc. It's loud and brazen, green as a lime; it's luscious, too, in its own tart, lean way. Nothing is complicated about it; it's just pure Sauvignon Blanc flavor, loud and clear. Prices for New Zealand Sauvignon Blanc are pretty steady; most good examples ask between $11 and $30.

Off the Vine

Don't be surprised if you find New Zealand Sauvignon Blancs sealed with screw caps instead of corks. The country has been one of the most enthusiastic adapters of screw caps, which are preferred by many vintners as a surer way to preserve the bright, fresh flavors of their signature Sauvignon Blancs.

New Zealand's wine regions.

South Africa's Stellar Sauvignon Blanc

South Africa gets a lot of press for its red wines, but to me, the country's Sauvignon Blanc is where it's at. The grape thrives in regions toward the southern end of the Cape of Good Hope, like Stellenbosch or Constantia, a rocky outcrop that juts into the sea. In these areas, the chilly breezes off the cold, salty water cool the vines so they ripen their fruit slowly, retaining acidity while piling on flavor. The result is wines that paint a liquid portrait of the place: sunny, stony, and cool with a warm heart. Talk about mouthwatering!

While some good South African Sauvignon Blancs cost from $8 to $10, the very best run $15 to $25 and can compete with like-priced examples from France's Loire.

Australia's Other White Wine

For years, most of Australia's Sauvignon Blanc provided a sharp, bright note in a sea of white wines made from blends of grapes, most of which come from the sprawling appellation of Southeastern Australia. These white blends still exist and at less than $15 can be terrific buys for summertime sipping and parties.

Off the Vine _____

Australia, like the United States, is still in the process of defining its wine-growing regions, but it has established a system of *Geographical Indicators (GIs)*, which are the appellations you'll see on Australian wine labels.

In the late 1990s, however, some gorgeous examples began emerging from South Australia's Adelaide Hills. This hilly, wooded region sits at a higher altitude than much of the surrounding land in South Australia, so it enjoys cooler temperatures than most of the generally warm region, yet it gets just as much sun. So the Sauvignon Blanc soaks up the sun and ripens slowly and completely, ripening from the more typical gooseberry fruit into green plum jam flavors. Rich as it is, it's not heavy: the acidity flows through it like a cool breeze on a hot day, invigorating, lively.

Quick Sips _____

Most of Australia's best Sauvignon Blanc wines come from the Adelaide Hills, where the altitude of the Mount Lofty Ranges keeps the vines cool.

A sea of Aussie Sauvignon Blanc sells for under $10, but the $11 to $16 range is a surer bet. It rarely costs more than $25.

South America's Best White Wine

Climate, culture, and history have dictated that South America's best wines are red. However, in the recent past, Chile has emerged with a white winner: Sauvignon Blanc. Not every part of Chile is as successful with the picky grape as others; in fact, most of the country produces Sauvignon Blanc that trades in the grape's hallmark flavors for undistinguished but affordable juice.

In Casablanca, the story's different. Long thought to be too chilly to grow grapes well, this coastal region was long ignored by vintners until Pablo Morandé came along. The winemaker, who'd worked for a bunch of the big wineries, suspected the region's cooler climate would be excellent for Pinot Noir. A few others followed him, and by the 1990s, the area was planted with grapevines thought to do well in cooler areas, like Chardonnay, Pinot Noir, and Sauvignon Blanc.

Today, Casablanca's Sauvignon Blanc is stellar, with smooth, ripe, almost guava-like flavors and refreshing acidity.

The region's success with the variety has inspired vintners to push into other coastal regions previously believed too cool to grow grapes well. Examples from the San Antonio Valley, especially the subregion Valle de Leyda, are showing great promise.

Overall, Chilean Sauvignon Blanc is a great deal; expect basic bottlings to run $8 to $15, with a few exceptional examples reaching into the $20s and low $30s.

U.S. Sauvignon

The backlash among wine lovers against Chardonnay in the 1990s was the best thing that ever happened to Sauvignon Blanc in the United States. Tired of heavy, buttery flavors, people began flocking to Sauvignon's greener pastures, newly appreciative of its lighter, brighter flavors.

As one of the most recognized grapes in the world, Sauvignon Blanc is grown all over the States, but it excels in only a few places: the cooler reaches of California and Washington State.

California's Sauvignon Blanc falls somewhere between New Zealand's and France's in terms of flavor. It's not as lean and minerally as in the Loire, nor is it as pungent and green as a kiwi. In the sunny warmth of California, it tends to be softer, smoother, more relaxed—perhaps just more Californian.

Many California vintners also age a small proportion of their Sauvignon Blanc in oak—a practice popularized by Robert Mondavi, who coined the name Fumé Blanc for his oaked Sauvignon Blanc in the late 1960s. The oak adds a toasty richness to the wine.

Quick Sips

In the United States, Fumé Blanc is synonymous with Sauvignon Blanc. It typically, but not always, indicates a wine that has had a little oak aging to give it a fuller, toasty flavor.

In California, Sonoma and Napa Valley claim most of the state's best Sauvignon Blanc, the cooler regions of both striking a balance between the grape's herbal characters and its richer, melon-ball side. Mendocino, California's most northerly appellation, puts out some good examples, often blended with grapes from the warmer Lake County farther inland to strike a balance between grassy and melony. Look also to Santa Ynez and Monterey if you like the herbaceous style and to Santa Barbara for the more lush, melony side of Sauvignon Blanc.

Just because Washington State is farther north doesn't mean it's a cool wine-growing area. In fact, most of the wine regions fall on the eastern side of the Cascades, where winters are frigid, but summers can be torrid and dry. Because of this, red varieties tend to stand out more than white (Cabernet Sauvignon, Merlot, and Syrah especially), but the Columbia Valley churns out some good Sauvignon Blanc. The best are lighter and brighter than many California versions, with lemony flavors and an herbal edge.

Prices for American Sauvignon are all over the board, and while you can find some good choices under $10, bottles that run $12 to $20 are a better bet.

Off the Vine

In addition to the Sauvignon Blancs covered here, check out Blanc from Northeastern Italy, especially if you prefer it clean and lean. Some of the best come from Friuli's cool climate. If you prefer a richer style, cross the border into Austria, where sunny Styria puts out Sauvignons that balance their rich, smooth fruit and grassy, bright acidity. Good examples of each tend to run $20 to $30.

Sauvignon's Soul Mate, Semillon

A significant proportion of the world's Sauvignon Blanc gets blended with other grapes, Semillon (sem-ee-*yon*, or, in Australia, sem-ill-*on*) most significantly. On its own, Semillon tends to be waxy and rather bland, like raw almonds, when young. As it ages, its satiny texture can develop luscious flavors of honey, figs, and roasted nuts, but few vintners these days make Semillon to age. Instead, they blend it with a little Sauvignon Blanc to add crispness and lively flavor to Semillon's lush texture.

The model for Sauvignon Blanc blends tends to be Bordeaux, France, where Sauvignon Blanc is often blended with Semillon, although some forgo the Semillon in favor of light, crisp, tart Sauvignon Blanc wines.

The most exalted examples come from Graves and its subregion Pessac-Leognan, where the Sauvignon Blanc–Semillon blends can age for years, taking on rich flavors of honeyed nuts and caramelized oranges that are worthy of fancy lobster dinners. As you might guess, the prices are as exalted. Most of us will spend more time looking for wines labeled Bordeaux Sec and Entre-Deux-Mers, most of which run a more reasonable $15 or less. Bordeaux Sec can be produced from Sauvignon Blanc and Semillon grown anywhere in Bordeaux; Entre-Deux-Mers grows between the Garonne and Dordogne rivers, as its name, Between-Two-Seas, suggests (rivers, seas: close enough); both seem designed to be drunk cold with a platter of seafood plucked from the local waters—or a cold salad on a hot day.

Quick Sips

Most white wines in Bordeaux are made from Sauvignon Blanc, sometimes in tandem with Semillon. You'll find them labeled by region: Bordeaux Sec, Entre-Deux-Mers, Graves, or its subregion, Pessac-Leognan.

Outside of France, Australia is the place to look for Semillon, on its own or in tandem with Sauvignon. The country's best Semillon age to a beautiful golden hue, redolent of figs, wax, and honey; in combination with Sauvignon, it makes easy-drinking, limey blends that rarely exceed $16.

In the United States, Washington State grows excellent Semillon, with a full, satiny texture and honeyed citrus flavors that blend well with the bright, green crispness of Sauvignon Blanc.

Tastings: Find Your Sauvignon Style

Every good Sauvignon Blanc in the world, regardless of where it's grown, has Sauvignon's hallmark green streak, whether the green is interpreted as fruit, herb, or vegetable. But the degree of greenness changes according to climate and style; it may be a background note, reflecting minerality, as in the Loire, or it may be front and center as in New Zealand.

All have their lovers, but which style is for you? Which one would you pick for oysters on the half shell, and which one for sipping *en plein aire?*

This array of tastings will help you determine the differences between one and another and to develop a grasp of the different styles. Any brands listed are only suggestions of wines that fit a style; any other wines in a similar style will do as well.

> **Off the Vine**
>
> Every year, Taylor Shellfish Farms in Shelton, Washington, assembles a panel of oyster-loving judges to find the best West Coast wine for West Coast oysters, like Kumamotos. And the winners in 2008 were? Note how many are Sauvignon Blanc:
>
> Amity Vineyards 2006 Pinot Blanc (OR)
>
> Chateau Ste. Michelle 2006 Columbia Valley Sauvignon Blanc (WA)
>
> Clayhouse Vineyard 2006 Sauvignon Blanc (CA)
>
> Clos du Bois 2006 Sauvignon Blanc (CA)
>
> Covey Run 2006 Fumé Blanc (WA)
>
> Dry Creek Vineyard 2006 Sonoma County Fumé Blanc (CA)
>
> Girard Winery 2006 Sauvignon Blanc (CA)
>
> Kathryn Kennedy Winery 2007 Sauvignon Blanc (CA)
>
> Robledo Family Winery 2006 Sauvignon Blanc (CA)
>
> Simi 2006 Sauvignon Blanc (CA)
>
> Van Duzer Vineyards 2007 Pinot Blanc (OR)
>
> Willamette Valley Vineyards 2007 Pinot Gris (OR)

France vs. New Zealand

A Loire Sauvignon Blanc, such as a Sancerre or a Pouilly-Fumé

A New Zealand Sauvignon Blanc

It makes no difference which wines you pick for this tasting; Loire and New Zealand Sauvignon Blancs are both considered archetypical styles, yet they are at such opposite ends of the spectrum that the differences will be clear regardless the exact bottling. Which one's for you?

Hold on! Before you taste these wines, stop and smell them. Which one smells like it'll be the stronger tasting of the two? The New Zealand Sauvignon jumps from the glass with bright green notes. The Loire Sauvignon, on the other hand, is more restrained and smells like it's from a cold place, all cold stone and taut, barely ripe fruit. To me, it recalls chalk and seashells.

Now taste, Loire first, as the aggressive New Zealand Sauvignon will out-shout the subtler Loire wine. Do you like its cold, minerally flavors? Imagine this wine next to a platter of cold oysters on the half shell.

Now taste the New Zealand Sauvignon Blanc. Is it more reminiscent of stones or of kiwis? Do you like its more generous flavors? Imagine it next to that same platter of oysters; does it work for you?

Fresh or Smoked?

Unoaked American Sauvignon Blanc, like Cakebread, Chateau Souverain, Frog's Leap, Matanzas Creek, or most other California bottlings

Oaked American Sauvignon Blanc, such as a Fumé Blanc from Chateau St. Jean, Dry Creek Vineyards, Grgich, or Robert Mondavi Winery

Most Sauvignon Blanc is made in stainless-steel tanks to preserve the grape's brightness and freshness. Some winemakers choose to ferment or age a portion of their wine in oak barrels to round out the wine's naturally sharp edges and give it a little more richness. Pour an unoaked and an oaked Sauvignon Blanc side by side and then smell them.

Can you tell which one has spent time in oak? While the oak notes may not be as obvious as the vanilla and toast scents that occur frequently in Chardonnays, oak typically gives Sauvignon Blanc extra richness compared to a sharp, grassy, unoaked Sauvignon Blanc.

Taste the wines, starting with the unoaked version. Which one's richer? Does the unoaked version taste crisper than the oaked version? Which one would you prefer on a hot day? On a cold day?

Differences Down Under

A South African Sauvignon Blanc, like Le Bonheur, Mulderbosch, Thelema, Vergelegen, or any other from Stellenbosch or the Western Cape

A Chilean Sauvignon Blanc from Casablanca Valley, like Casa Marín, Concha y Toro Terrunyo, Morandé, or Viña Leyda

> An Australian Sauvignon-Semillon blend such as Jacob's Creek, Lindemans, Tyrrell's, or any other

These two Sauvignon Blancs and one Sauvignon Blanc-based blend are all from the Southern Hemisphere. All three places are relatively new to their Sauvignon Blanc fame, and all have a characteristic style. Can you tell the difference among the three? Most of South Africa's Sauvignon Blancs come from the Western Cape, where cold breezes buffet vines that hang on to a stony plateau. Chile's best come from a maritime clime as well, although the chill isn't quite as dramatic. Australia makes some crisp, cold-climate Sauvignon Blanc, too, but blends of Sauvignon with Semillon are more popular. These tend to come from the warm flats of Southeastern Australia, where Sauvignon Blanc gets juicy with fruit flavors; Semillon's smooth texture accentuates the richness of the fruit with its own smooth texture.

Line the wines up and smell each of them. Does one smell less fruity and less ripe than the others? Is the Australian blend less distinctly green and Sauvignon-like?

Taste them now, South Africa first, the blend last. Can you feel the coolness of the vineyards in the mineral flavors and bright acidity of the South African wine? Does the blend taste softer in comparison? How about the Chilean wine? Can you taste the sun in the ripe green fruit, yet feel the sea breeze in the wine's bright acidity?

The Least You Need to Know

- Sauvignon Blanc makes white wines with high acidity and a hallmark green note—green fruit, herb, or vegetable.

- For lean, tart, minerally Sauvignon Blanc, look to colder climates, like France's Loire Valley, New Zealand, and Northern Italy.

- For richer, riper, rounder Sauvignon Blanc, look to California, Australia, Austria, and inland Chile.

- To find Sauvignon Blanc wines from France, look for wines labeled Sancerre, Pouilly-Fumé, Quincy, Reuilly, or Menetou-Salon, all of which are made from 100 percent Sauvignon Blanc.

- Fumé Blanc is another name for Sauvignon Blanc in the United States and is typically, but not always, used for oaked versions.

- Sauvignon Blanc is often blended with Semillon; in the New World, wine labels will say so, but in Bordeaux, the blend isn't mentioned on the label.

Chapter 6

Riesling

In This Chapter

- Riesling: the world's greatest grape?
- Riesling's remarkable acidity
- Places Riesling flourishes
- Finding Rieslings for you

Chardonnay may have the biggest fan club of all white wines, but Riesling has the most ardent. Riesling does strange things to people who fall under its spell; some have been known to demand Riesling at every meal. What is it about the nearly colorless wine from this cold-climate grape?

Riesling: The Acid-Head's Grape

Many people think of Riesling as a sweet wine, but there's a lot more to the story. Riesling can produce everything from stone-dry whites to honey-sweet elixirs. Its possible flavors span several octaves, from bass notes of slate to high-pitched lemon zest, with peach, pear, lime, apple—you name it—in between. Getting to know the grape and its habits will help you figure out what kind of Riesling is for you and how to find it.

Riesling's most remarkable trait is its acidity. Whether desert-dry or sweet as syrup, Riesling's acidity stays strong, providing a backbone for the wine's flavors that keeps them firm yet lifted, light on the tongue no matter how substantial. The grape is built like a long-distance runner: lean, lithe, and light, yet strong and built for endurance.

While the majority of Riesling is drunk within a year or two of its vintage date, Riesling's high acidity keeps it fresh and lively far longer than most white wines. The best can age for 20 to 30 years or more, their flavors turning darker, more nutty and mineral while retaining a fresh, lively feel.

A Spoonful of Sweetness ...

Of course, high levels of acidity could be mouth-puckeringly unpleasant without some flavor to balance it. Really dry Rieslings can actually be a little hard to take on their own. The acidity can be so strong it feels like it's etching the tongue. However, give that Riesling something else to sink its acidity into—say, duck or bacon-wrapped dates—and it'll cut right through the richness to relieve the palate for another bite. In this way, Riesling can go where few white wines dare: to rich, full-flavored dishes that are usually more red wine fare.

Since Riesling's acidity is so very high, many vintners will leave a little bit of sugar in the wine to take the edge off. This _residual sugar_ is barely noticeable in a wine with lots of acidity and flavor; it just tastes well balanced.

The Terroirist's Grape

Riesling is also revered by wine lovers who prefer wines that give a sense of a place—terroir—in their flavor. The grape, light and clear as its flavors are, excels in its ability to pick up intense mineral flavors, almost as if it's been fortified with vitamins and minerals. (It hasn't.)

These mineral flavors change with climate, region, even vineyard. Serious terroirists—those who consider terroir the vinous holy grail—debate the various qualities of Rieslings grown in adjacent vineyards in Germany and Alsace with the passion of rockers discussing recordings. Some frequently tossed-around connotations are slate, quartz, and loam. Another commonly heard term is petrol, which is British for gasoline. Petrol is more common to warmer-climate Rieslings than cooler climate ones (for instance, Alsace Riesling has more than those from the Mosel, in general).

Whether a person is a terroirist or a wine lover just looking for a refreshing drink, Riesling comes in styles for everyone. You just have to know where to look to find the one that fits.

Where Riesling Gets Racy

Sauvignon Blanc might like it chilly, but Riesling likes it downright cold. It thrives in places few other major grapes can hack—places where the first frost often hits in November. If the climate is too warm, the grape loses that acid backbone, without which you might as well suck on a lemon lollipop.

In cool places, though, the grape ripens slowly, holding on to its acidity while gathering up flavors. Some of the best come from …

- Germany.
- Alsace, France.
- Austria.
- Australia.
- New York State.

Riesling can also make exceptional sweet, dessert-style wines, some of the best of which come from Ontario, Canada (see Chapter 19).

Germany's Pride

German wines often get short shrift. One look at those gothic labels with all those umlauts on the long words makes most non-German speakers want to run away. But stick with me here. It's worth it because Germany makes arguably the best Riesling in the world. And as scary as the labels look, they aren't that hard to understand. Almost all carry the name of the grape on the label, as well as the name of the region in which it was raised and an indication of the ripeness of the grapes when they were picked—major clues to the style of wine inside.

> **Quick Sips**
>
> Almost all German varietal wines state the grape on the label; if a bottle doesn't list a grape, it's most likely a blend.

Germany's major winegrowing region is a mouthful: the Mosel-Saar-Ruwer—but pros just call it the Mosel. The Mosel is a river in southwest Germany, and the Saar and Ruwer are tributaries that flow into it. The vineyards that blanket the slopes of all three are some of the most dramatic anywhere in the world: steep and curvaceous, cold and covered in stone and vines. Riesling takes up almost every inch.

> **Off the Vine**
>
> It is three times as costly to tend vineyards as steep as the Mosel's as it is vineyards on flat lands.

The river plays an essential part in the climate of the region, reflecting its heat up the slopes to moderate the cold air. It also curves so dramatically that it nearly folds back on itself in many parts, creating south-facing slopes where vines can catch the sun's warming rays. This is important in a region where the first frost can strike as early as mid-November, when Napa Valley's vintners are still gardening.

The vertiginously steep slopes are slippery with slate, which covers the ground like a shattered blackboard. To climb them requires strength and no fear of heights, not to mention help from the extra-tall stakes used to hold the vines upright.

For the vines to hang on, they need to grow deep, strong roots that reach several feet into the earth. There may or may not be a correlation between the depth of a vine's roots and that of its flavor, but it often seems like there is, as the taste of minerals in good German Riesling is so strong. The slate also helps the grapes ripen, as it soaks up sun during the day to reflect its heat back onto the grapes in the chilly nights.

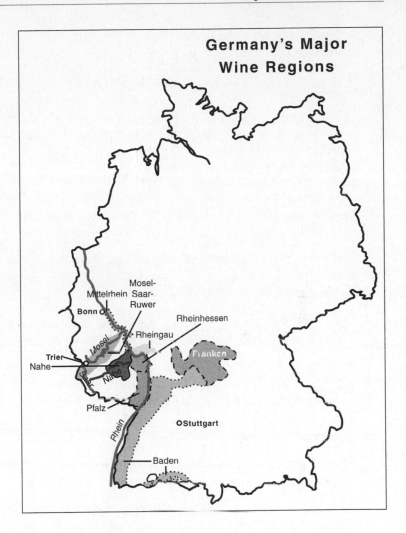

Germany's Major Wine Regions

Beyond the Mosel

While the Mosel is responsible for the majority of Germany's greatest Riesling, it doesn't hold an exclusive contract. Look also to …

◆ Baden.

◆ Franken.

◆ Mittelrhein.

◆ Nahe.

◆ Pfalz.

◆ Rheingau.

◆ Rheinhessen.

◆ Württemburg.

Baden's vineyards spread out through the warm south of the country and contain a cornucopia of grapes, white and red. Its Riesling tends to be simple and affordable.

Winespeak

A **Bocksbeutel** is a squat, round bottle traditionally used by vintners in Franken and northern Baden.

Franken wines are immediately recognizable by their squat, round bottles, called a *Bocksbeutel*. In the relative warmth of this region in central Germany, Riesling grows soft and rich—an easy choice for immediate drinking.

The **Mittelrhein** stretches northwest to southeast across the top of the Mosel region from near Bonn down to the Nahe; most of its vines are Riesling, which make cold, acidic wines in its very cool climate.

Nahe is a fairly large area that flanks the Nahe River. The size makes it hard to generalize, but in the best cases, Nahe Riesling has a warm, pleasant earthiness that distinguishes it from those of other regions.

Pfalz Rieslings are as gentle as the pastoral rolling hills of the region. The warmer weather here makes for ripe, peachy Rieslings with softer acidity than the Mosel's.

Rheingau challenges the Mosel for its Riesling throne. Most all its vineyards rise high above the Rhine on its north bank; a few lay on the lower, warmer south side. Its wines tend to fall somewhere between the Pfalz in fatness and the Mosel in steely minerality. They are at once dry, nervy, and powerful. Riesling is so predominant that many Rheingau vintners don't bother to list it on the label.

Rheinhessen is framed by the Rheingau to the north, Nahe to the west, and Pfalz to the south. It's a major source of bulk wines, but the few good Rieslings that emerge from its steeper vineyards offer a full, earthy flavor.

Württemburg Riesling tends to make country-style whites, easy and a little rough around the edges but delicious nonetheless.

Degrees of Ripeness

One more thing to learn about German wines that will help you choose the right one for you is how to decipher the *Prädikat*. The Prädikat is a measure of how ripe the grapes were when they were harvested. Only the highest level of wines sport a Prädikat; they are called Quality wines with Distinction (*Qualitätswein mit Prädikat* or QmP) to differentiate them from table wines (*Tafelwein*) and straight Quality wines (*Qualitätswein* or QbA). However, a lot of the German wines exported to the United States are QmPs, so it helps to know what the Prädikat signifies.

The Prädikat has five levels, from ripe to ripest:

- Kabinett

- Spätlese (*shpat*-layz-eh)

- Auslese (*ows*-layz-eh)

- Beerenauslese (BA)

- Trockenbeerenauslese (TBA)

Winespeak _____

Prädikat (*pray*-dee-cat) means distinction and signifies the ripeness of the grapes at harvest. It often, but not necessarily, corresponds to the sweetness of the final wine.

In general, the wines get sweeter as you move from Kabinett to Trockenbeerenauslese, but here's the catch: ripeness does not necessarily mean sweetness. That's because a high level of acidity can make a wine with a fair amount of residual sugar taste dry. Furthermore, a vintner can choose to ferment his grapes until no sugar is left, so that regardless how ripe they were, the wine ends up dry. So one winemaker's Spätlese can taste as dry as another vintner's Kabinett.

Sour Grapes _____

Many self-described wine connoisseurs turn up their noses at wines that have a little bit of sweetness. They are missing out. As long as a wine has plenty of acidity, a little sweetness can go far in making it a more friendly drink, rounding out its acid edges and bulking up its fruity flavors. Sweetness without acidity makes a wine feel flabby; sweetness with acidity makes a wine feel more powerful. And besides, slightly sweet wines typically have less alcohol than bone-dry ones—a boon when it comes to matching with spicy food. Don't fear sweetness; Spätlese wines are your friend.

How can you tell how the wine will taste? You can't without tasting it. Generally, you can bet that a Kabinett and Spätlese will be dry enough to drink with dinner, that an Auslese will be fairly sweet, and that most all BAs and TBAs are firmly in the dessert realm.

Off the Vine _____

Sometimes it pays to be late; it did for the messenger of the 1775 harvest, at any rate. Back then, so the story goes, the monks who tended the vineyards at Schloss Johannisberg in the Rheingau had to wait for the Abbot to tell them when they could start to pick the grapes. That year, the abbot was away during harvest, and his message to start picking came late. Though the vintners had been worried that the harvest would be spoiled, the riper grapes turned out to make such good wines that they began to purposely pick their grapes *Spätlese*—late.

If you want to be certain the wine you choose is stone dry, look for the adjective *trocken* on the label. It means dry and signifies that the wine has been fermented until it is dry, regardless how ripe the grapes were. But be forewarned: trocken wines in less ripe vintages can be almost painfully austere.

Winespeak

Trocken means dry and indicates that a wine is dry regardless of its Prädikat. **Halbtrocken** (half-dry) are not as bone-dry as trocken wines, but most have little to no perceptible sweetness.

Vineyards Matter

Okay, I lied; you might want to know one more thing about German wines. You know how I said earlier that Riesling has an extraordinary ability to pick up mineral tastes and other notes particular to a place? Well, it does this so well in Germany that Riesling from adjacent parcels can taste very different just because the soil is different or the slope is less steep or for reasons inexplicable to anyone. Because of this, Germans also label their best Rieslings with the name of the vineyard in which they grew.

Quick Sips

The German Wine Board has an impressively complete guide to the country's wine regions at www.germanwineusa.org. The Riesling Report no longer publishes regular issues, but its extensive, well-written glossary of German wine terms and guide to Riesling producers around the world is available at www.rieslingreport.com.

You can tell which words identify the vineyard on the label by finding the word that ends with er and is followed by one or more words: this is the name of the town where the vineyard is located (important in the case of popular vineyard names like *Sonnenuhr* or Sundial) followed by the name of the vineyard itself. For example, Wehlener Sonnenuhr means from the Sonnenuhr vineyard in the town of Wehlen.

The Mosel alone counts hundreds of vineyards; consider that each vineyard can have several different owners, each of whom makes his own wine from that vineyard and could make several different versions with different Prädikats. The possibilities could make the mind spin.

My advice: don't worry about it. When you find a German wine that you like, make a note of the vineyard it came from because the same producer's Riesling from a different vineyard won't taste the same. And explore: taste two wines from the same vineyard made by different people and see whose you prefer; taste two different vineyards and note the differences. You might discover, like many others, that getting to know the vineyards is an addictive and exciting pursuit.

The Cost of Ripeness

Those who are brave enough to wade into the world of German Riesling are amply rewarded with some of the best bargains in the wine world. Fresh, crisp, everyday QbAs go for just $10 to $15; some even impress mightily with their combination of delicate fruit and powerful minerality.

Kabinetts overlap with QbAs, most running $10 to $30 and most Spätlese runs $12 to $40, with a few reaching to $60 or more.

From there, prices rise faster because the longer the grapes hang on the vines, the fewer there are, as nature challenges them. Animals eat them; wind blows them off; rain pelts them; hail tears their skins; rot attacks. Depending on the difficulty of the vintage, an Auslese can cost from $25 to $80, BAs and TBAs much more.

Alsace's Elegant Examples

If you follow the Rhine River south from Germany's Pfalz region, you'll end up in Alsace, France. Alsace (*all*-sahs) became a part of France in 1648 and has been occupied by Germany twice in the past hundred years, so it's no surprise that the major grape here is also Riesling. Alsace is also one of the few places in France that labels its wines with the name of the grape when it's 100 percent of a single variety—like Germans do.

Only, tasting Riesling from Germany and Alsace side by side, it would be difficult to tell that they grow in close proximity. Alsace Riesling has a very different profile: richer, drier, and higher in alcohol. Like German Riesling, though, it's filled with minerality and an acidity that allows it to take on nearly any type of food. It lasts for decades in the cellar, too.

What makes Alsace's Riesling taste so different is no doubt culture and philosophy, but it's also a good measure of geography. Alsace's vineyards lie in a long, skinny strip along the eastern side of the Vosges mountains, where they get to bask in the sun most days of the year—while rain and clouds darken the western side. The combination of cool climate and lots of sun (it's one of the sunniest spots in France) makes for grapes that get slowly but abundantly ripe and wines that are rich and powerful in flavor and acidity.

Alsace calls some of its wines *Grand Cru.* Like the famed Grand Crus of Burgundy, France (see Chapter 4), Alsace's Grand Cru wines come from specific vineyards selected for the quality of the wines they have produced over the years. Wines coming from these 51 Grand Cru vineyards are subject to stricter yield regulations than other vineyards, the idea being that the fewer the grapes, the more concentrated the wines.

> **Winespeak**
>
> **Grand Cru** means great growth, indicating, in wine-speak, a vineyard that has proven over time to grow grapes that make exceptional wines.

As in Germany, Alsace makes excellent sweet Rieslings; however, the ripeness levels are less complicated. If a wine says *Vendange Tardive* or *Sélection de Grains Nobles*, it's most likely sweet enough for dessert. Otherwise, it's dry. (For more on Alsace's sweet wines, see Chapter 19.)

> **Sour Grapes**
>
> Alsace's Grand Cru system was put into place in only 1983—recent history in French winemaking—after a decade of discussion over which vineyards would be granted Grand Cru status. However, even after a revision in 1992, many vintners were dissatisfied with the system and to this day prefer to label their wines with proprietary names rather than vineyard names. So if a wine doesn't carry a vineyard name on it, don't dismiss it. It could be just as good as the Grand Cru sitting next to it.

Alsace Costs

There's little need to memorize Alsace's 51 Grand Cru vineyards; price will surely make it clear what's what from the vintner's point of view.

> **Quick Sips**
>
> Find everything you want to know about Alsace wines and much more at www.vinsalsace.com; for Austrian wines, look to www.winesfromaustria.com.

At the low end, $12 to $15, Alsace's Rieslings are some of the best bargains going: dry yet full of rich, appley flavor and minerality. They have the delicacy to pair well with richer fish, like skate or monkfish, but also the weight to take on choucroute, a local specialty of sausage and sauerkraut.

From there, prices rise quickly, with Grand Crus and their equivalents concentrated in the $25 to $60 range. Here, you can expect wines that impress with powerful fruit and earth flavors. These are special occasion wines, and most deserve time in the cellar to age before drinking.

Along the Danube: Austrian Riesling

You've probably noticed by now that Riesling has an affinity for rivers in cool regions—the Mosel in Germany, the Rhine in Alsace. It's little surprise, then, that you'll find Riesling vines out in force along the banks of Austria's Danube, too.

Summer can get very warm here, and as a result Austria's Rieslings tend to be more powerful than Germany's, with a flavor all their own. The grape is grown all over the country, with particularly great results in:

◆ Wachau (Vah-*khow*)   ◆ Kamptal

◆ Kremstal   ◆ Weinviertel (*Vine*-fear-tl)

And in every one of these regions, if a wine is made from Riesling, the label says so loud and clear.

Austria's Wachau

Just west of Vienna on the other side of the fast-running Danube, Wachau's vineyards soar up slopes almost as steep as those along Germany's Mosel. Facing south, the vineyards soak up long days of sun, plus get light and heat reflected up from the river.

At the same time, a chilly breeze whisks down the Danube, ruffling leaves as it goes. It cools the vines on hot days, and it regularly gets into the 80s in the summertime here. Together, the combination makes for long, slow ripening, leaving the grapes plenty of time to pack in all the flavors they can gather up.

Wachau wines are classified in three levels:

◆ Steinfeder (*schtine*-fay-der): the lightest wines, designed for immediate drinking, and most of them get drunk up in Vienna's wine bars before they have a chance to leave the country.

◆ Federspiel (*fay*-der-schpiel): a little richer, but still generally light and crisp; most run $12 to $25.

◆ Smaragd (smahr-*ahgd*): the most intense, ripe as a peach, as dense in flavor as an apricot, and as mineral-filled as the slopes they grow on. A Smaragd Riesling has the stuff to stand up to a leg of lamb or survive in a cellar for 20 or 30 years, brilliantly. Their quality earns their prices: $20 to $65.

Off the Vine

Smaragd, which designates the ripest wines of the Wachau, is the name of a little green lizard that lives in the Wachau vineyards. Like the grapes that get ripe enough to earn this designation for their wines, the lizard loves to bask in the warm sun.

Kremstal, Kamptal, and Weinviertel

Heading east from the Wachau, you'll run into Kremstal, named for its biggest town, Krems. It's warmer than most of the Wachau and less steep, so Kremstal Rieslings tend to be fruitier, softer, more opulent. Kamptal is right next door and shares so many similarities with Kremstal that some vintners think they should be considered one large appellation.

Weinviertel includes all the forest and vine-covered land north of Kamptal and Kremstal up to the borders with the Czech Republic and Slovakia. It's chilly up here, and the wines show it—Weinviertel Rieslings are light and acidic.

Off the Vine _____

Though Austria uses a ripeness designation system similar to Germany's, winemakers tend to leave it off the label unless the wine is sweet. Austrian dry wines tend to be much drier than their German counterparts.

New World Riesling

Recently, Australia has been gathering press for its Rieslings. They have a style all of their own (as you might expect from a country with kangaroos), tending to be lighter yet riper, with more fruit and less mineral, and more exotic flavors, like lime, lime blossoms, and ginger, maybe even peaches or passion fruit in the ripest examples.

The best Australian Rieslings come from the ocean-chilled vineyards of Western Australia, which produce lean, austere Rieslings, or from cool enclaves of South Australia such as the Clare and Eden Valleys, where German settlers planted Riesling more than a century ago and the vines produce riper, friendlier Rieslings. Expect to pay $12 to $25 for good examples.

The West Coast has never had much luck in growing great Riesling, although Washington State puts out a few solid, affordable examples. That could be changing; recently Mosel vintner Ernst Loosen joined forces with Chateau Ste. Michelle to produce Riesling; Eroica is one of the best on the West Coast. And although California isn't known for great Riesling, a few devoted vintners stand out for the quality of their wines. Look for Claiborne & Churchill, Navarro, Smith-Madrone, Trefethen, and Stony Hill.

Idaho winery Ste. Chapelle also makes terrific lean, lemony Riesling from its vineyards on the slopes of the Snake River.

In the United States, the best Riesling is made in New York State's Finger Lakes District, America's little Mosel. Along the stony slopes of Seneca, Keuka, and Cayuga Lakes, Riesling vines find just enough sun and warmth to make it through the harsh, snowy winters and produce Rieslings surprisingly like Germany's own, with lean, crisp fruit and lots of smoky mineral flavor. There's not much of it yet as the wine industry here is young, but should you find Rieslings from Dr. Konstantin Frank, Fox Run, or Hermann J. Weimer, the most established producers, they will be worth every penny of the $11 to $30 spent.

> **Off the Vine**
>
> One California winemaker figured out how to get around the dearth of great Riesling grown in his home state: import the wine in bulk containers. In his Pacific Rim Riesling, vintner Randall Grahm blends Washington State Riesling with a good dollop of Riesling shipped over from Johannes Selbach of Selbach-Oster in Germany's Mosel for a Riesling with the friendly fruit of the New World and restrained finesse of the Old.

Tastings: A Matter of Style

No white wine grape comes in as many styles as Riesling. From soft, simple California Rieslings to stony, austere Mosel wines to rich, opulent Alsace bottles, feather-light Austrian versions, gingery Australians, and more, there's a Riesling for every man, woman, and meal. It's just a matter of figuring out which one fits your tastes and needs. These tastings might help.

Extreme Contrasts: California vs. Germany

A German QbA Riesling, around $12, such as Dr. Loosen, Dr. L, Lingenfelder Bird Label, St. Urbans-Hof, or any others

A California Riesling, such as Beringer, Fetzer, Turning Leaf, or any other that's $10 or less

Here are two flights of Rieslings; pick one from each. The suggested wines are easy to find and about as basic and affordable as Riesling gets in their respective countries, but feel free to substitute like wines. The differences between them will demonstrate some of the basic differences in style between the two countries.

Smell them. Which smells fruitier? Which would you guess comes from a warmer region? (Hint: the warmer the region, the riper the fruit flavors in the grape, and generally, Germany is colder than most of California's grape-growing regions.)

Taste them; try the German wine first. How does it taste? Is it fruity, or is it more stony? Can you taste the cool climate in the wine's acidity? Now taste the California Riesling. Is it fruitier, like it came from riper, sweeter grapes? Go back to the German Riesling. Does it taste drier than the first time you tasted it? Often, a dry wine tasted after a sweeter one will seem even drier than it is simply because of the contrast.

Two Hallmarks, Two Expressions

A German Kabinett Riesling from the Mosel-Saar-Ruwer, like one from C. von Schubert, Dr. Loosen, Kerpen, Selbach-Oster, or any others under $20

A Riesling from Alsace under $20, like the basic bottlings from Dopff & Irion, Hugel, J.B. Adam, Paul Blanck, Trimbach, or others

Alsace and Germany produce Rieslings thought of by Riesling-ophiles as hallmarks of the style, and yet they are very different. These are some affordable examples of both. Choose one of each, and pour them side by side. Smell them; which smells richer, more sun-filled? Which smells colder, more minerally? Taste them. Was your guess correct? I bet it was. Alsace's warmer, sunnier vineyards make for very different Rieslings than those grown along the cold Mosel.

Alsace Ease and Complexity

A basic Alsace Riesling, like any from the previous tasting

A Grand Cru or equivalent Alsace Riesling, like Domaine Weinbach Grand Cru Schlossberg, Josmeyer Grand Cru Hengst, Trimbach Clos Ste-Hune, anything from Zind-Humbrecht, or whatever you can afford

Alsace makes good Riesling at both ends of the price spectrum, yet what you get for the money is pretty different. Most basic Alsace Rieslings are blended from a variety of vineyards to make a smooth, easy, ready-to-drink wine, the sort you'd like to have on hand for impromptu parties and simple dinners. High-end Alsace Rieslings typically show off a particular terroir, whether a Grand Cru vineyard or an area the vintner finds stands out. Smaller parcels mean less wine, which often translates into higher prices, but that's not all. Compare a basic Alsace Riesling with a high-end one.

Which smells more striking and why? Does one smell softer, fruitier than the other? Taste them. Which feels more acidic, more concentrated, more powerful? Can you imagine the more expensive one developing even more flavor with a few years in the cellar and drinking the other one while you wait for the more expensive bottle to age?

The Difference Down Under

> A Riesling from South Australia, such as Yalumba South Australia Y Series, Jacob's Creek Barossa Valley Reserve Riesling, or Clare Valley Riesling, like Annie's Lane, Grosset Polish Hill, or Pikes
>
> A Riesling from anywhere else in the world, your call

Australia makes Riesling like no one else does. It's dry, limey, tropical, gingery, and delicious. Check it out next to a dry Riesling from anyplace else to get a feel for the Aussie Riesling style.

These are just a few of the tastings you can make to help define Riesling's wide range of expressions. Keep experimenting: try Australian Riesling next to Austrian Riesling or Germany versus New York State. Play with Rieslings of different ripeness levels. And try Rieslings with food; you might be surprised what Riesling can take.

The Least You Need to Know

- Wines made of Riesling almost always say so on the label, regardless where they are from.

- Some Rieslings are sweet (see Chapter 19), but many, and all in this chapter, are dry.

- Riesling likes a cold, hard life, growing on stony slopes in places like Germany, New York State, and Idaho.

- If a Riesling says *trocken* on the label, it's dry; believe it.

- Ripe doesn't necessarily mean sweet, so a wine that says Spätlese could be stone dry or slightly sweet.

- Riesling's naturally high acidity makes it extremely flexible with a wide range of foods, from fish to fowl and even red meat.

7

Pinot Grigio/Pinot Gris

In This Chapter

- ◆ The taste of Pinot Grigio
- ◆ Where to look for snappy Pinot Grigio
- ◆ The lushness of Pinot Gris
- ◆ Grigio's cousin, Pinot Bianco
- ◆ Which Pinot when?

There was a time not so long ago when Pinot Grigio rarely appeared outside Italian restaurants. Now it belongs to the regular roll call of white wines served by the glass at the bar, sounding sexier and more exotic than the ever-popular Chardonnay and Sauvignon Blanc.

Pinot's Many Faces

In its Italianate version, Pinot Grigio is loved for the taste of *la dolce vita* it offers; it's simple, giving, and easy to drink, requiring nothing of its drinker but an open mouth. Sure, its pear and hazelnut flavors whet the appetite, and its light, refreshing acidity makes it a good pour on its own or with salads. But its real strength is its ability to transfer just enough delicious flavor to please but not interrupt the conversation.

The French version often tastes like something else completely; Alsace vintners label theirs Pinot Gris and make them lush and opulent, with a satin feel and the flavor of crushed almonds.

Oregon vintners make Pinot Gris, too, but theirs taste different yet again, falling someplace between Italy and Alsace with hazelnut flavors carried on a smooth yet light texture. It's the same grape; how could this be? Ah, it's the joy of wine: so many choices, even within a single grape.

What's in a Name

Pinot Grigio, Pinot Gris, Tokay Pinot Gris … these are all the same grape, a mutation of the red grape Pinot Noir, named *grigio* or *gris* for the pale, smoky color of its skin. The different names simply depend on where the grapes are grown.

Off the Vine

Grigio and *gris* mean grey, a reference to the grape's skin, which varies between smoky pink to a pale purple-blue. Usually, its wine is fairly colorless, but some Pinot Grigios will even have a pink cast.

As with all grapes, climate, tradition, style, and the winemaker's whims all play into the sort of wine that Pinot Grigio makes, but the language used provides a bit of a clue. Since Italy's Pinot Grigio tends to be much lighter than France's Pinot Gris, the names have developed certain connotations; for instance, if a California winemaker calls his wine Pinot Grigio, it's probably made in the lighter Italian style.

Quick Sips

However you say it, it's all Pinot Grigio:

Pinot Grigio: Italian name, adopted by winemakers all over the world.

Pinot Gris: French name, also used worldwide.

Tokay Pinot Gris: Old name in Alsace, France, for Pinot Gris. It was outlawed in March 2007, although it appears on wines made before then.

Grauburgunder/Ruländer: German names.

Italy's Pride and Shame

When most people think of Pinot Grigio, Italy's is the model: light, crisp, and affordable. It's a favorite house pour in homes and restaurants around the world.

The grape grows all over the country, most especially at the top of the boot, but like Chardonnay, because wine drinkers love it so, it's often grown anywhere grape growers can find space.

The overproduction that results is Pinot Grigio's downfall; a focus on quantity rather than quality never makes for great flavor. Too warm a region and Pinot Grigio loses its nerve, the acidity that gives it a refreshing feel; too many grapes per acre, and the wine that results tastes like little more than water.

Unfortunately, way too much dull, lackluster Pinot Grigio is out there as wineries churn it out by the bucketful, hoping to make money on the grape's cachet alone.

Where can you find the good stuff? In vineyards far to the north, where cool air lets the grapes ripen in their own time, and from wineries concerned with quality as much as they are with making a buck.

> **Off the Vine**
>
> Pinot Bianco is another Pinot you might see on white-wine shelves. The white Pinot isn't the same as Pinot Grigio, but it's close, just another variation of the mother of them both, Pinot Noir (black Pinot). Although it tends to have a little less overt flavor than Pinot Grigio, its richer texture and weight can provide a luxurious background for baked fish or other delicate dishes.

Chilling Out

The little bit of Pinot Grigio grown in Southern Italy soaks up the sun and heat, creating some nice, ripe, peachy-sweet wines that tend to sell for little more than $10. The only thing lacking is a little of the acidity that would make them refreshing, but give them a hard chill and they'll be fine for the beach or backyard.

For the whole package, go north, to the Veneto or higher, into Trentino-Alto Adige or Friuli. Way up here in the hinterlands of Italy, the Alps and the Dolomites provide plenty of slopes for vines to hold on to, where they'll be well-drained, protected from the freezing winds by the mountain's back, and able to soak up the sun for long hours every day. Here, Pinot Grigio ripens more slowly than it does in the warmer south, taking on peach and almond flavors while retaining its all-important acidity.

Most Italians also prefer their Pinot Grigio crisp and refreshing, so they vinify it in stainless-steel tanks. Steel doesn't lend the wine any extra flavors, and it can be chilled to keep the grape juice cold and fresh.

A Quick Lesson in Northern Italian Geography

Most wine experts would have a difficult time telling a Trentino Pinot Grigio apart from a Veneto version, but a little geography would at least give you an idea of why the place name is on the wine label.

- **Veneto:** the Veneto is responsible for a good portion of Italy's bargain-priced Pinot Grigio. Here, the fertile Po Valley produces a veritable sea of it, much of which is unremarkable except to say that it's white and wet. There are always exceptions, of course, but you can generally count on the Veneto to provide party Pinot Grigio at $15 or less.

- **Trentino–Alto Adige:** this region falls along the Adige River. Trentino is the lower half of the region, where it's flatter and warmer; its wines often taste like Veneto's. Move north into Alto Adige (called Südtirol by some locals, a clue to how close it is to Austria in more than just geography) and the vineyards climb higher off the riverbanks. It's cooler here, so the grapes hold on to more of their acidity; the Pinot Grigio from Alto Adige can be very fine, with delicate fragrance and lively, crisp, apple-like flavors. The difference often shows up in price, too: Alto Adige Pinot Grigio ranges up to $30 or so per bottle.

- **Friuli:** this region, officially called Friuli-Venezia Giulia, though that's rarely heard, is squashed between the Alps to the north and the Gulf of Venice to the south. The mountains act like a baseball mitt here, catching the cold alpine winds and holding them over the vineyards. It's cool, especially at night in some higher elevations, which makes for Pinot Grigio with cool, clear, pear-like flavors and more vivacious acidity than most. Also, there's the matter of style: like Alto Adige, Friuli was part of the Austro-Hungarian Empire until 1919, and the taste here runs to high-acid whites more so than in more southerly regions. Generally regarded as some of the country's best, Friuli Pinot Grigio can demand up to $40 a bottle, though most run $12 to $25.

Quick Sips

Collio means hills; Collio and Colli Orientali del Friuli are hilly subregions within Friuli that stand out for fragrant, high-acid white wines.

Alsace's Opulent Gris

Italy's snappy Pinot Grigios are only one interpretation of the Pinot Grigio story. Alsace offers a different take altogether, one that many wine lovers would argue convincingly is the best in the world. They are the richest and most opulent by far.

As with Alsace's Riesling, Pinot Gris (as it's called here, in parlance and prominently on wine labels) enjoys its enviable position next to the Vosges mountains, which protect them from rain and clouds. The grape seems to soak up the sun and its warmth like a super-absorbent sponge, becoming as densely flavored as a handful of golden raisins.

At its simplest (around the $10 to $15 mark), Alsace's Pinot Gris offers a lot of wine for the money, its rich, waxy texture typically laden with dry honey and pear flavors. It's a terrific alternative to Chardonnay when you're looking for a wine that's rich yet free of the weight and sweetness of oak that's so common to Chardonnay in this price range.

Quick Sips

Alsace used to call Pinot Gris "Tokay Pinot Gris," but no longer. Concerned that buyers would confuse Alsace's Tokay Pinot Gris with Hungary's esteemed Tokaji wines (see Chapter 19), the EU has banned the use of "Tokay" for Alsace wines as of 2007.

Great Pinot Gris grown in Alsace also seems to soak up flavors from beneath, drawing the earth's minerality into its core. It can taste distinctly spicy, smoky, and stony. Because of this, Pinot Gris is one of the four grapes eligible to use the Grand Cru designation on the label if the wines come from Grand Cru vineyards (see Chapter 6). The resultant Pinot Gris are white wines with weight and gravitas, about as different from Italy's party pours as imaginable. The price will make this difference clear, as well; great Alsace Pinot Gris goes for $20 to $50 or so.

In the Alsace section of the wine store, you'll likely see many wines labeled *Pinot Blanc* next to the Pinot Gris. It's not the same grape, but cousin Pinot Bianco under its French name. The best Pinot Blanc can match the region's Pinot Gris in breadth and richness, though they typically offer less interesting flavors. It's frequently used as a base for blending with other varieties to create affordable, everyday wines. These blended wines will not bear the name of any grape on their label; many are terrific, flexible drinks at affordable prices.

Oregon's Stealth Grape

One more place in the world makes exceptional Pinot Gris, and it's right here in the United States: Oregon. The state hasn't been at it for that long; it was just 1967 when David Lett of Eyrie Vineyards planted the state's first Pinot Gris on a hunch that it might do well in the cool Willamette Valley.

Today, Oregon's Pinot Gris is second only to its Pinot Noir in both quality and quantity. The state's style runs from light, crisp, and mineral (not unlike Italy's, but with a little more weight and flavor) to rich with spicy, nutty, honeyed pear flavors.

Quick Sips _____

If you get hooked on Oregon Pinots, you may want to subscribe to Cole Danehower's newsletter at www.oregonwinereport.com. You'll also find a lot of free information at www.winepressnw.com.

Some of this variety depends on where the grapes are grown, but most of all it has to do with winemaking style. To make an Alsatian-style Pinot Gris, vintners often work their vineyards so they get low yields and pick the grapes when they are very ripe. Often, they'll put the wine into oak barrels instead of stainless steel, too, to add a toasty, spicy, vanilla richness to the wine. And the wine will also be put through a second, malolactic fermentation (see Chapter 4), to transform the crisp, sharp malic acid into gentler lactic acid and help give the wine its luxurious texture.

It's difficult to tell which style of wine is in the bottle unless the winemaker has been thoughtful enough to tell you on the back label, but price is often a giveaway. Light, everyday wines sell for everyday prices ($10, give or take $3), while Pinot Gris fit for King Salmon averages around $20 to $30, with some examples double or triple that.

Pinot Gris Around the World

Inspired by Pinot's performance in Italy, Alsace, and Oregon, winemakers everywhere are giving it a shot. New Zealand may be the biggest up-and-comer: the country's Pinot Grigio plantings increased 16-fold between 1998 and 2008. And look for great grigio in the following places as well.

Slovenia

Here's something unusual: if you take a walk in the vineyards of Collio in far northeastern Italy, you could find yourself in Slovenia without knowing it. The border is only political, after all; pre-1919, these vineyards were all in the same country. (See the map of Northeastern Italy.)

Slovenia's wine industry, however, fell into grave disrepair under Communism, and it's only since 1991 that Slovenians have been able to work at turning the vineyards around. They worked fast; today, Slovenia boasts Pinot Grigio as good as Northern Italy's, with sharp mineral flavors, bright, snazzy acidity, and lots of pear and hazelnut flavor. The best range from $12 to $30. Of course, some amount of Pinot Grigio from Collio, Italy, takes grapes from vineyards that are officially in Slovenian territory, too.

Austria

Head north over the mountains from Italy, and you'll land in Styria, a region of low, rolling hills in southeast Austria. Here, Pinot Grigio is called *Grauburgunder*, and it soaks up the warmth to make bigger, richer wines than those of neighboring Italy, yet still has enough acidity to hold up all the flavors.

Better yet are the region's wines made from that Pinot Grigio cousin, Pinot Bianco, here called *Weissburgunder*. Austrian Weissburgunder can pack a wallop, with nearly 14 percent alcohol and enough flavor to take on a lamb chop, though fish napped in a mushroom cream sauce would probably be more appropriate. All that flavor costs; the few found in the United States run around $15 to $30 but can be stunning dinner companions.

> **Off the Vine**
>
> The German names for Pinot Gris and Pinot Blanc, *Grauburgunder* and *Weissburgunder*, hint at the vine's origins in the Burgundy region of France, where the red grape Pinot Noir, the vine's parent, holds sway. Today, however, few Pinot Gris and Pinot Blanc vines remain as Chardonnay has long taken over as the white wine grape of choice.

Tastings: Picking Pinot Grigio

So what'll it be, Gris or Grigio? Both have their considerable virtues; it's just a matter of time and place. Here are a few examples of the differences.

Shades of Grey

An under $15, Italian Pinot Grigio from Venezia, such as Lagaria, Pighin, Tieffenbrunner, or Zenato

A basic Alsace Pinot Gris, like one from René Barth Trimbach, Willm, or others less than $16

Italy and Alsace share the renown for the best wines from this grape, and yet their wines are as different as sliced apples are from an apple pie. One is fresh, crisp, bright, just steps away from the taste of a grape straight from a vine; the other is warm, unctuous, full of pear flavor yet dry. Have someone pour you these wines without telling you which one is which. You might be able to tell from smell alone which is lighter, crisper, more Grigio than Gris. Taste them. Feel the difference between the two?

Gris with an American Accent

Inexpensive Pinot Grigio from California, like Forest Glen, La Famiglia di Robert Mondavi, or Meridian

Inexpensive Pinot Gris from California, such as Gallo of Sonoma Reserve, Joseph Swan Vineyards, or Navarro Vineyards, or any others you can find under $30

Same grape, same country, yet one winery has chosen to call its wine by the Italian name, Pinot Grigio, and the other labels its wine Pinot Gris. What's the difference?

Sometimes not much, but in general, winemakers who emulate the Italian style of Pinot Grigio—light, fruity, easy to sip ice cold on a Friday afternoon—use the Italian. Those who make a richer style, more like the wines that come out of Alsace, where the climate makes for Pinot Grigio with rich, peachy flavors and a broad, satin texture, tend to use the French name. Does the California Pinot Gris seem richer than the Grigio? Which one of these wines would be more refreshing on a summer evening? Which style is easier to imagine next to pasta in a mushroom cream sauce?

Oregon's Pinot Blancs and Gris

Oregon Pinot Blanc, like Adelsheim Vineyard, Erath, Foris, Yamhill, to name just a few

Oregon Pinot Gris, such as Chehalem, Cristom, Firesteed, King Estate, Sokol Blosser, or others

To get a feel for Oregon's prowess with the white-wine side of the Pinot family, pick a Blanc and a Gris. Start with the Blanc; it's usually the less expressive of the two. Smell them; taste them; roll them around in the mouth to get familiar with both grapes. It might be hard to tell the difference, especially after only two samples, but it is easy to tell that they both make for delicious wines.

The Least You Need to Know

- Pinot Grigio and Pinot Gris are the same grape.

- Rock-bottom prices usually buy rock-bottom Pinot Grigio—fine for parties, perhaps, but a few extra bucks goes a long way.

- Reach for Italy's Pinot Grigio when you want a wine that's light and crisp; the best come from the northern regions of Veneto, Trentino-Alto Adige, and especially Friuli.

- Pull out Pinot Gris from Alsace when the mood calls for rich opulence.

- Look to Oregon for the best American pinots, whether blanc or gris (or even noir).

- Pinot Bianco/Blanc is a close relative worth checking out for its rich, round texture and pineapple fragrance.

Chapter 8

Cabernet Sauvignon (and Its Progenitor, Franc)

In This Chapter

- The taste of Cabernet
- Best places for Cabernet
- The cost of Cabernet
- About that Franc
- A comparison of Cabernet styles

If a grape could be king, it would be Cabernet Sauvignon. It can be gentle and authoritative—both at the same time. It has sex appeal in its rich black fruit, but it's also a little distant, its tannins holding it back like a body-guard. It plays well by itself, creating varietal wines that are some of the world's favorites, but it plays even better with others, offering the sort of support that allows other grapes to shine along with it.

With a profile like that, who wouldn't like to have some of it in their vine-yard? Vintners do, all over the world. And the more you know about it, the more you might find to like about it, too, so read on and let's see.

Cabernet's Hallmark Flavor

One of the remarkable things about Cabernet Sauvignon is how much it tastes like Cabernet anywhere it is grown. California, France, Australia, and Lebanon all make different versions, but at the heart of it, good examples all taste clearly like Cabernet Sauvignon.

And what's Cabernet's hallmark flavor? Black currants—and if you don't know what they taste like, get thee to the jam section of the grocery store and pick some up. It'll be sweetened, of course, but it'll also give an idea of how unsweet this fruit is in its natural form. Black and juicy yet tart and slightly bitter, their flavor comes closest to something like Cabernet Sauvignon.

Cabernet also frequently has a green edge, something like bell peppers, herbs, or pleasantly foresty pine depending on how ripe it gets and where it's grown. And it always has tannin, the drying elements that give wines structure and help preserve them over years. Tannin comes mostly from a grape's seeds (pips) and skins, and Cabernet Sauvignon has thick skins wrapped around small berries full of seeds, so it's considerably tannic. That tannin is what helps many Cabernet Sauvignons age so well and long. It's also what makes Cabernet a popular steakhouse pour. Tannin actually bonds with proteins, so when a tannic Cabernet meets a steak, the tannin bonds with it rather than your tongue.

Quick Sips

Cabernet Sauvignon at a glance: lots of tannin—the stuff that dries out your mouth—and lots of dark color; flavors of black currant, black plum, bell pepper; often, wood tones of cedar, sandalwood; sometimes earthy notes like lead pencil, minerals.

The Grapes Behind Cabernet

Behind every great chef, there's a battery of cooks helping to realize his potential. It's the same with Cabernet; it's irrefutably a great grape, but it almost always gets a little help from other grapes, even when those others aren't listed on the wine label. (For instance, California winemakers can include up to 25 percent of other grapes and still call a wine Cabernet Sauvignon.) Cabernet's challenge is its lean fruit and heavy tannins, which can make for a wine that tastes unforgivingly austere. Merlot helps out most frequently, its soft, jammy fruit adding padding; though Cabernet Franc, Petit Verdot, Syrah, and others are popular ameliorators depending on who's making the Cabernet Sauvignon.

In most cases, however, Cabernet Sauvignon still stars, and the other grapes are almost invisible. I tell you this only to give credit where credit is due.

> **Off the Vine** _____
>
> Most grape varieties are results of mutations and accidental crossings of grape varieties in the vineyard. (Hybrids are the exception: these are crosses between two species of vines and are usually instigated by man.) For instance, Cabernet Sauvignon was the result of a tryst between the red grape Cabernet Franc and the white Sauvignon Blanc, according to DNA analysis performed at the University of California, Davis.

Bordeaux, Cabernet's Kingdom

Do you ever wonder what sort of wines can possibly fetch thousands of dollars per bottle? Or hear a wine bore go on about the 1982 vintage of Château Frou-Frou? It's likely that those bottles would be Bordeaux. Not all Bordeaux are so fancy (most aren't, in fact), but the _crème de la crème_ have made Bordeaux very hot property.

Bordeaux is the name of a city on the Atlantic coast of France, and it's also the name of the wines that come from the vineyards surrounding it. As with most French wines, the Bordelais (the people from Bordeaux) don't bother putting the grape on the label; for them, the place says it all.

Besides, most all Bordeaux's wines are blends of grapes, with Cabernet Sauvignon and Merlot playing starring roles supported by some combination of Cabernet Franc, Petit Verdot, Malbec, and Carmenère. But even in combination with other grapes, Cabernet's strong flavors shine, providing the model for Cabernets around the world. To find these Cabernet-based Bordeauxs, you need to know your Banks.

Know Your Left from Your Right (Bank)

Bordeaux has two major parts: the Left Bank and the Right Bank. The Right Bank is the land on the eastern side of the Gironde River, and Cabernet Sauvignon doesn't ripen so well in the clay soils that make up much of its land. Instead, Cabernet mainly plays a supporting role to Merlot (see Chapter 9).

On the Left Bank, gravelly rises provide a warm, well-drained environment for Cabernet Sauvignon. In the wines of this side Cabernet has earned its fame, making lean, tannic reds that can keep for years (and indeed, many of them need years before you should go near them or the tannin will glue your mouth shut).

Unfortunately, Bordeaux wines don't indicate from which Bank they hail. To find Cabernet-based Bordeaux, you need to know the appellations of the Left Bank.

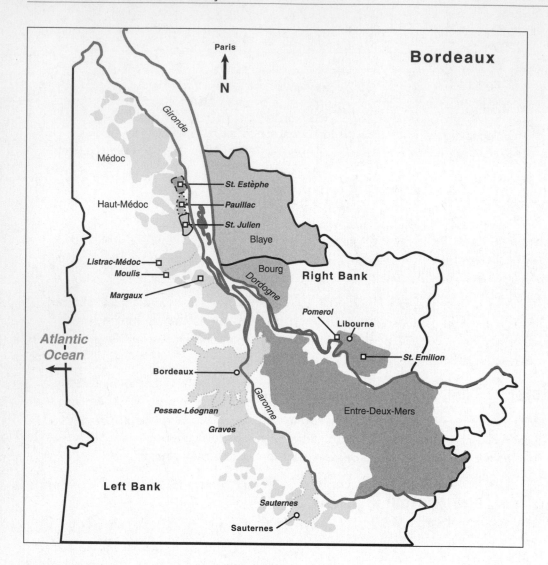

The Left Bank's Exalted Appellations

You can find some good deals in wines labeled simply Bordeaux or Bordeaux Supérieur, but the best wines come from smaller areas within the Left Bank. To begin with, the Left Bank is divided into three main areas: the Médoc to the north, Graves to the south, and the Haut-Médoc in the middle.

While there are some good buys in the Médoc (Château Potensac and Rollan de By, for instance), the Haut-Médoc is where most of the action is. The area boasts six appellations that stand out for the quality of their wines. They are:

◆ Listrac-Médoc: lesser-known appellation giving angular, earthy, and black-fruited wines

◆ Margaux: the gentlest of the Left Bank wines, rose-scented and soft-fruited

◆ Moulis: represents good value with firm yet velvety and succulently fruity wines

◆ Pauillac: the most famous (think Châteaus Lafite, Latour, and Mouton-Rothschild), with big, brooding, tannin-filled monsters that take years to tame

◆ St-Estèphe: austere, hard, lean Cabernet

◆ St-Julien: graceful, firm yet friendly Cabernet

Graves is unusual in that the region puts out a little bit of white wine in addition to lots of red. Its best reds come from Pessac-Léognan, an appellation formed in just 1987 to highlight the concentration of great estates here. If you've heard of Château Haut-Brion, you know of a wine from Pessac-Léognan.

Quick Sips

The most esteemed Cabernet-based wines in Bordeaux come from Margaux, Pauillac, Pessac-Léognan, St-Estèphe, and St-Julien.

Cru Cuts

When shopping for Bordeaux, you might notice that many of the expensive ones sport a line on the label that reads "Premier Cru" or "Deuxième Cru." The translation is First Growth and Second Growth, but to understand its importance, you need a little history.

Bordeaux is unusual in that its wines have historically been important as an item of trade. Unlike other regions that made wine mostly for themselves and only recently (in the last 50 years or so) began exporting them on a large scale, Bordeaux's position as a major port made it easy for the producers to sell to outsiders. For this reason, it gained fame early on.

Sour Grapes

As if it weren't complicated enough, Bordeaux considers "Premier Cru" the highest honor, while in Burgundy wines, Premier Cru is a step down from Grand Cru. It's an important detail, but if you forget it, the prices of the wines will probably trigger your memory.

It also inspired a classification scheme unlike any other to make some sense of the huge amount of wines the region produces. It's called the 1855 Classification, and it's a list of 61 estates grouped according to their track record and the prices they fetched that year.

The top five were deemed "Premier Cru," or First Growth; the second best were ranked "Deuxième Cru," or Second Growth, and so on down the line to Fifth Growth.

This list applies only to the wines of the Haut-Médoc (save for Château Haut-Brion in Graves and Château d'Yquem in Sauternes, which were included in the original classification). Graves received its own classification in 1953, and St-Émilion in 1955.

The strange thing about the 1855 Classification is that only one change has been made since it was drafted: Mouton-Rothschild was promoted to a Premier Cru in 1973. Though many of the classified wineries have changed much since 1855, the wineries at the top level still tend to bring in the highest prices. Often the quality of their wines warrants it, but the rank is no guarantee.

Also, many wineries that didn't make the classification are today making great wines—better wines even than some of the classed growths. Don't be afraid to look outside the classified estates for great wines, because they do exist.

Bordeaux on the Cheap

The prices of the Bordeaux wines that attract the most attention are enough to make all but the most deep-pocketed run the other way, but there's no reason to spend that much if you just want to get a taste of Bordeaux Cabernet Sauvignon. Most of the expensive wines, in fact, are mean and tannic when first sold; they are meant to be cellared for years so that their tannins have time to soften.

When you want a Bordeaux to drink tonight, look for something simpler and kinder, like ...

◆ Unclassed estates: excellent estates have appeared or massively improved since the classification. To find out about these estates, ask a retailer who loves Bordeaux wines. Chances are he's selling the high-flying names and drinking lesser-known treasures.

◆ Wines labeled simply Médoc or Haut-Médoc or the smaller, lesser-known appellations Listrac and Moulis.

◆ Second-label wines, which are wines made by great estates from grapes that didn't make the cut for the estate's flagship wine. While they are simpler wines, they offer a taste of the estate's style at a significantly lower price. To find them, ask your retailer.

The range of possibilities in these three categories is huge, but you can have good, everyday Bordeaux for as little as $12; $15 to $30 can buy excellent wines to drink today or age for a few years.

California Cab

California is famous for its Cabernet Sauvignon, and rightly so. First, there's a lot of it: it outpaces plantings of other red wine grapes by 25,000 acres or so. More importantly, it makes wines that range from juicy, herb-scented $8 drinks to intense, smoky, densely fruited, and mineral-studded monsters that last for years and fetch hundreds of dollars.

California Cabernet is typically more friendly and juicy than Bordeaux's austere Cabernet-based reds, and yet it's also firm and tannic, giving it a sophisticated, restrained feel (compared to other red wines from California, at least). The state's best come mostly from Napa and Sonoma valleys; the Santa Cruz Mountains south of San Francisco have long put out some outstanding examples, too.

Quick Sips

If a California wine contains at least 75 percent Cabernet Sauvignon, it can be labeled as such. If it's less than 75 percent Cabernet Sauvignon but blended with other varieties common to Bordeaux, the wine is often called a Meritage blend (see Chapter 2).

Napa's Fame

Cabernet grows all over the state, but the most outstanding examples come from regions where it's not too hot (as in the flat, sun-baked interior) and not too chilly (as it can be by the coast).

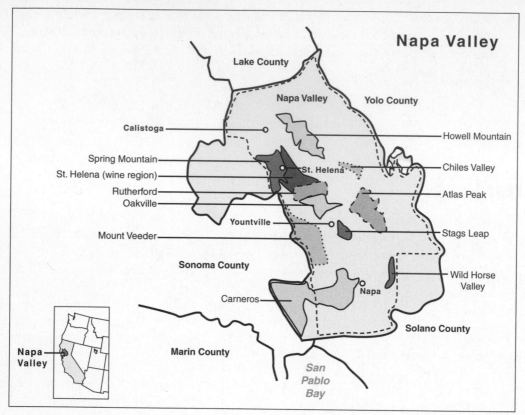

Napa's Cabernet strongholds.

The epitome of the California style comes from Napa Valley, a long, thin valley framed by San Pablo Bay to the south and the Mayacamas Mountains to the west. Here, different AVAs or defined areas give different styles of Cabernet Sauvignon. Some of the best versions come from mountain vineyards, where the ruggedness of the rocky land keeps yields lower than on the fertile valley floors and where the combination of high-altitude coolness and intense sun leads to intensely ripe, full-flavored wines. Then again, parts of the valley floor have soils that make outstanding Cabernets, too. Some AVAs to look for are:

♦ Diamond Mountain: a rocky outcrop of the Mayacamas in the north of the valley, this warm, high area is known for tannic, long-lived Cabernet Sauvignon.

♦ Howell Mountain: the highest Napa AVA, hot summers and cold winters on volcanic soil make for rugged Cabernet thick with black fruit and strong tannin.

◆ Mount Veeder: west of Yountville, rising 400 to 2,677 feet, Mount Veeder Cabernet gets ripe and tannic from the combination of hot sun and cool, high-altitude air. It often takes on a foresty quality, too.

◆ Oakville: the valley floor around the town of the same name gives almost Bordeaux-style wines with red fruit flavors kept lean and elegant with gravelly tannin.

◆ Rutherford: north from and slightly warmer than Oakville, Rutherford's part of the valley floor is said to lend a dusty, dry character referred to as "Rutherford Dust" to its blacker-fruited wine.

◆ Spring Mountain: another peak of the Mayacamas mountain range west of St. Helena that gives powerful Cabernet Sauvignons.

◆ Stags Leap District: the combination of warm heat reflected off the soaring Stags Leap Palisades and the cool ocean air that gets sucked up from San Pablo Bay through the valley in the evening makes for rich-textured, full-fruited, firm yet hedonistic Cabernet Sauvignons.

Sonoma: Napa's Competition

Sonoma County gets more recognition for its Chardonnay than its Cabernet Sauvignon, but some of its warmer, fog-free areas make excellent Cabernet. Look to the following AVAs:

◆ Alexander Valley: bordered by the cool Russian River Valley to the south and cooler Mendocino to the north, this would seem an unlikely place to ripen Cabernet, but in fact, it beds down in the valley's warm, gravelly loam to make plush, rounded wines.

◆ Knights Valley: east of Alexander Valley and heading into the Mayacamas, this is the warmest part of Sonoma County, and makes the richest, darkest Cabernets—perfect for the beef raised around here.

◆ Sonoma Mountain: these south- and east-facing vineyards on the West side of the Mayacamas rise far enough above the fog line that they stay warm enough to ripen, yet cool enough to enjoy a long season in which they can develop fragrant, rich Cabernet Sauvignon.

The problem with California Cabernet is that it's hard to find a good example for $10 or less that doesn't taste like jam and vegetables. The safest bet is the $12 to $25 category, though you could spend a lot more and be quite happy with the results.

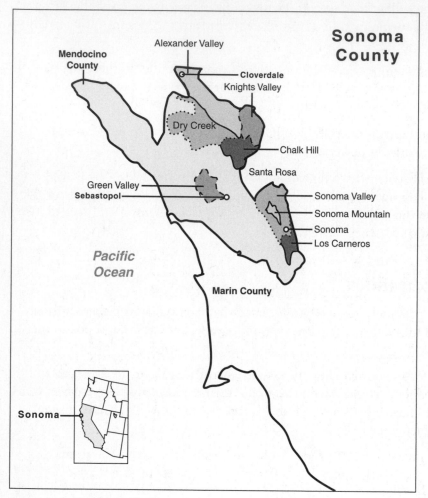

Sonoma's Cabernet strongholds.

Cab Down Under

If Cabernet Sauvignon could ever make it out from the shadow of Shiraz in Australia, more people might realize just how great the grape can be here. As in the United

States, the array of styles is enormous, from juicy, easy-drinking Cabernet Sauvignon from the warm flatlands of southeastern Australia to lean, forest-scented Cabernets from the wild edge of Western Australia.

If there's one region that stands out above all others for its Cabernet Sauvignon, though, it's Coonawarra.

Coonawarra's *Terra Rossa*

South Australia offers a variety of good Cabernet Sauvignon. Styles differ from area to area: McLaren Vale, for instance, is known for its rich, almost jammy Cabernet Sauvignon; Barossa Valley's are even bigger and chunkier. The most remarkable, however, come from Coonawarra.

On the surface, there's little remarkable looking about this long, thin strip of land in South Australia save for just how flat it is. Dig down a few feet, though, and you'll find soil as red as rust.

This is Coonawarra's famed *terra rossa*, and it's what's credited with giving Coonawarra Cab its telltale ferrous (iron-like) flavors. Some amount of Shiraz is also grown in the terra rossa, but the earthy character it gives shows best in Cabernet Sauvignon.

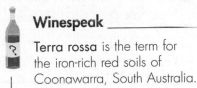

Winespeak

Terra rossa is the term for the iron-rich red soils of Coonawarra, South Australia.

To taste the difference for yourself, get a few wines together from different parts of South Australia, and taste them side by side. You can buy good examples, such as Wynns Coonawarra Estate, Penley, and Rosemount Show Reserve, for $12 to $25.

Windy Western Australia

Western Australia deserves credit for its Cabernet Sauvignon, too. The region's vineyards are concentrated in the far southwest corner of the state. In the most inland vineyards, it can be hot—hotter than any other wine-growing region in the country, actually—which isn't great for Cabernet. Move out toward the ocean, though, particularly along the Margaret River, and you'll find some of Australia's best Cabernet.

Here, breezes off the Indian Ocean cool the sun-soaked vineyards, allowing Cabernet Sauvignon to ripen more slowly than in other regions. The result is restrained Cabernet that has more in common with Bordeaux than it does the rest of Australia's.

These are lean and slightly tannic, with ripe black currant flavors and a foresty green note around the edge. Their restraint is a shocker to some who are used to the big, honkin' reds of South Australia and a relief to others.

Good Western Australia Cabernets do come at a price; start at $20 and work up for better examples.

The Rest of the World

Chile and Argentina make more than just bargain-priced Cabernet Sauvignon. Chile's best come from Maipo, a region that surrounds Santiago, where Cabernet Sauvignon has been growing since the mid-1800s. All along the Maipo River, peaks and valleys and the moderating effects of the ocean and the river itself draw out the ripening season, allowing Cabernet to ripen slowly, retaining its structure while packing on the rich, ripe fruit. Some of the best come from Macul, an area that pushes into the stony foothills of the Andes and gives tense, minty, earthy Cabernet; further south and closer to the river, there's Puente Alto, which gives dark, structured Cabernet. There are other good Cabernets in Chile, but Maipo boasts most of the best.

Argentina's Cabernet Sauvignon is bested by its Malbec (see Chapter 17), but its best are worth a taste. Most come from cooler elevations of Mendoza, such as Agrelo and Lunlunta. In these regions, the little bit of elevation makes the difference between simple, jammy reds and lushly ripe Cabernet with structure and acidity.

In Europe, few serious Cabernet Sauvignon strongholds exist outside of France. Spain makes a little of it, but Italy makes the most of it, especially in Tuscany. Here, Cabernet Sauvignon has long been used in the chewy, tannic wines of Carmignano, a small region west of Florence. Cabernet really took off in Tuscany, after Mario Incisa della Rochetta released a wine called Sassicaia in the late 1960s. Made from Cabernet he grew in the moderate climate of Bolgheri on the coast of Tuscany, that wine kicked off the craze for *Super Tuscan wines*, wines made from varieties considered nontraditional to the region, like Cabernet. Now Cabernet shows up in many Super Tuscans as well as in Chiantis, where its black currant fragrance and tannin provide extra flavor and support. You can find simple Cabernet-Sangiovese blends for as little as $10, but expect to pay double or triple for richer, more structured reds, and even $100 or more for some Super Tuscans.

Winespeak

Super Tuscan wines employ techniques or grapes, like Cabernet, that are considered nontraditional to Chianti, Tuscany's most famous wine region.

Meet Franc, Cabernet Sauvignon's Father

You might think that the parent of Cabernet Sauvignon would be revered, but instead Cabernet Franc is largely and unfairly ignored. Its flavors are very much like those of Cabernet Sauvignon, full of lean, black currant–like fruit and considerable tannin, but it tends to taste a little lighter and to have a more distinct foresty or herbal flavor.

Few places in the world specialize in Cabernet Franc, and they are worth searching out—especially since they tend to be cheaper than Cabernet Sauvignon.

The Loire Valley, Franc's Kingdom

Inland from the Atlantic, along the Loire Valley, Cabernet Franc makes up quite a few wines, though the grape isn't mentioned on the wine labels. To try Loire Cabernet Franc, look for wines from the appellations:

♦ Anjou

♦ Bourgeuil

♦ Chinon

♦ Saumur

In these cooler areas, the grapes don't get very ripe, and so the resulting wines can be very light in color and taste, with a green scent that, in poetic moments, can recall picking berries in a cool forest. (Other times, it tastes simply green and black.) The richest wines come from Chinon, which can be black in color, but still retain an acidity that makes them feel light and fresh, perfect for picnics with cold sliced ham or cheese. All tend to be great bargains, with lighter wines starting at $11 and moving up in cost and density to around $30 for some special bottlings. Names to look for are Baudry, Breton, Couly-Dutheil, Joguet, Mabileau, and Olga Raffault.

California

California puts out few Cabernet Francs, and the best tend to come from cooler areas of the Napa Valley, where the grape ripens to a black richness yet retains its herbal acidity. Good examples tend to run about $20 to $50; look for Lang & Reed, which specializes in Cabernet Franc, as well as Cabernet Sauvignon producers who make Franc on the side, such as Peju Province, Reverie, and von Strasser.

Long Island, New York State

This young wine-growing region is only beginning to figure out what it grows best and where, and Cabernet Franc seems promising. The region has many similarities to Bordeaux, actually, being flat, temperate, and Atlantic Ocean–influenced, and the best examples get ripe enough to balance their herbal edge with rich black fruit. Schneider Vineyards is the role model.

Off the Vine

Cabernet Franc also plays an important part in many blends, most famously on the Right Bank of Bordeaux, where it gives structure and aroma to the Merlot. It's also grown in Washington State, where it appears on its own and more often in blends, and in Ontario, where it's made into an unusual (some would say bizarre) dessert wine.

Friulian Franc

Northern Italy also puts out some Cabernet Franc and labels them as such. In the region's cool climate, its wines tend to be lean, dark-fruited, and very tannic, more for steak than for sipping casually. Some suspect that what Friuli calls Cabernet Franc is actually another Bordeaux-based grape called Carmenère, but until that's determined, you'll still find them labeled Cabernet Franc.

Tastings: Cabernet Comparisons

So you're off to the store to pick up a bottle of Cabernet. What will you choose? A lightly tannic, aromatic Bordeaux fragrant with black currants and cedar notes, or a big, mouth-filling Napa Cab? If it's summertime, maybe the lighter weight of a Loire Cabernet Franc would be more appropriate. Take a look at these tastings to get a better idea of how Cabernet grown in various places differs. I offer some suggestions for wines to look for, but, as in all the tastings, they are only meant to be jumping-off points. Use what you can find that fits the category being tasted; or skip the wines and follow along in your mind.

Dour Bordeaux, Sunny California

Any Left Bank Bordeaux wine, $15 and under

Any California Cabernet, $15 and under

Pick any Left Bank Bordeaux and any California Cabernet for this exercise. Pour them side by side and look at the difference. Bets are on that the lighter one is the Bordeaux. Smell them. Which smells more herbal, stonier, less about fruit? Bingo, the Bordeaux. Taste them. Can you taste the cool, gravelly rises of Bordeaux that Cabernet prefers? Does one taste riper, fatter, like its been fed on California sun? Which do you prefer? Which would you prefer with coq au vin and which for a back-yard barbecue? Either fits; it's all about what you prefer.

Australia's Extremes

Margaret River Cabernet, such as one from Cape Mentelle, Leeuwin Estate, Moss Wood, or Vasse Felix

Coonawarra Cabernet, such as one from Lindemans (St. George), Parker, Penley, or Wynns Coonawarra Estate

Margaret River is in the far western corner of Australia, where gale-force winds off the ocean keep Cabernet vines cool; Coonawarra is a flat rectangle of iron-rich soil in warm, dry, and sunny South Australia. They produce such different Cabernet Sau-vignons that you'll probably be able to tell one from the other in just a couple whiffs. Try it, starting with the Margaret River wine. It's lean and dry, with an appetizing herbal edge. Now try the Coonawarra Cabernet. Wow, there's dense fruit in here, and instead of herbs there's a dark mineral edge. Taste them. Both are tannic, but feel how much more fruit flavor pads the tannin in the Coonawarra Cabernet. Can you taste the coolness of Margaret River in the leanness of the fruit? Can you taste Coonawarra's red soils in the earthy notes of the wine?

Get Frank with Franc

A Chinon, such as one from Baudry, Breton, Couly-Dutheil, Charles Joguet, or Olga Raffault

A California Cabernet Franc, such as Lang & Reed, Peju Province, Reverie, or von Strasser

A Long Island Cabernet Franc, such as one from Pellegrini, Schneider Vineyards, or Wölffer

Now you have three different takes on Cabernet Franc; to begin, just smell them and see if you can guess which one came from the coolest place. Does one smell like it was made from grapes that were less ripe than the others? A little less fruity, a little more peppery, a bit more acidic? That would be the Chinon. Now taste them in the order listed, and note how they feel. Can you feel the cool air in the tense acidity of the Chinon and the tighter feel of the fruit, like black currants on the edge of ripeness? Move to California and see how the wine feels softer, as if it's been fed by the sun—and yet it still has Cabernet Franc's telltale foresty green notes. Now try the Long Island wine, and see if you can imagine the hot summers that get the grapes so ripe and the cool breezes off the Atlantic that cool them down so they can hold on to that acidity.

If you have any Cabernet Sauvignon left from the previous tastings, pull it out to taste it alongside the Francs. Notice the lighter texture, the blacker fruit, that foresty green character? That's what's so cool about Cabernet Franc. And the fuller, more tannic flavors of Cabernet Sauvignon? That's part of what makes that variety so irresistible.

The Least You Need to Know

- For Cabernet Sauvignon–based wines in France, look to Bordeaux's Left Bank, particularly the appellations of Médoc, Haut-Médoc, Graves, Listrac-Médoc, Margaux, Moulis, Pauillac, Pessac-Lèognan, St-Estèphe, and St-Julien.

- California regions that stand out for Cabernet Sauvignon are Napa Valley and parts of Sonoma County, like Alexander and Knight's Valleys.

- In general, the more expensive a Cabernet, the more tannic it is, and the longer it needs to age before drinking.

- When a Cabernet Sauvignon is super tannic, pull out some rare beef or strong cheese like cheddar; the tannin will bind with the protein and leave your tongue alone.

- Cabernet Franc, a close relative to Cabernet Sauvignon, makes wines with similar but blacker fruit flavors and a green, herbal/foresty edge.

- To taste Cabernet Franc, look to France's Loire (Anjou, Bourgueil, Chinon, Saumur); California's Napa Valley; Friuli, Italy; and Long Island in New York State.

Chapter 9

Merlot

In This Chapter

- ◆ Merlot defined
- ◆ The tastes of Merlot
- ◆ Places Merlot thrives
- ◆ Finding your Merlot style

Merlot is to red wines what Chardonnay is to white: a grape as easy to love as it is to hate. Simple to pronounce and brimming with soft, plummy flavor, the variety took off in the 1980s, particularly in the United States.

Not long ago, however, Merlot was overplanted, overproduced, and over-exposed. Wine lovers who subscribed to the *Anything But Chardonnay* club typically eschewed Merlot, too.

Today, a lot of crappy Merlot is still around, but what was good is even better, and when Merlot is good, you'd have to be some curmudgeon not to admit it's delicious.

Where Merlot Grows

Merlot grows just about everywhere, but that's only because the demand is so high. The grape ripens relatively quickly, so it can take cooler temperatures than Cabernet Sauvignon, but not too cool. Northern Italy is about as cold as it wants to get, and even those Merlot wines tend to be an acquired taste.

Quick Sips

Merlot at a glance: a hedonist's grape, with soft fruit that ranges from red cherries to purple plums, and gentle tannins. It's often blended with a little Cabernet Sauvignon to give it more structure.

Merlot also can't take it too hot, or the grapes get ripe so fast their juice tastes more like melted grape jelly than wine because they become so devoid of acidity. If it's so hot that the grape sugars soar but the rest of the grape's elements (its tannins and other phenolics) haven't had a chance to develop, the wine can taste like roasted root vegetables: sweet and vegetal.

When it finds a place that's just right, Merlot ripens to the perfection of an August plum, plump and soft and giving, with enough acidity to feel bright and fresh and tannins that gently, smoothly grip the tongue. Some of the grape's favorite spots are …

- ◆ Bordeaux, France.
- ◆ Washington State.
- ◆ Napa and Sonoma Valleys.
- ◆ Parts of Italy.

Bordeaux, France (Again)

If you read the Cabernet chapter (Chapter 8), you know Merlot plays an important part in the wines of Bordeaux. The grape takes up more land there than any other, and the Bordeaux wines that are most in vogue today tend to be the ones with a preponderance of Merlot in their blends. That's because compared to the Left Bank's austere, Cabernet-concentrated reds, the Right Bank's Merlot-saturated reds are downright cuddly.

To find Bordeaux Merlot, look to the Right Bank of the Gironde River (see the map in Chapter 8). There the soils are heavy with clay, which holds a damp chill longer than the gravel of the Left Bank. Cabernet can't hack cold, damp feet, but Merlot does fine; in fact, here it's an advantage as the Right Bank is warmer than the Left, and the cool soils help Merlot to ripen slowly and fully.

There are areas of gravel and sandy soil, however, so Merlot does share Right Bank vineyard space with Cabernets Sauvignon and Franc. These Cabernets provide Merlot with needed tannin and acidity and add some different flavors. So just as Cabernet Sauvignon on the Left Bank often gets help from Merlot and other grapes, on the Right Bank, Merlot gets a hand from the Cabernets Franc and Sauvignon.

Of course, Bordeaux wine labels don't say Merlot or Right Bank. To find Merlot-dominated wines, look for …

- Pomerol.
- St-Émilion.

And their lesser-known neighbors …

- The Côtes de Bourg, Blaye, Castillon, and Francs.
- Fronsac (and Canon-Fronsac).
- Lalande-de-Pomerol.

The first two claim the most sought-after wines of the Right Bank. Pomerol's wines, which don't have any classifications beyond Pomerol, are known for lush flavors that hold a deep mineral note, said to be from the iron content in the soil.

St-Émilion is known almost as much for the beauty of its little hill town as it is for its plummy wines with their sweet core of Merlot. Its wines are classified in a scheme similar to that of the wineries of the Médoc

> **Off the Vine**
>
> Another thing to know about Merlot is that Merlot loves oak. Or, more accurately, many wine drinkers love Merlot that's been aged in oak barrels because the oak's vanilla-spice notes send the already friendly wine right over into the world of seriously hedonistic drinks.

on the Left Bank, except that it is amended every decade or so to take into account any changes in the region's wineries. It also terms its levels slightly differently: the top wines are called *Premiers Grands Crus Classés*, and the next level is *Grands Crus Classés*, followed finally by *Grand Cru* without the Classé.

Pomerol and St-Émilion hold many more tiny estates than the appellations of the Left Bank. It's often easier to find a decent wine for less than $30 over here, though prices rise into the triple digits to match those of the Left Bank, too. To find a good, everyday-priced Merlot-based wine, it's worth looking to the small, lesser-known appellations. While few of the wines will have the finesse and the longevity of the best wines from Pomerol and St-Émilion, many are delicious in their own soft, juicy Merlotian way.

Washington State

Merlot: here's a category where Washington soars past California in quality. It's not that California doesn't have some spectacular Merlot; it's just that the quality isn't as uniformly high. Washington State's Merlot also tends to be more elegant, with ripe black cherry and chocolate flavors held in check by acidity.

All the state's Merlot comes from the eastern side of the Cascades, in the Columbia Valley. Here, it's dry and sunny, since the mountain peaks hold the clouds at bay, forcing them to drop their rain on the western side. The vines also get long hours of sunlight during summer ripening season since the region is so far north. With a little irrigation pulled from the Columbia, Snake, and Yakima rivers, it's grapevine bliss.

Washington's AVAs

The Columbia Valley AVA covers 11,500,000-some acres east of the Cascades, dipping into Oregon. That's a large area, so to recognize particular microclimates within the region, the valley has been broken down into several subappellations. The standout AVAs are:

◆ Horse Heaven Hills

◆ Red Mountain

◆ Walla Walla

◆ Wahluke Slope

◆ Yakima Valley

Horse Heaven Hills: the Columbia River defines the southern border of this 570,000-acre AVA. The best Merlot vineyards are planted close to the river, where the vines can enjoy the water's moderating effects on temperatures, which spare them from winter freezes and summer's torrid heat spikes. Together with the clay soils, Merlot can ripen evenly, taking on a velvet texture. Not every part of this large appellation is as good as the next for Merlot; look particularly for Merlot from Canoe Ridge and Champoux, two vineyards from which several vintners make wine.

Red Mountain: at a max of 1,500 feet, it's more a hill than a mountain, but this area within the Yakima Valley has about 4,000 acres of very dry, gravelly, sun-soaked slope that are credited with some of the state's most powerful Merlot. In particular, wines from Ciel du Cheval, Kiona, and Klipsun vineyards stand out.

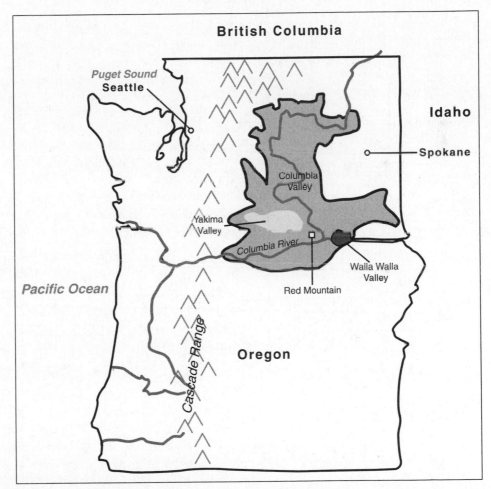

Washington State wine regions.

Wahluke Slope: right in the middle of Columbia Valley and far north of the rest of these AVAs, this very warm, arid AVA slopes from the Saddle Mountains south to the Columbia River. It was made an AVA only in 2006, so you should be seeing more wines labeled with this AVA over time.

Walla Walla: Walla Walla's 1,200 acres straddle Washington and Oregon with silty, basalt-rich soils edged by the Blue Mountains. It's significantly wetter (by 4 inches or so of rain a year) than Red Mountain, and the wines tend to be less powerful and more graceful. L'Ecole No. 41, Leonetti, and Pepper Bridge make fine examples.

Yakima Valley: this cooler region covers 11,000 acres that follow the Yakima River, including the higher elevations of Rattlesnake Hills, Red Mountain, and Horse Heaven Hills. The climate tends to make for lighter, finer Merlot than those from farther inland. Look particularly for wines from Boushey and DuBrul vineyards, such as Fidelitas (Boushey) or Owen Roe (Dubrul).

Are Merlot wines from these more specific areas better than those from the larger Columbia Valley AVA? Not necessarily. Winemakers who have access to land in different areas often blend grapes, using their differences to create a wine with different flavors and better balance. For a case in point, look to the Columbia Valley Merlots from Chateau Ste. Michelle and Columbia Crest, whose perennial popularity attests to the power of blending. The choice just depends on whether the winemaker wants to accent the flavor of Merlot particular to an exact place or the potential of the variety.

> **Off the Vine**
>
> You don't necessarily need to grow your own grapes to make great wine. You can buy them from a great grape grower. That's why you'll sometimes see the same vineyard name on wines from different wineries. For instance, McCrea and Betz both make wines from Boushey Vineyards in Yakima Valley.

Whether from a small AVA or the encompassing Columbia Valley, good Washington Merlot starts at about $10 and gets better at $18 to $35 or more.

California Merlot

California's Merlot is some of the most popular around and for good reason. The state pumps out gallons of sunny, plummy juice, ranging in price from $2.99 to more than $100.

Unfortunately, Merlot's quick ascent to popularity in the 1980s also provoked plantings that would have been better off left to pasture. When Merlot is bad, it's about as appealing as month-old vegetable stew. So how do we find the good stuff? Stay out of the hot Central Valley appellations and head to cooler, hillier land.

Degrees of Difference

Merlot doesn't like it too hot nor too cold. Where does that leave us? North of San Francisco, for the large part. Napa's Merlot tends to get overshadowed by its sought-after Cabernet Sauvignon; still the region is responsible for most of the state's most structured, concentrated Merlot. (It usually has a little help from Cabernet Sauvignon or Franc, as in Bordeaux.)

Over in Sonoma, Merlot finds its best homes in the region's warmer areas, where it makes big, rich reds that are generally slightly lighter than Napa's.

Typically, the warmer the region, the richer and riper the wine. So when you want a more restrained Merlot, look to cooler regions like Carneros or the Russian River Valley; for bigger Merlot, try Stags Leap, Howell Mountain, Rutherford, or Alexander Valley. Either way, expect to pay for the good stuff. Though you can buy decent party-quality Merlot with a basic California appellation, the great stuff runs $20 and higher.

Italian Merlot

Italy, the land of high-acid spaghetti reds, seems a strange place to find rich, soft Merlot, but it turns out to be well equipped for the variety. There are two major styles: light and acidic, and rich as any Napa Merlot. Each comes from different areas of Italy.

Light and Frisky

Merlot has a long history in northeast Italy, up in the Veneto, Trentino, and Friuli regions. In the chilly but sunny air, the grapes get ripe—but barely. That means they taste like juicy plums, but lightly so, with lots of palate-invigorating acidity. And Merlot from these regions is easy to spot as it always carries the name of the grape on the label. It tends to run $10 for easy aperitif-type reds to $20 to $30 for more structured wines. Check out Livio Felluga, Rocca Bernarda, and Villa Russiz for good examples.

> **Off the Vine** _____
>
> Head over the Alps from Italy into Switzerland and you'll find that not only has the language made it over the pass, but so has the Merlot grape. In the southern, Italian-speaking canton of Ticino, Merlot takes up the most vineyard space. It's chilly here, so Merlot del Ticino (as the wines are labeled) are more in the light, bright style of northern Italy than the lush, languid style of Tuscany.

Rich and Tuscan

Merlot is relatively new to Tuscany, but it's taken off in a big way since the so-called Super Tuscan wines proved its possibilities. Inspired by Bordeaux's blends, Tuscan winemakers often blend Merlot with Cabernet Sauvignon, which gives the grape a little more shape in the form of tannin and acidity. Some others feature the grape on its own, showing off just how richly ripe it can get in the warm hills of Chianti and its environs. Avignonesi, Castello Banfi, Frescobaldi, and Ornellaia make sought-after examples; prices start at $45 and rise into the triple-digits.

> **Off the Vine** _____
>
> Not so long ago Tuscan wines made from grapes like Merlot and Cabernet Sauvignon, considered foreign to the region, could only be labeled with the lowly *vino da tavola* moniker, and no reference to where or with what it was made. However, after many Tuscans went ahead and made very good, very expensive wine with them, the government established a new designation in 1992 called an IGT, or Indicazione Geografica Tipica, that allows Super Tuscan wines to claim Toscana, their origin, on the label.

The Rest of the World

Merlot is right up there with Chardonnay as a favorite among wine lovers and so is found just about everywhere. Not all Merlots are created the same, though, so proceed carefully. In these places you might find excellent examples.

Long Island, New York State

Long Island's cool, Atlantic Ocean–influenced vineyards bear some similarities with Bordeaux, Merlot's home, so it's little surprise that the grape does well here. Long Island Merlots aren't the bodacious beauties of California, though; instead, they offer some restraint and herbal flavors.

Chile's Merlot and Carmenère

Chile also makes some delicious Merlot. Here in Chile's Central Valley, which spreads around Santiago and stretches south, Merlot thrives in the abundant sun and warmth of the valleys between the mountains and the sea. Gallons of Merlot come from the warm flats of subregions Curicó, Maule, and Rapel, and most of this makes plummy, easy-drinking reds that sell for $6 to $13. To get firmer, more structured examples, vintners head up into the hills; some of the best Merlots come from the higher elevations of Cachapoal and Colchagua, particularly in Apalta, which Casa Lapostolle has made famous with Clos Apalta, a Pomerol-like blend of Merlot with other Bordelais grape varieties.

Quick Sips _____

Spanish-speaking Chilean wine lovers should check out www.planetavino.com for extensive coverage of the current South American wine and food scene (and lots more; in Spanish).

However, a lot of what was thought to be Merlot turned out to be another Bordeaux variety called Carmenère.

The Chileans are still sorting out which vines are Merlot and which are Carmenère, but now many vintners are bottling pure Carmenère—and some are still bottling Merlot that's made up in part or in whole of Carmenère. What's the difference? They have a similar feel, with round, rich, plummy fruit, but Carmenère is slightly smokier, with foresty, peppery flavors and a little more tannin. Some versions are bottled under the name Grand Vidure, an old Bordeaux synonym for Carmenère.

Off the Vine _____

How can winemakers not know what grape is growing in their vineyard? Well, because sometimes it's obvious—the leaves are shaped differently, or the grapes are a different shade of blue–purple. Other times, the differences are very hard to perceive by the eye alone, especially when there's nothing around to compare it to. Often, grapevines traveled from one place to another so many centuries ago their origins are lost, and the locals have devised their own names and ways of growing the grapes. In the case of Carmenère in Chile, everyone called it Merlot; there was no apparent reason to question it. That is, until a Bordeaux viticulturalist mentioned that this Merlot actually looked more like Carmenère to him. Years of investigation ensued, and still continue, but it has been determined that at least some of what was being called Merlot is indeed Carmenère.

Price-wise, if it's under $10, you can bet it'll be light and simple, like a similarly priced Merlot. At more than $10, it'll often offer more than a Merlot at the same price, with equal concentration but more smoky, interesting flavors. Rare bottles hit $20, and usually earn it with graceful, structured, concentrated flavors. Names to look for are Concha y Toro Marques de Casa Concha, Cono Sur, Montes, Santa Rita, and Terranoble.

Languedoc Value

When you're looking for very affordable Merlot for a backyard barbecue, this is where to head. The sprawling Languedoc region of southern France is home to many hundreds of acres of Merlot, which ripens quickly and easily in its sunny, low hills and flatlands. The results range from stinky, vegetal reds to hedonistically jammy, juicy drinks. Fortant de France, Lurton, Robert Skalli, and Tortoise Creek offer reliable buys for about $10.

Tastings: Merlot Matters

So now it's time to grab some bottles of Merlot and find out what style, if any, is to your taste.

Merlot, American-Style

A Merlot from Sonoma Valley, like Gallo of Sonoma, Clos du Bois, or Simi

A Merlot from California's Napa Valley, such as Cosentino, Duckhorn, or Swanson

A Merlot from Washington State's Columbia Valley, such as Chateau Ste. Michelle, Seven Hills, or Woodward Canyon

These three Merlot wines are from three places well respected for their take on the grape. Can you tell a difference between them? Line them up, and smell them. Keep in mind that Sonoma lies on the west side of the Mayacamas Mountains, within reach of cool air currents channeled off the ocean and San Pablo Bay. Over the mountains in Napa Valley, the only relief from the sun's beating heat is the coolness of altitude; altitude, however, requires digging deep roots to climb rugged, soil-poor mountain slopes. Washington's Columbia Valley can get just as warm, but the temperature plummets at night, giving the vines a few extra hours to relax and slow down the ripening process. Columbia Valley also gets more hours of sun per day than northern California—allowing the grapes to soak up extra sweetness.

So keeping this geography in mind, can you guess which wine was cooled by maritime breezes? Which struggled up the side of a hot valley? Which took its own sweet time over long, sunny days and cold nights to reach lush ripeness?

Battle of the Bordeaux Banks

A Left Bank wine, such as Château Coufran Haut-Médoc, Château Greysac Médoc, or Mouton Cadet Médoc Réserve

A Right Bank wine, like Château Cap de Faugères in Côtes de Castillon, Château Tayac in Côtes de Bourg, or Château La Rivière in Fronsac

If you have the bucks to splurge on wines from Bordeaux's big-name appellations, go for it; even so, you might want to check out these wines, all of which are both affordable and ready to drink, although none would suffer from a few years in the cellar, either. Pick a wine from the Right Bank that relies heavily on Merlot. Pick another one from the Left Bank that stresses Cabernet Sauvignon. Smell each of them. Can you smell Cabernet's lean, gravelly, pencil- and pepper-like tones? Does the Merlot wine smell fruitier, more giving? Does one smell a little bit more like black currants than black plums? Taste them. Can you tell which one is made from leaner, more tannic Cabernet, and which one depends on Merlot for its rounder, juicier feel?

Off the Vine _____

The best values in Merlot tend to be from Chile, where $10 can buy a super example. The fanciest, most impressive, and most expensive Merlots tend to come from Napa and Bordeaux, France.

Italian Examples

Northern Italian Merlot, like Sartori from Friui (under $10), Keber from Collio, or Doro Princic from Friuli

Tuscan Merlot, like Castello di Ama, Avignonesi, Ornellaia, Petrolo, or Falesco from Lazio, farther south

Here's an obvious pairing. Pick one from each category, and smell each of these. Can you guess which one is from the cooler, more northern area? Does it smell a little bit sharp and green in comparison to the Tuscan example? Taste them; bet you were right.

The Least You Need to Know

♦ Merlot is like the littlest of the three bears when it comes to where to grow: not too cold, not too warm, but just right.

♦ The warmer the growing region, the richer the Merlot; for lighter, tighter Merlot, look to regions like Northeastern Italy, Switzerland, and Long Island.

♦ In the United States, Merlot excels in Washington State, but Napa puts up stiff competition, and Sonoma offers some good examples, too.

♦ In Bordeaux, look to the Right Bank for Merlot-heavy wines, particularly St-Émilion and Pomerol at the top end, and Fronsac, Lalande de Pomerol, and the Côtes de Bourg, Blaye, Castillon, and Francs for more affordable options.

♦ Check out Carmenère (also called Grande Vidure), a variety long confused with Merlot in Chile, for wines with similar plummy flavors but more structure and spice.

Pinot Noir

In This Chapter

- ◆ Defining Pinot Noir
- ◆ Explaining the cost
- ◆ Where to find the best
- ◆ Pinot choices

Pinot Noir grabs wine lovers' hearts like few other grapes. Part of the attraction is its seductive fragrance, an ethereal mix of fresh and dried cherries, damp forest, and sweet spice. The other part is its texture, light and acidic yet filled with staying black fruit flavor. The grape's fickle personality is enough to dissuade most right-minded vintners from trying to grow it, yet the Pinot-committed will go to great lengths for their fix.

What's the Big Deal?

In the current craze for full-throttle reds, it might seem surprising a grape with a light color and ethereal flavor steals so much attention. But Pinot Noir is proof that size isn't everything; unlike Cabernets and Merlots that often earn points for depth of color and taste, Pinot's beauty lies in its delicacy and grace. The grape's thin skin doesn't offer lots of color-giving pigments, so rather than the deep, dark bordeaux color of Cabernet Sauvignon, Pinot Noir usually has a slightly earthy-looking pale burgundy cast.

Pinot Noir's flavors typically match its color in density, too, but whatever they lack in weight, they make up for in complexity. That means that in addition to light cherry flavors, Pinot Noir can offer an array of other notes, from spices to herbs to animals. With Pinot Noir, *barnyard* is actually frequently heard to describe its sometimes earthy, funky fragrance.

That weightless flavor is not only seductive, even addictive, but it also makes it exceedingly easy to match the wines with food. If you're at a table with a fish eater, a steak lover, and a vegetarian, Pinot Noir is the wine that will make peace with all three of them.

In general, the cooler the source, the lighter and more acidic the Pinot Noir; the warmer and sunnier, the riper and darker. But there's such a short limit to Pinot Noir's tolerance on either end that it's surprising so many people have tried to grow it over the years. The grape is one of the few major red wine grapes that prefers a pretty chilly climate; its natural habitat is Burgundy, France, and it's found in parts of Germany, too. However, unlike other grapes that simply make decent-but-not-great wine when grown in places that are a little too warm, too cold, too dry, or too wet, Pinot Noir fails miserably unless it's in a favorable place. If it's too cold, the wine tastes like an unripe plum: hard, green, no reason to take another bite. Too wet, the grapes rot. Too hot, the wine tastes like melted lollipops, devoid of the acidity and detail that give it grace and interest.

Pinot Noir also doesn't often make very good wine until the vines are at least a decade old. That gives Burgundy, France, where the vine has been growing for centuries, a nice head start.

So where does Pinot Noir succeed best? It's a short list of places:

◆ Burgundy, France

◆ Oregon

◆ New Zealand

A few other places put out some good Pinot Noir, but for now, let's look at these places to see what Pinot Noir lovers get so excited about.

Burgundy: The Pinnacle of Pinot Noir

France's Burgundy region has been hallowed for its fine Pinot Noir for centuries. It typically grows well along the region's chilly limestone ridge, although even here it can be too cold or too rainy to ripen the Pinot Noir thoroughly. The region depends on the variety for all its red wines (save for Beaujolais, which uses Gamay). And when it's good, it's easy to understand why; few wines in the world can claim such arresting scents and flavors and simultaneously feel so light and gentle as red Burgundy.

That transparency of flavor is key in Burgundy because a major element of its wines' attraction is their sense of terroir, the taste of the place where the wine was grown. Burgundians take the concept of terroir further than anyone else, dividing their vineyards into smaller and smaller parts based on geographical differences they find make a difference in the wines. The differences can be tough to spot, but it's a delicious task to try.

 Off the Vine

Even though red Burgundy looks and feels very light, the wine has the stuff to age well for years, becoming even more suffused with pleasantly earthy, truffly scents and flavors.

 Quick Sips

All red wines from Burgundy (except for Beaujolais) are made from Pinot Noir, though they do not say so on the label. And if the wine isn't from the French region called Burgundy, it isn't Burgundy, regardless of what the label says.

Burgundy's Varied Geography

Let's start with the big view; the most basic wines are labeled simply *Bourgogne*, French for Burgundy. A *Bourgogne Rouge* can be made from grapes grown anywhere in the Burgundy region. Typically, they are light, simple wines that run $10 to $25, the sort you'd find poured by the glass in French bistros.

From here, talk of red Burgundy usually revolves around three major areas, listed here in descending order of importance:

Winespeak

Bourgogne Rouge is French for red Burgundy, a Pinot Noir wine; *Bourgogne Blanc* means white Burgundy, a wine made from Chardonnay.

- Côte de Nuits
- Côte de Beaune
- Côte Chalonnaise

The Côte de Nuits is the northern half of the Côte d'Or, which is the heart of Burgundy; it is devoted almost solely to the Pinot Noir grape, unlike the other regions listed that share land with Chardonnay.

The Côte de Beaune is the southern part of the Côte d'Or; it claims more Chardonnay land than Pinot Noir but still offers some excellent Pinots.

The Côte Chalonnaise is farther south yet, between the Côte d'Or and the Mâconnais, and produces little red wine.

Each region is divided into many different communes, or villages, each of which has its own particular personality depending on its position, microclimate, and soils.

Here's the catch: wines from villages carry only the name of the village on the label; to know it's a Burgundy wine, the buyer needs to know the village is part of Burgundy.

My advice: make a cheat sheet to stick in your wallet. Look for these names, listed geographically from north to south so you can follow along on the map:

Red Wine Villages in the Côte de Nuits:

Marsannay	Vougeot
Fixin	Vosne-Romanée
Gevrey-Chambertin	Flagey-Échezeaux
Morey-St-Denis	Nuits-St-Georges
Chambolle-Musigny	

Red Wine Villages in the Côte de Beaune:

Pernand-Vergelesses	Ladoix-Serrigny	Aloxe-Corton
Savigny-lès-Beaune	Chorey-lès-Beaune	Monthélie
Pommard	St-Aubin	Auxey-Duresses
Beaune	St-Romain	Volnay

Red Wine Villages in the Côte Chalonnaise:

Mercurey   Rully (only tiny amounts of red)

Givry

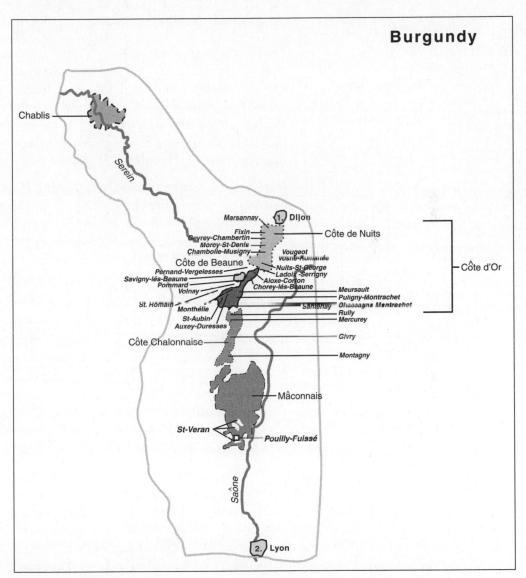

Burgundy's Pinot Noir regions.

It takes years of drinking Burgundy to distinguish the differences between wines from different villages, and there are always exceptions, but in the most general terms, the simplest wines come from villages such as Marsannay, Santenay, Auxey-Duresses, Monthélie, St-Romain, St-Aubin, and Rully; and the richest come from Gevrey-Chambertin, Morey-St-Denis, Nuits-St-Georges, Aloxe-Corton, Pommard, and Volnay.

Sour Grapes

Don't confuse Burgundy's designations with those of Bordeaux. In Burgundy, Grand Cru signifies the top wines, and Premier Cru is a step down; in Bordeaux, it's the opposite.

Quick Sips

Grand Cru Burgundies list nothing but the name of the Grand Cru vineyard on their labels—not even the term Grand Cru.

However, and this is a big however, the Burgundians have also declared 561 of their vineyards as *Premier Cru*, first growth, and another 30 even higher, as *Grand Cru*, great growth. If the wine is from a Premier Cru vineyard, it will carry both the name of the village in which it was grown and the vineyard name, followed by Premier Cru or *1er Cru*.

If the wine is from a Grand Cru vineyard, it will say nothing more than the vineyard name: no village name, no Grand Cru hint, nothing but the name of the vineyard. However, for better or worse, the price is usually a clear tip-off that you've ventured into Grand Cru territory; these easily hit $100 and keep moving up from there.

You don't have to spend a bundle to try a Pinot Noir from Burgundy, though. The most affordable Burgundies are labeled simply Bourgogne, which indicates that the grapes could have come from anywhere within the entire region; light and lively, they can be good buys at $10 to $25. Wines labeled with regional appellations within Bourgogne, such as Hautes Côtes-de-Nuits and Hautes Côtes-de-Beaune, offer good value for about $15 to $30, and many simple village wines (the ones labeled with the name of a village) can be had for about the same. If it's a special occasion, you might splurge on a $30 or $40 bottle. Anything above that should be darn special, and you might not want to drink it right away.

High-level Burgundian reds might seem tame in comparison to big, tannic Cabernet Sauvignons, but they hide considerable tannin and acidity within their delicate façade. Sock even a village Burgundy into the cellar for five years, and it will begin to take on complex flavors of nuts and spice; lose a Grand Cru in there for a decade or many more, and its velvet texture will take on beguiling notes of dried cherries, damp, forest earth, even truffles. Opening a Burgundy before its time is like cutting into a pear that isn't ripe: it's okay, but it would have been a lot better had you waited.

Oregon's Out Front

Oregon is far simpler to parse than Burgundy. The state makes extraordinary Pinot Noirs and lists the grape and the region from which it came clearly on the label.

Two regions in Oregon stand out for Pinot Noir. They are:

◆ Willamette Valley

◆ Umpqua Valley

Oregon's major wine regions.

The Willamette Valley (pronounced will-*am*-ette) is Oregon's most famous region for Pinot Noir. Situated in the northwest corner of the state, framed by mountains on three sides and the Columbia River to the north, its 100-mile length is Oregon's coolest grape-growing area, making it well suited to cold-loving grapes like Pinot Noir. Its Pinot Noirs tend to have a little more fruit flavor and a little less earth than Burgundy's, and yet the best share the delicacy and fragrance that makes Burgundy the model. They also happen to match excellently with Pacific salmon.

Off the Vine

For those who can't get enough Pinot Noir, many Pinot Noir festivals are held around the world. The Hospices de Beaune in Burgundy may be the most famous (www.hospices-de-Beaune.com/fr) followed closely by the International Pinot Noir Celebration (www.ipnc.org) in McMinnville, Oregon. If you can't make it, then www.princeofpinot.com will keep you up to date on recent Pinot news and events.

To the south, the warmer, drier Umpqua Valley produces Pinot Noir with a little more weight in fruit and texture. If Willamette Pinot Noir is built for salmon, Umpqua Pinot Noir is the answer for turkey, duck, or game birds.

Regardless of region, expect to pay at least $15 for good Oregon Pinot Noir and up to $75. Most run $20 to $30—a bargain compared to similar-quality red Burgundy.

New Zealand's Primo Pinot

New Zealanders originally pinned their red winemaking fame on Cabernet Sauvignon, but the exceptional Pinot Noir that began to emerge in the early 1990s spawned enough interest to make it the most planted red grape on the two islands by 1997. The sort of Pinot Noir New Zealand makes, though, can't be compared to Burgundy; it's a wine unto its own, darker and richer than most any others, filled with black raspberry and even licorice flavors. What keeps it in the Pinot Noir realm is the grape's hallmark acidity, which it retains in the country's cooler climates and which gives the wine's richer, darker flavors a pleasant lift. The regions of the country that particularly excel in Pinot Noir are as follows:

Off the Vine

Pinot Noir also plays a major part in sparkling wines. For more information, see Chapter 18.

- ◆ Wairarapa

- ◆ Martinborough

- ◆ Canterbury

- ◆ Central Otago

While each place gives its own character to Pinot, winemaking style has as much to do with the differences, so explore, and keep a running list of favorite names.

Off the Vine

New Zealand takes the lead in quality Pinot production in the Southern Hemisphere, but others are following, with good results. Check out Australian Pinot Noir, particularly from the very cool climes of Tasmania and the Yarra Valley; also look to Chile, which has been planting Pinot Noir in chilly places such as Casablanca and even Bío Bío in Patagonia to good effect.

A Few Far-Flung Pinot Posts

So far, we've concentrated on places that excel at Pinot Noir on a regular basis. Their lead has inspired plantings around the world, with mixed success. Here's a rundown of some of the more promising areas in which to go Pinot-seeking.

California

California's warm, sunny climate is exactly what sent vintners enamored with Pinot Noir running for the cool, cloudy reaches of Oregon. However, perseverance paid off for some who stayed—after they found cool pockets where the grape would grow well. If you're looking for good California Pinot Noir, look to these regions:

- ◆ Sonoma Coast

- ◆ Russian River Valley (including Green Valley and Chalk Hill)

- ◆ Carneros

- ◆ Northern Central Coast

- ◆ Santa Barbara (including Santa Ynez and Santa Maria valleys)

Sonoma Coast is one of the broader AVAs of California, stretching from Marin to Mendocino along the coast, but the vineyards that do actually come within spitting distance of the coast, or feel the breezes hard and cold, at least, make some of the most elegant, structured Pinot Noir in the United States.

The Russian River Valley sits up in the western reaches of Sonoma County. It's named for the Russian River, which pulls cool air up its length from the freezing waters off Jenner. It rarely gets really cold here, though, so the grapes have a long, slow growing season over which time they can pack themselves with spiced cherry flavor. The Russian River Valley also includes the Chalk Hill AVA and the even cooler Green Valley AVA.

Carneros lies farther south, straddling Napa and Sonoma counties where they run into San Pablo Bay. The bay sets this area apart as it sends fog rolling over the vineyards, where it acts as a shield to the sun and keeps the vines cool until late morning. There's also the wind, a stiff, cold breeze off the water that keeps the vines cool when fog isn't protecting them. The growing season is long, extended by the moderating influence of the bay in the autumn, so Pinot Noir can ripen slowly and coolly. A number of sparkling wine producers also take advantage of Carneros' cool climate to grow Pinot Noir for sparkling wines (see Chapter 18).

The northern Central Coast runs from San Francisco Bay to south of Big Sur and includes many AVAs. The areas where Pinot Noir thrives are in the cool, breezy mountain peaks, whether in among the cool, wooded Santa Cruz Mountains, the chilly eastern side of the Santa Lucia Range (where Santa Lucia Highlands clings), or further inland in the warmer Gavilan Ranges, where the tiny Chalone and Mt. Harlan AVAs lie.

Santa Barbara County is far south down the coast, just two hours north of Los Angeles. It might seem sensible to assume it'd be warmer down here—and in places, it is—but anywhere the sea breezes and fog whoosh in can be chilly, even colder than it gets in the Russian River Valley. And at this latitude, the growing season stretches even longer. The resulting grapes make some of California's most intense Pinot Noirs, at once concentrated and fragrant yet light and airy due to their acidity. Some vintners here label their wines by the county's AVAs, Santa Maria Valley or Santa Ynez Valley.

Quick Sips

Santa Maria Valley and Santa Ynez Valley are AVAs within Santa Barbara County.

Loire Valley

Burgundy isn't the only area of France that grows Pinot Noir; the Loire Valley grows a little bit of it, too, mainly in Sancerre. (See the map of France's Loire region, Chapter 5.) In this cool climate—most famous for its cool, crisp, mineral-laden Sauvignon Blanc—Pinot Noir makes pale, mineral-tinged reds with high acidity and earthy cherry flavors. These wines will not list the grape on the label.

> **Quick Sips** _____
>
> France's best Pinot Noirs come from Burgundy, but good versions are made in Sancerre, too. They tend to be lighter on the palate and the wallet.

Italy's Pinot Nero

In northeast Italy, where wines are typically labeled by their grape variety, some wines bear labels that say *Pinot Nero*. It's the same grape as Pinot Noir, just the Italian name. And as you might expect in these cold reaches, the resulting wines have bright, sharp acidity enlivening their earthy black cherry flavors—better suited for local game and wild mushroom dishes than for sipping on their own.

Germany's Spätburgunder

Late Burgundy is how *Spätburgunder*, German for Pinot Noir, translates. That seems strange, as the grape is considered an early-ripening variety, but in many of Germany's main growing regions, the season is too short for the grape to ripen fully. However, in warmer regions like the Pfalz, Pinot Noir ripens to a light, truffled cherry flavor. The last few years have even been warm enough to allow the Pinot Noir to attain fairly full black cherry richness. If global warming continues at the same pace it's been moving, we might well start seeing more and better German Pinot Noir.

> **Winespeak** _____
>
> In Germany, Pinot Noir is called *Spätburgunder;* in Italy, it's called *Pinot Nero.*

New York State

There's not much of it, but if you happen upon a bottle of Finger Lakes Pinot Noir, snatch it up. The cool, short summer here makes it tough to ripen the grape completely, but it also makes for nervy, frisky Pinot Noir that recalls some of Burgundy's most delicate.

Tastings: Picking Pinots

Listen to hard-core Pinot Noir lovers talk, and you might think that Pinot Noir is only found in expensive, unattainable reds from the hallowed vineyards of France's Burgundy region. Thank Bacchus there are more options than that. If you look around enough, you'll find everything from light, easy, affordable Pinot Noirs for summer sipping to weightier reds with enough spiced cherry fruit to stand up to a winter stew. In any category, Pinot Noir impresses with its combination of power and grace. Let's taste how many ways it can express itself.

Region vs. Village vs. Vineyard

Why do the Burgundians break their wine-growing regions into smaller and smaller parts? It's not just to be obtuse, and this tasting will help demonstrate that.

Here's the challenge (and you can get help from your local retailer): find a winery that makes a basic Bourgogne, a village wine, and a Premier Cru or Grand Cru wine. What you get will depend partly on availability of all three, and partly on what you can spend. If you can afford Domaine de la Romanée-Conti, go for it, but if you're like me, you'll be looking more for wines from more affordable wineries like Tollot-Beaut, Jadot, Domaine Bouchard Père et Fils, J. M. Boillot, or Antonin Rodet.

Line them up, from most general to most specific appellation. From the color alone, you'll probably be able to see that the wine from the most general appellation, Bourgogne, is the palest. Smell them. Do you detect a difference as you move from one to the next? Do the wines smell richer or more mineral? Taste them. Which one is the simplest? Which one packs more details into its flavor, as if it were describing a specific place? Which one would you guess would last longest if you were to put it in the cellar? Which one would you rather have for a fancy dinner?

Coming to America

> Domaine Drouhin Oregon
>
> Joseph Drouhin France

Here's a fun pair. Joseph Drouhin is a well-established Burgundy producer in Beaune. In 1987, Domaine Drouhin bought land in the Willamette Valley and began Domaine Drouhin. Today, Frédéric Drouhin oversees the domaine in France and his sister Véronique makes the wines in Oregon. So both wines are informed by a French point of view; the major difference is the land on which the grapes grow. Pour the wines side by side and see whether you can tell from color alone which is the American wine. Then smell. Can you smell the sun more in one than in the other? Taste them. Pretty different, hmm?

Of course, you don't have to use these two wines to make a comparison. You could compare any French red Burgundy with a California Pinot Noir. This pair is simply interesting because it puts the wines on a more even footing.

American Pinot Noir, North to South

> An Oregon wine, such as Domaine Serene, Rex Hill, or Benton-Lane
>
> A Sonoma County wine, such as Dutton-Goldfield: Flowers, Merry Edwards, Siduri, or Williams-Selyem
>
> A Santa Barbara County wine, such as one from Au Bon Climat, Miner, Sanford, Taz, or Testarossa

I picked these wineries not only because they make excellent Pinot Noir but also because they all make wines that hover somewhere around $30, so you don't have to spend a fortune. Whatever wines you do decide on, make sure they're around the same price so you're not comparing wines at wildly different levels of finesse.

Pick one of each, and line them up. Smell them. Do any smell lighter, more herbal, or spicier than the rest? Taste them. Does the scent bear out what it suggests in taste? It's going to be tough to tell one from another, to tell the truth, but it just goes to show you how much good Pinot Noir we have in the United States.

Differences Down Under

Australian Pinot Noir, such as Coldstream Hills, Nepenthe, Dromana, Ninth Island, or Yarra Yering

New Zealand Pinot Noir, such as Brancott, Craggy Range, Felton Road, Matua Valley, or Saint Clair

Both these countries are still new to the Pinot Noir game, but both have made impressive inroads in the last decade. Their styles tend to be very different, though, with New Zealand Pinot Noir offering denser, darker flavor and Australia holding more to a Burgundian ideal of heady but translucent flavor. Smell them both and taste them. Does one seem heavier to you? How would you characterize the difference?

The Least You Need to Know

◆ Pinot Noir is hard to grow, so expect it to be expensive.

◆ To find Pinot Noir in France, look for red wines from Burgundy; all except Beaujolais are made entirely from Pinot Noir.

◆ Although California and Washington State make some excellent Pinot Noir, neither beat Oregon for sheer concentration of top-notch Pinot Noir.

◆ For the best California Pinot Noir, look to the coast, specifically the Sonoma Coast and Central Coast appellations, such as Santa Cruz Mountains; or follow the fog into the Russian River, Santa Maria, and Santa Ynez valleys.

◆ If you're looking for a richer Pinot Noir, check out New Zealand.

◆ Because of Pinot Noir's light texture and high acidity, this red wine can go with fish as well as red meat.

Chapter 11

Syrah/Shiraz

In This Chapter

- Syrah, Shiraz, Sirah—which is it?
- The best Syrah spots
- The lowdown on Petite Sirah
- Finding your style of Syrah

Syrah and Shiraz are different names, but it is the same grape with the same luscious blackberry and spice flavors. Syrah (sir-*ah*) is the name of the grape in France, the source of most of the Syrah vines around the world today; Shiraz (shir-*ahz*) is what it was called after it arrived in Australia in the 1800s.

Today, Shiraz vines outnumber all other varieties in Australia's vineyards, and the variety continues to spread around the world. It's loved for its spicy fruit flavor, softer and richer than Cabernet Sauvignon but with more ummph and structure than Merlot. It comes in myriad styles, too, from barbecue reds to white tablecloth pours.

Sirah, on the other hand, is short for Petit Sirah, a completely different grape. We present it in this chapter anyway as it's worth checking out for its brooding black flavors.

France's Northern Rhône

Head south from Lyon along the gracefully curving Rhône River, and gradually the industrial suburbs will fade away into steep slopes covered with vines. It's here that Syrah attains a grandeur that long ago placed it among the world's most revered wines.

In the Northern Rhône, which stretches from Lyon down to about Tain L'Hermitage, Syrah is the only red grape grown. The grape never appears on the wine label, though. Instead, you'll need to look for wines from …

Quick Sips

Syrah at a glance: plums and blackberries, sweet spice and black pepper, and often a note of eucalyptus and a streak of vanilla, coconut, or dill from American oak barrels.

Quick Sips

For great Syrah, look particularly to France's Northern Rhône Valley, Australia, California, and Washington State.

- ◆ Côte-Rôtie.
- ◆ St-Joseph.
- ◆ Hermitage.
- ◆ Crozes-Hermitage.
- ◆ Cornas.

If a red wine comes from any of these appellations, it's made from Syrah. Each region, however, offers a slightly different take on the grape due to its microclimate and geography. Generally, moving north to south the vineyards get warmer and less steep, making for richer, softer wines. But there's a little more to it if you're interested in terroir, the particulars inspired the creation of these appellations, so I've broken it down for you.

Côte Rôtie

The Roasted Slope, as this appellation translates, is as far north as Syrah ventures in France. It's chilly up here—remember, it's not far from Lyon, famous for its hearty, stomach-warming food. This slope on the western side of the river is steep and stony—terrific for forcing the vines' roots deep into the earth and allowing the grapes to soak up long hours of sunshine. So the grapes get ripe but take their time, making for Syrah with spicy, restrained, roasted fruit flavors, and deep, earthy tannin. Most are so tannic that it's best not to open them for at least five years from the vintage.

Some vintners add a touch of Viognier, a white grape with an exceptionally floral fragrance, to their Côte Rôtie, which adds a delicate note to the brooding, tannic wine.

Either way, tending vines on slopes so steep takes courage, muscles, and a degree of insanity, so the wines aren't cheap. Expect good Côte Rôtie to start at $35 and soar upward.

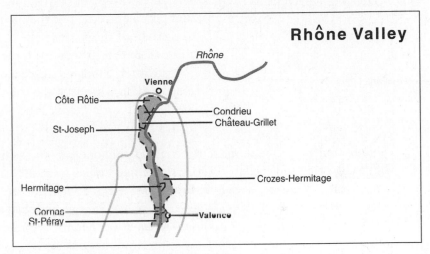

Wine regions of the Northern Rhône Valley.

St-Joseph

Continue south from Côte Rôtie on the same side of the river and the slope will gradually widen out, becoming the region of St-Joseph. It's an enormous appellation with many different microclimates, so it's a little hard to generalize about the style of wine it produces, but typically, St-Joseph's warmer climate and gentler landscape makes for warmer, gentler Syrahs—perfect for drinking while you're waiting for a Côte Rôtie to come around. The most expensive can offer lush berry fruit made more complex with earthy spicy notes, but most hover between $15 and $30 and offer soft, delicious spiced berry flavors.

Hermitage

Look across the river from St-Joseph and you'll see a monumental, balding hill topped with a little chapel. This is the small but revered appellation of Hermitage, named for a hermit who inhabited the chapel in the thirteenth century. The steep slopes around it are covered with vines. From their vantage point, the vines can watch the sun rise and set, enjoying every moment of its warmth.

As on most famous wine-growing hills, grapes grown in different parts give different flavors. Wines from the very top of the hill, where the dirt has eroded leaving nothing but hard stone, are the most austere and tannic, tasting as if they sucked up the power and flavor of the stone itself. In the middle of the hill, where there's more soil, the wines tend to be a little fatter, though still plenty mineral-filled and *peppery*. The bottom of the slope, where all the eroded soil settles, makes the plushest, most giving wines of all.

Some vintners choose to make wines from only one part of the hill and put the name of the plot on the wine label. Others combine grapes from different parts of the hill to present a balanced, liquid picture of Hermitage in its entirety. Both tend to be high quality (the appellation is just too small to bother with bad wines), though the single parcel bottlings tend to be more expensive, upwards of $80, as the parcels can only provide so many grapes. Like Côte Rôtie, Hermitage wines deserve a few years (or decades) in the cellar before opening.

Crozes-Hermitage

Crozes-Hermitage sprawls around the base of Hermitage. Its size makes it unpredictable; if a vintner pulled his grapes from the foot of the Hermitage hill where there's still a little bit of a slope, the wines tend to be more structured and interesting than those grown on the high-yielding flatlands farther inland. Unfortunately, there's no way to tell what part of Crozes-Hermitage a Syrah came from. The best bet is to spend $12 or more, unless a cheaper bottling comes highly recommended. The best Crozes-Hermitage reds taste like diminutive Hermitage reds, ready to drink far sooner but just as spicy and solid.

Cornas

The southern edge of St-Joseph gives way to the rugged granite slopes of Cornas. With the warmth of the southern Rhône at its feet and the chill of the Northern Rhône at its back, the region's 100-percent Syrah wines tend to be some of the most intense examples of Syrah in the region. Traditional examples needed years in the cellar before they became pleasurable drinks; modern producers such as Allemand and Jean-Luc Colombo are making friendlier versions that are approachable when young yet age well.

Following the Rhône South

Syrah continues to follow the Rhône River south, only it's joined by many other grapes as it goes and recedes into blends made up of many different grapes where it's valued for its dark, rich color, flavor, and tannic backbone (see Chapter 14).

It's not until Syrah hits the Languedoc, a large area along the Mediterranean, that it's showcased again, mostly in simple, easy-drinking reds labeled Syrah from the large appellation Vin de Pays d'Oc. These can be great buys at around $8 to $12.

Australia's Claim to Fame

Syrah was one of the first European vines to arrive in Australia, brought by nineteenth-century settlers who wanted a taste of France's Rhône back home. Though Rhône was the model—so much so that 50 years ago, Syrah wines were still being called Hermitage—Australians soon developed their very own style, informed by geography, climate, and of course the Australians' own attitude.

The grape grows in just about every wine-growing region of the continent, which means you have many different styles from which to choose. Most all, however, offer some degree of sun-soaked, dark plummy fruit, many with a streak of eucalyptus as if they've absorbed the sap from the surrounding trees. Here's a quick rundown of what to expect where.

Quick Sips

James Halliday, one of Australia's most respected wine writers, offers scads of information on Australian wine at www.winecompanion.com.au and subscribers gain access to tasting notes and more. Also check out www.wineaustralia.com, which holds a wealth of basic Aussie wine information.

Australia's wine regions.

South Australia

There's an Australian candy bar called Cherry Ripe, a heady combination of cherries and coconut wrapped in dark chocolate. Imagine that, and you have an idea of the character of South Australia's Shiraz.

Shiraz arrived here in the mid-nineteenth century, along with early settlers who found the fertile rolling hills around the bay to be prime farmland. You can still spot some cattle and vegetable plots between the vineyards, but today, Shiraz is so popular that grapevines compete mainly with suburban sprawl for land.

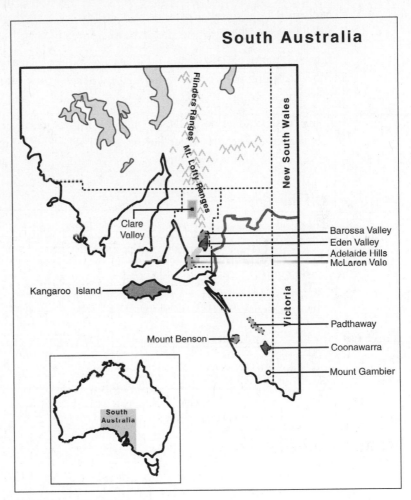

South Australia's wine regions.

It's easy to see why the wines are so popular, too; in this sunny, warm clime, the Shiraz is dark as black licorice and plump with juicy, plum and blackberry flavors. Often, too, Aussie vintners put their Shiraz into American oak, which gives the wines a distinct sweet vanilla cast.

Shiraz differs slightly from area to area in South Australia, which is why the government granted the region many different GIs (Geographical Indicators). They might be difficult to discern at first, but with practice, you might notice the following differences:

- McLaren Vale: excels in the lush-'n'-heady style of Shiraz in vogue these days, full of those Cherry Ripe flavors with some spice and tannin for extra spunk.

- Barossa: particularly warm and boasting some of Australia's oldest Shiraz vines, Barossa is known for Shiraz built like a Mack truck, densely ripe and packed with spicy, jammy fruit flavor.

- Clare Valley/Adelaide Hills: the slightly higher, cooler elevation of these two GIs makes for slightly finer Shiraz, still packed with black fruit flavor but with more acidity and less alcohol.

Off the Vine

Shiraz wasn't always popular in Australia. In the 1980s, a wine glut dropped the price of Shiraz grapes so low they were used in muffins rather than wine. In an effort to correct the oversupply, the government paid people to rip out their vines. The old vines that remain today are highly prized.

Victoria

The wine-growing regions of this state to the east of South Australia are far cooler than its neighbor, and its Shiraz is likewise leaner, spicier, and more obviously tannic. The wines fall someplace between South Australia and France in style.

Western Australia

Chardonnay and Cabernet attract most of the attention in Western Australia, but GIs like Margaret River far out on the cool western tip of the continent and Great Southern to the south produce lean, peppery, black-fruited Shiraz more similar in style to Rhône Syrah than most Australian Shiraz.

New South Wales

Shiraz is grown with increasing frequency all over New South Wales, but its stronghold is the Hunter Valley just north of Sydney. The region's hot, humid climate makes for Shiraz with a particularly earthy (some would say sweaty) flavor, an acquired taste perhaps but deeply loved by those who have developed it. Ripe and tannic, Hunter Shiraz usually benefits from a few years in the cellar to mellow out.

Southeastern Australia

This catchall appellation takes in many warm, high-production flatlands, and so it's synonymous with the Aussie idea of a good drink: simple, thirst-quenching, and affordable. Expect Shiraz labeled Southeastern Australia to cost no more than $12, while good examples from the country's smaller appellations tend to congregate in the $15 to $25 range, with special bottlings ranging from $60 to more than $100. More money usually means even more pleasure, but even at the low end, Australia Shiraz packs in a lot of value.

Shiraz–Viognier Blends

Lately, a lot of Australian wines have been showing up on the shelf trumpeting themselves as Shiraz–Viognier blends. It might sound strange to blend a white grape—especially one as floral as Viognier—with a dark red grape, but the combination is a long-held tradition in France's Côte Rôtie, where that little bit of white grape adds a discreet delicacy and brightness to a tannic, heavy wine. It does the same when added to Australia's Shiraz, only the addition is often more obvious—sort of like a clutch of white lilies floating on a dark sea of ripe, sweet fruit. To me, this is a delicious combination, but that's me. Try it for yourself.

California's Rhône Rangers

After spending years trying to make wines to compete with those of France's Burgundy and Bordeaux regions, a group of California vintners woke up and noticed how similar their land felt to that of the Rhône Valley. The group, formed in the 1980s, began looking into planting Rhône grapes like Syrah in California's more Mediterranean climates.

Off the Vine

It was clear the Rhône Rangers weren't nuts to plant grapes common to France's Rhône Valley when the Perrins, owners of Châteauneuf-du-Pape's esteemed Château de Beaucastel, set up shop in California's Central Coast. Today, the Perrins make excellent Rhône-style wines under the label Tablas Creek.

Today, there's a bevy of excellent Syrahs coming from all up and down California's length. The best come from the cooler corners of the state, taking on more spice and structure to complement their plummy fruit. Some standouts:

◆ Santa Barbara County, about two hours north of Los Angeles on the Pacific Coast, is a hub of Syrah production. Numerous microclimates give way to different styles of Syrah, but for the most part, expect dense yet juicy Syrah with black fruit and even black olive flavors and firm tannin.

Winespeak _____

Hang-time is how long grapes hang on the vines before harvest.

◆ Santa Ynez Valley is a cooler region of Santa Barbara County, north of the city of Santa Barbara. The climate allows the grapes a longer _hang-time_ here, and the longer the grapes hang on the vines, the more ripeness is possible, so expect succulent, sweet-centered Syrah with lots of spice and earth tones.

◆ Santa Maria Valley is also within Santa Barbara County. The valley sucks Pacific breezes up its length that cool the vines and let the grapes slowly ripen. The best Syrahs from Santa Maria combine the minerality of Rhône wines with the sunny fruitiness of California wine, with a kick of spice in the end.

◆ Napa Valley's best sites are mostly given over to Cabernet Sauvignon, so Syrah tends to get the warmer pockets of the valley, where it gets ripe and chunky.

◆ Sonoma County's cool corners, like the Russian River Valley, often give restrained Syrah, with frisky fruit and peppery spice.

◆ Mendocino County, just above Sonoma, tends to produce lighter versions of California Syrah, with spicy red cherry flavors and lots of acidity.

Quick Sips _____

If a California wine calls itself Shiraz, you can bet it's been made with the Australian style in mind: rich, ripe, and sweetened by the vanilla tones of American oak.

Regardless where Syrah comes from in California, expect $6 to $12 bottlings to be pretty simple, juicy, and light, with the sort of spicy cherry-berry flavors that complement a roast chicken. A few dollars more buys significantly more concentration—enough for a steak—and complexity, while $20 to $50 bottlings should offer minerality, earthy flavors, and a sense of a place as well as concentrated, lip-smacking fruit flavor.

Washington State

Syrah grown in Washington's sun-soaked Columbia Valley is some of the sexiest around, saturated with soft, ripe, even chocolaty fruit flavor yet firm with acidity and tannin. And Washington hasn't even been at it that long: the first Syrah vines were planted in 1985. Today, it's the third most-planted red wine grape (after Cabernet Sauvignon and Merlot), and the wines keep getting better and better.

As with Merlot (see Chapter 9), the warmer the region, the denser the Syrah. Look to Walla Walla and the Yakima Valley for some of the most graceful. High demand and low supply mean that you'll pay for the best, though; good deals are hard to find for less than $18, and wines can easily command $30 or more, especially for single-vineyard examples. Columbia Winery started the trend; Cayuse, K Vintners, and McCrea have become specialists in the variety.

Petite Sirah's Not-Petite Pleasures

Despite the name, there is nothing petite about Petite Sirah. It's not a diminutive version of Syrah or even a relation. It's a very old French grape that has nearly disappeared from France but has found a good home in California's warm climate. Its black, tannic profile makes it a good-blending grape; on its own, it's intense, with the sort of dark, teeth-staining flavor that requires a haunch of venison or other large, impressive hunk of meat to feel at home. Eos, Foppiano, Rosenblum, and Stag's Leap Winery make good examples.

Tastings: What's Your Syrah Style?

Do you want a light, easy-drinking bistro red? Syrah's your wine. Or do you prefer a meaty, spicy red with the guts for steak? Syrah's your wine again. Are you yearning for a lush, chocolaty red with more structure than most Merlot but a similar juicy richness? Syrah answers. Syrah's many interpretations ensure there's a Syrah for just about every taste. The only challenge is deciding which one you want now.

France's Hills and Vales

A Crozes-Hermitage from Delas Frères, Dard & Ribo, or Yann Chave

A Côte Rôtie from E. Guigal, Eric Texier, or René Rostaing

Do this tasting when you're feeling spendy, as Côte Rôtie always costs a small bundle (and good Crozes isn't cheap, either). It's a good idea to have a leg of lamb on hand, too, as it would be a shame to open these bottles and not show them in their best light, which is next to hearty, meaty food.

Start with the Crozes; it will be fruitier than the Côte Rôtie but less tannic. Smell them both; note the earthy tones of the Côte Rôtie. Then taste them. Note the smooth richness of the Crozes, especially next to the Côte Rôtie. Notice the earthy, almost rust-like character in the Côte Rôtie and its firmness, and think of the steep, sun-baked, rocky slope it grew on. Can you imagine it? Which one would you want with a roast chicken and which one with steak and fries?

All Across Australia

Western Australian Shiraz, such as Cape Mentelle, Howard Park, or Vasse Felix

A Victorian Shiraz, such as Jasper Hill, Rufus Stone, or Taltarni

A McLaren Vale Shiraz, like Coriole, d'Arenberg, or Rosemount Estate

A Barossa Shiraz, like one from Barossa Valley Estates, Elderton, Peter Lehmann, or Wolf Blass

Here's a short tour of Australian Shiraz, from the cool climes of Margaret River in Western Australia to the warm, sunny Barossa Valley in South Australia. Line them up. Do they look darker as you go down the line? Sniff them. Can you tell which one is lightest and which is richest? Taste and imagine what you'd want to eat with each one of them. And while you're at it, snack on some bread or crackers; these wines can pack a wallop of alcohol, reaching nearly 16 percent.

Down America's West Coast

Washington Syrah, like Betz, Cayuse, Columbia Crest, K Vintners, or McCrea

Mendocino Syrah from wineries such as Bonterra, Fife, McDowell, or Patianna

Santa Barbara County Syrah from Babcock, Fess Parker, Lincourt, Qupé, or Taz

The West Coast of the United States provides almost as many interpretations of the grape as France's Rhône Valley, maybe more. Which one should you pick? Well, do you want a Syrah that's ripe yet still holds on to enough acidity that it feels light, spicy, even a little frisky as if it would like some food alongside? An American bistro red?

Or would you rather have a Syrah that's dense with fruit from plums to olives, tannic and concentrated as if by the sun? Or how about something in between, like a version that's enjoyed long hours of sun as well as some cool, season-lengthening nights? Smell them. The Mendocino wine's acidity should make it smell lighter and brighter than the others. Taste them, Mendocino first, and notice how they feel. Is one denser, thicker than the other as if concentrated by the sun? Which feels more velvety (less acidic)? Which would you rather drink on a cold evening by the fire, and which on a sunny Sunday afternoon?

Que Syrah Sirah?

Rosenblum Cellars Dry Creek Valley Petite Sirah

Rosenblum Cellars Sonoma County Syrah

Or

Stags Leap Winery Napa Valley Petite Syrah

Jade Mountain Napa Valley Syrah

This first pairing is meant to give you the opportunity to taste a Syrah and a Petite Sirah side by side to compare the grape varieties without worrying about winemaking differences. The second gives an alternative should you not be able to find one or both of the Rosenblum wines. Feel free to substitute others; just make sure you have one of each grape variety. Pour the wines and give them a swirl. Can you smell the blackness of Petite Sirah's fruit? Can you feel Petite's harder, firmer tannins?

The Least You Need to Know

- Syrah and Shiraz are the same grape; Petite Sirah (and that's the correct spelling, though it's spelled Petite Syrah sometimes, too) is a different, more tannic, grape.

- The most Syrahs are from France's Northern Rhône Valley, labeled by village: Cornas, Côte Rôtie, Crozes-Hermitage, Hermitage, or St-Joseph.

- Wines labeled Shiraz are usually made in the big, buxom Australian style, with liberal fruit and vanilla flavors from American oak.

◆ Australia's most outstanding Shiraz regions are Barossa Valley, Hunter Valley, McLaren Vale, and Victoria.

◆ For great American Syrah, look to Washington, particularly Columbia, Walla Walla, and Yakima valleys, as well as to California.

Chapter 12

Zinfandel

In This Chapter

- California's hallmark grape
- The lowdown on white Zinfandel
- The range of red Zinfandel
- Italian Zinfandel

If importance is estimated by the number of places where a grape appears, Zinfandel falls low on the scale. If it's judged on how essential it is to a place, though, the grape is off the charts. As much Chardonnay, Cabernet, and Merlot as California grows, Zinfandel is is the grape identified most strongly with the state.

However, the grape didn't begin its life in America. As a *Vinifera* vine, the type that makes the best wines, it had to be imported. So how did it get here, and how did it manage to steal our hearts away from better-known imported grapes? That's a story long and exciting enough to fill a book (in fact, several have been written), but I'll give you a short lowdown. First, though, grab a glass of red Zinfandel; its spicy, juicy, jammy flavors may be all you really need to know.

Zinfandel's Origins

The question of how Zinfandel got to California has dogged historians since the late 1880s, and only recently has some of the story been cleared up. As Charles Sullivan accounts in his book *Zinfandel: A History of a Grape and its Wine* (University of California Press, 2003), Zinfandel enjoyed immense popularity in the 1830s and 1840s—as a table grape grown on the East Coast. But then the Concord, the big, juicy, purple grape made famous by Welch's grape jelly, pushed it out, and Zinfandel was largely forgotten until the 1880s when winemakers up and down California's coast were planting and praising it as a wine grape.

By then, no one knew exactly where it had come from, though ideas of its origins instigated passionate arguments. Most of them rotated around Arpad Haraszathy's claim that his dad, Agoston, had imported the vines from Hungary, a myth that lasted more than a century. It was thrown off track several times, but most radically in the late 1960s when an American visiting Apulia, Italy, discovered a vine the locals called Primitivo. It looked like Zinfandel and made wines that recalled Zinfandel.

It took another two decades to prove conclusively with DNA analysis that indeed Primitivo and Zinfandel are genetically identical, but it still wasn't clear where the grape originated. Researchers eventually traced Zinfandel to the coast of Dalmatia, where it's called Crljenak Kastelanski.

Off the Vine

So is Zinfandel originally from Dalmatia? It's impossible to say, though researchers believe that there's a better chance it originated there than in Apulia since so many related vines are living nearby. Why do we care? There may be much to learn from the way others grow and make their Zinfandel, and they may have better clones of Zinfandel than exist today in California. It gives winemakers a wider range of sources from which to pull knowledge and material.

As for how it came to be called Zinfandel in the United States, the jury's still out. (At least it's easier to pronounce.) Stay tuned for the next installment of the Zinfandel drama. In the meantime, check out the wine's many faces.

Zinfandel's Many Faces

For a grape that's so purple it looks almost black, it's a little surprising that the most famous wine it makes is pink. White Zinfandel, the pink version, is one of the most popular wines in the United States.

However, Zinfandel's proudest form is as a red wine. Its rich, black fruit flavors provide a wallop of juicy, friendly flavor—so much so that it's sometimes turned into a mouth-filling Port-like dessert wine (see Chapter.19 for the dessert styles).

Quick Sips

Zinfandel at a glance: red grape rich with spicy, blackberry flavor and high acidity. The wines often attain high alcohol levels (14–16 percent). It's made into popular pink wines as well as hefty reds.

"Blush" on Many Different Levels

With Zinfandel fan clubs and bottles that sell for more than a hundred bucks, it's hard to believe that just 30 years ago, California winemakers couldn't even give away the grapes. In desperation or brilliance, Bob Trinchero of Sutter Home Winery in California drew some of the "free run" juice, the juice that flows from the grapes simply due to their own weight, from his wine and bottled it separately as a pink wine. That was in 1972; by 1987, Sutter Home's white Zinfandel was the most popular wine in the United States; soon enough, a dozen other bottlings came to compete with it in the marketplace.

Today, in this decade of big reds, white Zin is often looked upon as some pansy pink wine. Some of it is extremely frivolous, with light, sugar-sweet flavors tasting vaguely of watermelon bubblegum. But better, drier white Zin, like DeLoach, can be a terrific aperitif chilled well on a warm day. Sweeter versions can be great foils for spicy takeout Chinese or Thai food, too. The sweetness of the wine complements the sweet notes in the food and blankets the fiery spice. And they rarely cost more than a carton of lo mein; $10 is about as pricey as white Zinfandel gets.

Hearty Reds

The wines that inspire Zinfandel's cultlike following are red. They come in all sizes and styles, from easy-drinking $3 bottles (no joke) that make good party wine or burger accompaniments, to $60 bottles of tannic black juice with as much detailed flavor as any other fine wine.

Off the Vine

Every January, Zinfandel lovers can take refuge from the winter cold at the annual ZAP (Zinfandel Advocates & Producers Association) festival in San Francisco. More than 200 producers pour their wines for a crowd of more than 9,000. If you can't make it but share the obsession, check out www.zinfandel.org.

No matter the price or style, Zinfandel's personality comes through. These are no shrinking violets; nor are they showy in the refined way of a Bordeaux or Barolo. They are more like pedigreed puppies, at once gorgeous and well bred yet exuberantly friendly, even boisterous, with lively, spicy, juicy flavors.

The Deal Behind "Old Vine"

Many California Zinfandels sport the phrase "Old Vine" someplace on the label, typically used to imply that what's in the bottle is an intense, concentrated wine. As the term has no legal meaning, this isn't always the case. However, when vines become truly old, let's say 60 years or older, they become less productive. Their roots grow deeper, their vigor diminishes, and they produce fewer grapes. By the time they are 80, they are barely eking out any grapes, but what grapes they do put out tend to benefit from the concentration of effort.

Sour Grapes

Though "Old Vine" is typically used to indicate wine that has come from truly old— we're talking 70, 80, 100 years old—the term has no legal meaning anywhere in the world. That means that the wine you pick up that says old vines could come from vines that aren't old at all. How can you avoid this? You can't, unless the winery discloses the age of the vines on the back of the bottle, or you can ask them directly.

Remember, though, that not all wines made from old vines say so on the label and that it doesn't have to be made from old vines to be good. Careful work in the vineyard can also ensure concentrated flavor. Drink what tastes good to you.

Zinfandel's Purview

Vintners in France, Australia, and other places now grow Zinfandel, but no place grows it as well as California. Here's a place-by-place breakdown of Zinfandel's strongholds.

Central Valley Zin

The Central Valley is the wine sea of California. Hot, flat, and fertile, its 25,000 square miles grow literally tons of grapes, not to mention artichokes, garlic, lettuce, and more. Much of the Zinfandel grown here is treated as workhorse variety—that is, it's there to grow lots of grapes to make into lots of affordable wine. Much of it goes into making white Zinfandel.

There are pockets of the Central Valley, though, that produce distinctly higher quality Zinfandel, like Lodi.

Lodi, Mother Lode of Zin

East of the Sacramento River and north of Stockton, Lodi's flat acres look like much of the rest of the flat Central Valley, but some miracle of geography—here, the delta—pulls an uncannily cool breeze off the ocean and through the area. This keeps it cool enough to produce grapes that have more complex flavor as well as prodigious amounts of sweet fruit. Most Lodi Zins run $10 to $20 and top out at $30.

Head east, and there's more Zin in the hills—the Sierra Foothills.

Sierra Foothills Zin

East of Lodi and into the Sierra Foothills, Zin rules the land, particularly in the AVAs Amador, El Dorado, Fiddletown, and Shenandoah. This has been Zin country since the Gold Rush, and there are some very old vines to show for it. Together with the warm, rolling hills, Sierra Foothills Zins tend to be very ripe, peppery, and generously fruity. They also tend to be a bit more expensive than Lodi Zins, with most of the best examples running $20 to $30. Names to look for are: Renwood, Shenandoah Vineyards, and Sobon Estate.

Off the Vine

If you're not sure what Zin to buy, look for the Rs. For whatever reason, many of Zinfandel's most famed producers begin with R: Rabbit Ridge, Rafanelli, Ravenswood, Renwood, Ridge, and Rosenblum.

Paso Robles Zin

Over in San Luis Obispo County, the Paso Robles AVA produces Zinfandel that defines the slurpy, super-rich style of Zinfandel. It's very warm here, but with coastal breezes and a short climb into the Santa Lucia Range that creates a large drop in nighttime temperatures, the grapes can ripen fully and slowly, creating a core of sweet cherry flavor surrounded with plump, rich, plummy fruit. Some of the best come from Eos, Eberle, Peachy Canyon, Rabbit Ridge, and Rosenblum.

San Francisco Bay Zin

The areas around San Francisco were some of the first to be planted by immigrants, and thus are the source of some excellent old-vine Zinfandel. It's here in Contra Costa County that Zin specialists Rosenblum and Cline Cellars get old-vine Zinfandel for some of their most intensely black and jammy Zins.

The most acclaimed Zinfandels, however, come from farther north, in Sonoma, Napa, and Mendocino.

Napa Zin

As long as Napa Cabernet Sauvignon gets all the attention (and its grapes go for twice the price of Zinfandel), its Zinfandel will be a comparative bargain. It's not cheap (some examples hit $70), but it doesn't taste cheap, either. As with Napa Cab, Napa Zin is rich and tannic, built to be impressive and live long, especially when it's grown in the mountain appellations like Howell Mountain, Diamond Mountain, or Mt. Veeder. Check out Chateau Potelle, D-Cubed, Howell Mountain Vineyards, or Storybook Mountain for good examples.

Napa's stiffest competition when it comes to high-class Zinfandel is its neighbor, Sonoma.

Off the Vine

The ATF (Bureau of Alcohol, Tobacco, and Firearms) is notoriously difficult when it comes to getting a wine label approved. It has turned down labels that show nudity (even when the nudity is a famous artist's rendering on a bottle of Mouton-Rothschild, like the 1993 label designed by Balthus) or contain anything that might be considered remotely offensive. Abbreviations seem to be oblique enough to pass through without objection, though, if Chateau Potelle's Zinfandel is any indication. It's called V.G.S., short for Very Good, um, Stuff.

Sonoma Zin

Sonoma leads the way in fine Zinfandels. Not only is there more than twice as much of it here as in Napa, but there are also more old vineyards, a legacy of Italian settlers, that put out intensely flavored fruit.

The warm, ruddy soils of Dry Creek Valley produce the most hallowed Zinfandels, dark and brooding with black fruit, black smoke, and black spice flavors, smooth and lush. Some of Zinfandel's most famous names make wines from Dry Creek Valley Zinfandel, like Dashe, Quivira, Ridge (Lytton Springs), Rafanelli, Rancho Zabaco, and Ravenswood (Teldeschi Vineyard).

Russian River Valley is no little shakes either; its cooler climate produces livelier, bright, spicy Zinfandels, like those of DeLoach, Dutton-Goldfield, Limerick Lane, and Martinelli.

Alexander Valley turns out chocolaty examples, too, as bottlings from Alexander Valley Vineyards (SinZin), Rosenblum, and Seghesio show. Most of the best Sonoma Zins run $20 to $40.

Mendocino's Slim Zin

Mendocino's Zinfandels are overlooked in this era of bigger-is-better reds. In this cool, northern region, Zinfandel gets less sugar-sweet and more spicy, creating a lean powerhouse of a wine. The style is great for more delicate red meat dishes, as well as any time you don't feel like getting hit over the head with your red. Look for wines like Edmeades, Fife, and Lolonis.

Zinternational

The positive publicity, high scores, and high prices that Zinfandel has achieved over the last two decades have attracted attention from all over the world. Though it's still difficult to find a bottle outside the United States, winemakers in other countries are beginning to experiment with it. The grape has made its way to Mexico, where Château Camou makes a spicy Baja version, as well as across the ocean to Domaine de l'Arjolle in France's Languedoc. Kangarilla Road Vineyard also makes a rich, smooth version from Zinfandel grown in South Australia's warm McLaren Vale region.

The biggest plantings of Zinfandel outside the United States are those that have been grown in Apulia, Italy, for centuries under the name Primitivo.

Italy's Primitivo

It's true that Primitivo is essentially the same grape as Zinfandel, but that doesn't mean it tastes the same. It tastes similar, to be sure, plump with juicy black fruit and spice, but it doesn't taste American.

Some of that is no doubt because of where it grows, in the hot, sunny western side of the heel of Italy's boot, where the grapes ripen quickly and sometimes even get a little sunburned. Much of it has to do with a comparative lack of technology. And there's just the simple fact that it's made by Italians, and so Primitivo naturally has Italian soul.

So when you're looking for something dark and juicy to go with your sausage and broccoli rabe or just something like Zinfandel but a little more Italianate, check out Primitivo. It's easy at the prices, which rarely go over $20, even for the best examples, which are usually those labeled with the DOC Primitivo di Manduria, the name of a region on the west side of the boot's heel. Look for examples from A-Mano, Botromagno, Ca'ntele, Casa Catelli, and Palama to check it out.

Tastings: Shades of Black

Many people think of Zinfandels as all tasting the same: black. But there are many shades of black. Here are some tastings you can do to show up those differences and hone your red Zinfandel I.Q. I'll leave any white Zinfandel tastings up to you.

Zinfandel's Reach

A Mendocino bottling from Bonterra, Carol Shelton, Edmeades, Fife, or Lolonis, for instance

A Paso Robles bottling from the likes of EOS, Eberle, Rabbit Ridge, Peachy Canyon, or Wild Horse

Pour one of each of these into two glasses. You'll probably be able to see a difference; not many wines are thicker than Paso Robles Zin. Now swirl the wine in the glass, and watch it drip back down into the bowl. Is the Paso Robles wine more coating than the other? Now swirl and sniff. Which smells spicier, like it comes from a cooler climate, and which smells more like a jam pot, like it's been made from fruit that has warmed long in the sun? Does the taste prove your guess out? Which one do you like better? Which one would you rather have with your Thanksgiving turkey, and which one requires a T-bone steak?

Napa's Mountains and Sonoma's Valleys

A Zinfandel from Sonoma's Dry Creek Valley; Bella, Ridge, Dashe, Murphy-Goode, and Roshambo are just a few good examples

Napa Mountain Zinfandel, like Chateau Potelle, D-Cubed, Green & Red, Howell Mountain Vineyards, or Storybook Mountain

First, consider the geography and its effects on a grapevine. Mountain vineyards are typically steep (hard to hold on to), the soil has eroded away (hard to gather nutrients to grow), and there are lots of warm sun (sun means sugar) and cool air (coolness slows down ripening). If any vine is going to survive here, it's going to hold on tight, soak up all the sun it can get, and yet grow its fruit slowly and with restraint

Valleys, on the other hand, tend to be more like cradles, areas that catch the sun and the soil that erodes off the side slopes. Dry Creek's low, soft slopes have mineral-filled red soils that soak up the abundant sun.

Which one is going to make the more tannic, stony, determinedly concentrated wine? Which will make the softer wine with gentle, generous rolls of mineral-laden fruit? Wine often mimics the land in its flavor, so taste one each of these and see whether you can imagine where it came from.

Zinfandel vs. Primitivo

A Primitivo from Italy, such as A-Mano, Ca'ntele, Casa Catelli, or Palama

An equally affordable ($10 to $15) California Zinfandel, such as Angeline, Rosenblum, Screw Kappa Napa, or Sobon Estate

Pour one of each of these side by side, and they'll probably look much the same. Distinguishing between them in smell might be pretty tough, too. But now taste them. Can you taste the baking sun in one of them more than the other? Does one taste somehow more Italian than the other? Some people think so, some people don't; these sorts of differences cause long arguments in the wine world.

The Least You Need to Know

◆ Red Zinfandel and white Zinfandel (a pink wine) are made from the same grape, Zinfandel.

◆ Wine snobs love to poke fun at white Zinfandel, even though it is hugely popular in the United States, so if you like it, don't let anybody tell you you're wrong.

◆ Italy's Primitivo and California's Zinfandel are genetically identical, though they taste different.

◆ For lighter yet still-gutsy Zinfandel, look to cooler appellations like Mendocino, but for the biggest, richest Zinfandel, check out those from California's warmest wine regions, like Lodi and Paso Robles.

◆ For Zinfandel that can age like fine Bordeaux, check out the reserve bottling from Napa and Sonoma.

◆ Overall, it's pretty difficult to find truly bad Zinfandel at any price, even $3.99.

Part 3

Regional Specialties

We've covered the big grapes, the most popular and wide-ranging varieties, but sticking to those constantly is like listening to Top 40 radio these days: eventually, you get tired of the same songs. Sometimes you need to flick the dial and find something different, more exciting, more soothing, or more exotic. These six chapters offer another world of wines to explore.

We start with some whites that'll add an exotic note to any day: fragrant Chenins, spicy Gewürz, luscious Viognier. We delve into France's southern Rhône and sunny Languedoc for spicy reds and summery whites. We explore Spain, Portugal, and Italy, and we even go to South America and cover places we haven't even skimmed. Grab a glass: we're going for a spin.

Chapter 13

France's Fragrant Whites

In This Chapter

- ◆ Seductively scented varieties
- ◆ Where these grapes grow
- ◆ When you'd want to drink these wines
- ◆ How much you should expect to pay

It's amazing how much fragrance a pale liquid can hold. Flowers, fruit, spice, honey … a fragrant white wine can transport you to a garden, an orchard, a spice market, or just provide an exotic note. The white wines in this chapter tend to pack more heady fragrance into every sip than any others.

The grapes used for these wines are often made into sweet wines, but we'll leave those for later (see Chapter 19) and, here, talk only about the savory versions. You'll want to know about these wines when you're looking for a conversation starter, an intriguing aperitif, or just a delicious, unusual dinner companion. You've probably heard this before, but that's only because it's so true: the spicy, exotic flavors of these wines make them ace pairings with the complex flavors of many Asian dishes. If you like Chinese takeout, you'll want to have a store of these in your fridge.

Chenin Blanc

Chenin Blanc (*shen*-in blahnk) is a strange and wonderful white grape. In most places, it makes plonk—really lackluster white wines, simple sippers at best. But every once in a while and in one particular place with amazing regularity, it turns out rich wines fragrant with the scent of honey, quince, almond blossoms, and spice.

Quick Sips

Chenin Blanc at a glance: light and floral at least, lush with honey, quince, and mineral flavors at best, with lots of invigorating acidity.

Chenin Blanc also has plenty of acidity, though it's typically not very obvious. Good versions can age for decades, taking on deeper, richer, spicier flavors.

Its hallmark flavor, however, is a strange one and more appealing in experience than in theory: a lanolin scent, like the smell of sheep's wool. People who haven't spent time shearing sheep (I have) might think of it as hay or beeswax. You'll just have to try it to see what I mean. Where can you find it? France, South Africa, and occasionally, California.

Loire Lushness

France's Loire Valley makes definitive Chenin Blanc. In the maritime climate of the western Loire Valley (the opposite end from where the lean and sharp Sauvignon Blanc grows), the grape takes on flavors of quince, apple blossoms, spice, nuts, and that hallmark lanolin character, plus lots of minerality.

Quick Sips

Some great names in Loire Chenin are Chidaine, Closel, Laureau, Huet, Joly, and Soulez.

Loire wines made from Chenin Blanc won't say so on the label. Instead, you'll have to look for white wines from …

- ◆ Anjou.
- ◆ Savennières.
- ◆ Saumur.
- ◆ Vouvray.

Saumur tends to offer the lightest, crispest, and most affordable Chenin Blanc, with Anjou right behind. Vouvray and Savennières vary widely in style, from quince-flavored wines with cutting acidity to marzipan-rich, long-lived treasures that can command $80 or more. Savennières also claims one of the smallest appellations in France, the 17-acre Savennières–Coulée de Serrant, which is owned in its entirety by Nicolas Joly (pronounced jo-lee), who bottles wines under his own name.

Loire Chenin Blanc is also turned into an array of sparkling wines (see Chapter 18) and sweet wines (see Chapter 19).

South Africa's Sipper

Chenin Blanc is to South Africa as Chardonnay is to California: an all-purpose grape, grown everywhere and turned into wines that range from mindless quaffs to pricey splurges. It's so popular there that it's hard to find South African Chenin Blanc outside the country because they drink most of it up. But when you do find one, give it a try. It might be labeled *Steen*, the South African name for the grape; otherwise, it will say Chenin Blanc on the label. Versions under $10 will be simple, aperitif-style wines with light, gentle, honeyed apple flavors. Over $10, the wines should approach the Loire's in richness and style. Rudera, Raats Family, and Man Vintners all make good examples available in the United States.

California Chenin Blanc

Chenin Blanc is grown in the United States, South America, and Australia, but most of it is farmed to produce tons of grapes, which makes for tons of innocuous juice. California claims a few standouts, however, that are among the greatest values in the state. As unlikely as it sounds, some of the best come from Clarksburg in the warm, damp Sacramento River Delta; Dry Creek Vineyards and Pine Ridge set the model. Also check out Chappellet in Napa Valley. With dry, floral honey flavors and bright acidity, these wines show Chenin to its best advantages.

Gewürztraminer

Gewürz (geh-*vurtz*) means spice; Traminer is a family of grapes, of which this is the most famous. It's not that the other family members aren't good; it's just that *Gewürztraminer* (geh-*vurtz*-tra-*mean*-er) is hard to ignore. It's the Carmen Miranda of grapes: fruity, spicy, and outrageous.

Winespeak

Gewürz (geh-*vurtz*) means spice in German; it's also shorthand for *Gewürztraminer*, the grape or the wine.

Its fruit flavor is often described as lychee, which is amazingly accurate if you know what those fruits smell like. Think, too, of Damask roses, the heavily perfumed kind, and of the spices in a spice market—sweet cinnamon, pungent turmeric, piquant peppers. It's all there in Gewürz.

The only thing that the grape often lacks is acidity, but when the acid is there, Gewürztraminer can make some lively, exotic whites that can age for years. Where can you find good ones? Alsace, in particular, and a few other areas.

Unbridled Alsace

For the best examples of Gewürztraminer, head straight for Alsace. (Just don't look for the umlaut on the *u*, because this is France, and the French don't use them.) Here along the cool, sunny ridge parallel to the Vosges Mountains, the grape soaks up the sun and translates it into sugar and spice.

Quick Sips _____

Gewürztraminer at a glance: pale to deep golden in color, with exotic, rich, spicy scents and flavors of lychees, grapefruit, roses, and sweet and bitter spices; often low in acidity.

Though elsewhere in the world Gewürztraminer can make light, aperitif-weight wines, Alsace's versions are almost always heady and rich, with sweet flavors even when they are stone dry. That richness, along with an almost bitter edge of spice, makes them seem particularly suited to the region's sausage-and-sauerkraut cuisine. Then again, they go well with spicy Thai food, too, matching spice with spice and blanketing pepper-induced fires with their satin texture. Look to Kuentz-Bas, Trimbach, Weinbach, and Zind-Humbrecht for some of Alsace's best examples.

Elsewhere, an Exotic Alternative

Those who find Alsace's Gewürztraminer too heady and heavy might want to look to California and Washington. Few examples are available (Handley is one standout), but those that are tend to be lighter and fresher—a great aperitif or match for spicy cuisines. They also tend to be far less expensive than Alsace's versions, which can easily hit $50 and rise from there.

Off the Vine _____

White wines can be tannic, though it's rare. Gewürz is one of the few white wines that commonly has noticeable tannin; to buffer the bitter edge of the tannin, vintners often make the wines with a touch of sweetness.

Muscat

Not sure whether to bring flowers or wine to a gathering? You can bring both in one bottle when you bring Muscat (*mus*-kat). Wines made from this grape—and there are many, as it grows everywhere—are immediately recognizable by their pretty floral scent, paler and more delicate than Gewürztraminer's and without the spice.

The grape grows everywhere; in fact, there are a number of different kinds of Muscat, the major two being Muscat Blanc á Petit Grains and Muscat of Alexandria. The former is said to be finer; the latter, heavier with sweet, musky flavor, but most of the time the label won't tell you which sort of Muscat is in the bottle anyway.

Most Muscat grown around the world is made into sweet wine, but if you see one in the dry white wine section, pluck it out. Light, simple, and typically less than $10, dry Muscat can be a lovely white wine to have on hand for drop-by guests or Sunday brunches. Some great dry Muscat producers to search out are Boxer, Deiss, Dirler, Schlumberger, and Zind-Humbrecht in Alsace; Heidi Schröck in Austria; Navarro in California; and Theo Minges in Germany.

If any place excels in dry Muscat, it's Alsace. There's not much, but what it produces tends to be delicious, dry as stone but fragrant with orange blossom scents. It makes a lovely aperitif, or accompaniment to light fish and vegetable dishes. Look also to nearby Germany, where the grape goes by Muskateller. Just be forewarned: high-quality dry Muscat can run $20 to $80.

Quick Sips

Muscat at a glance: pale color with light, sweet, green-grapey fruit, a delicate flowery fragrance, often like orange blossoms, and low acidity. Most Muscat is best drunk young.

Whether Muscat, Moscato, Moscatel, or Muskatollor, it's all Muscat.

Moschofilero

Greece also grows Muscat, but the country's most interesting dry wines come from Moschofilero (moss-kho-*fee*-lair-oh). It's not related to Muscat, but its flowery fragrance has strong correlations; some of the best versions (Tselepos, Spiropoulos, Nasiakos) also have a spicy quality that brings to mind Gewürztraminer.

The grape has taken off in popularity in the last decade, but its stronghold remains Mantinia, a high, cool plain in the Peloponnese. Wines labeled Mantinia must be made from Moschofilero; they may or may not bear the grape's name. Most run about $15; a couple near $30.

Viognier

Peaches, cream, and honey—what's not to like about Viognier (vee-o-*nyay*)? The grape makes some of the most hedonistic wines out there, rich and pillowy with stone fruit flavors and aromas. It gets so ripe it's often made into dessert wines, so when it's vinified to dryness, it often comes packed with alcohol, too; 14 percent is common.

Quick Sips

Viognier at a glance: gold hue; heady, rich peach and apricot flavors and aromas; low acidity.

In good versions, the alcohol is barely noticeable; in fact, the grape needs it to hold up all its ripe fruit flavors because it doesn't have much acidity. Although there are some light, airy Viognier wines, mostly from young vines, most are winter whites, pendulous with the warming flavors of summer sun and August fruit and ready to match a veal stew or shrimp risotto. Where can you find the best? In a word, Condrieu (con-dree-*uh*).

Condrieu Is King

If you want to taste Viognier at its most exalted, head straight to the French section of the store, and pick up a bottle of Condrieu. Make sure your wallet's fat, though, for these aren't cheap wines by anyone's estimate.

Quick Sips

All Condrieu is made from Viognier, though it won't have the grape on the label.

The issue is this: Viognier is a lush. If it could, it would soak up all the sun it could, give up all its acidity, and offer up blowsy, overbearing flavors saturated with alcohol.

In this little pocket of France's northern Rhône Valley, though, cool weather and the steep, rocky slopes the vines cling to keep the grape in check so that it produces richly ripe yet shapely, graceful flavors. The best even have underpinnings of mineral flavor that firm them up.

Off the Vine

Château-Grillet is a tiny appellation within Condrieu defined by the steep terraced slopes surrounding the area. With only nine acres and one owner, Château-Grillet doesn't put out much wine, but it's revered for its nutty, more restrained flavors and its ability to age.

The challenge of picking wines on these vertiginous slopes (one vineyard is called The Gates of Hell), the low yields, and the capriciousness of the variety all lead to high prices for the wine: $25 and up. But if you like peaches and honey, you'll love Viognier, especially over lobster tails on a date.

Languedoc Alternatives

If you can't afford Condrieu or you want its flavors in a lighter version, head down river to the Languedoc. Producers across this sprawling band along the Mediterranean Coast have planted Viognier in the last decade. Whether due to the youth of the vines or higher yields, Languedoc Viognier tends to be very light, with soft peach flavors and a floral scent. It makes a pretty aperitif or summertime refresher. It's also easy to find, as Languedoc producers put the name of the grape on the label, and it runs $15 or less.

West Coast Viognier

Shortly after the "Anything But Chardonnay" phase many wine lovers went through, Viognier moved into the limelight. Its richness wasn't unlike that of Chardonnay, and its flavors were a nice change.

The craze was short-lived, in part because the first attempts at making Viognier just weren't that great. It's a challenging grape at best, and it was new to the States. Now, with the heat off and a chance to perfect it, there are some excellent California Viogniers.

Quick Sips

Very good Viognier comes from Cuilleron, Guigal, Vernay, Villard in Condrieu; Yalumba in Australia; Alban, Calera, Peay, Qupé in California; and Horton in Virginia.

Most of the best (and almost all) come from the Central Coast, down by Santa Barbara. In the California sun, the grape tends to get riper than it does in its homeland of Condrieu, with bigger, richer honeyed peach flavors and often very high (more than 14 percent) alcohol. Showy and delicious, California Condrieu can make a terrific match to Pacific Rim–style dishes, where tropical fruits and other elements of sweetness echo with the fruit intensity of the wine.

Do expect to pay for the show of flavors the best put on; light, aperitif versions run $10 to $15, while rich Condrieu competitors reach into the $40s and beyond.

The Least You Need to Know

- If you'd like a fragrant white wine, try wines made from Chenin Blanc, Gewürz-traminer, Muscat, Moschofilero, or Viognier.

- If you want a bargain, look for examples of these grapes from the United States, where the grapes aren't widely recognized.

- If you're looking for a fragrant white for a special occasion, check out more expensive versions from Alsace, the Loire Valley, or Viognier from Condrieu.

- To find Loire Chenin Blanc, look for wines labeled Anjou, Saumur, Savennières, or Vouvray.

- All white wines from Condrieu, France, are made from Viognier; any other Viognier wines list the grape on the label.

The Rhônely Hearts Club

In This Chapter

◆ The power of blending

◆ The satin pleasures of Marsanne and Roussanne

◆ Grenache panache, moody Mourvèdre

◆ Syrah revisited

◆ Australia's GSMs

So far, most all the wines we've discussed have been varietal wines—that is, they contain only one grape variety or so little of others that it's not considered an identity issue.

With few exceptions, such as Burgundy and Alsace, varietal wines are the province of the New World, of countries relatively new to wine that need to break it down, test out one variety at a time, and see what works best where.

In most of the Old World, the part of the world that has been making wine for eons, winemakers tend to work with what they have, which is often a jumble of varieties. They mix and match: use this grape for its acidity, that one for color, and a few others for a variety of complementary flavors.

Blending creates complexity in a similar way to the layering of colors in a master painting. We might not be able to tell what went into making it, but there's definitely more to it than a straight coat of red.

A variety of grapes also provides the more practical advantage of stability. Different grape varieties ripen at different rates, leaving them susceptible to inclement weather at different points. If one variety gets wiped out one year, other varieties may be able to fill in for it.

We've already covered one major region where blending is the norm: Bordeaux, where Cabernet Sauvignon and Merlot predominate. If there were another major area in France for blended wines, it would be the Southern Rhône.

While Syrah dominates the red wines of the Northern Rhône and Viognier takes all the credit for the lush whites of Condrieu, a bevy of other grapes join these main ones as the vineyards move south. Let's start at the top of the Southern Rhône and follow the river down toward the Mediterranean, beginning with white wines and moving to reds, touring all the major regions you might find listed on a wine bottle in your local store.

The Misses Rhônely Hearts, Marsanne and Roussanne

Remember Viognier, that lush, honeyed, peach-filled grape that makes up the elixirs of Condrieu in the northern Rhône? As we move south from Condrieu, this grape gives up space to two other white wine grapes, Marsanne and Roussanne.

Off the Vine

You didn't know France's Rhône Valley even made white wines? You're not alone and for good reason; only about 5 percent of the entire valley's wines are white. Nonetheless, they are worth seeking out for their smooth, almondlike flavors and floral scents.

Easier to grow, Marsanne is the more popular of the pair. Its broad marzipan richness and honeydew flavors are delicious on their own, but they also provide an excellent backdrop for the headier flavors of Roussanne, a grape that gives deep golden juice filled with aromas of straw, honey, beeswax, quince, flowers, and spice. Because of this, the French typically blend the two together.

They don't, however, tell you this on the label. In fact, in France, you rarely see Marsanne or Roussanne on a wine label; instead, you see the name of a place that excels at growing them. Those places are …

◆ Côtes du Rhône.

◆ Hermitage (er-me-*tahzhe*).

◆ St-Péray (sahn-pear-*ay*).

◆ Crozes-Hermitage (crowz er-me-*tahzhe*).

◆ St-Joseph (sahn-jho-*sef*).

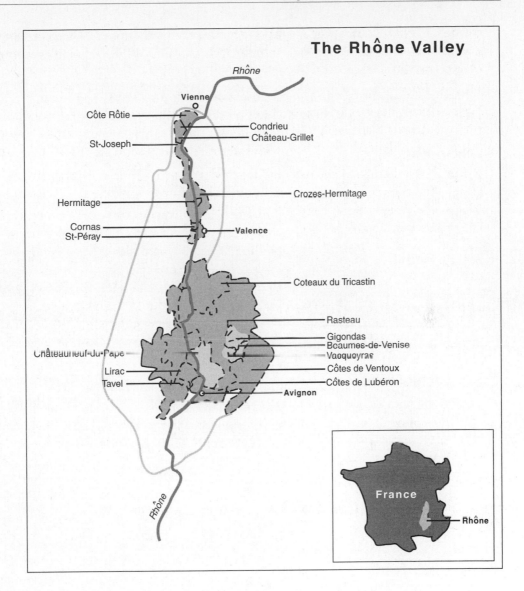

St-Péray is the only one of these four appellations that devotes all its land to producing white wines; the other four grow more red wines than white. While they are harder to find, they are well worth seeking out. Côtes du Rhône and St-Péray tend to offer the lightest wines of the bunch, pale whites filled with delicate peach and floral scents that make great starter wines and easy summertime pours. The white wines of Crozes-Hermitage and St-Joseph are richer, but, like the reds from those regions, they vary widely in concentration and quality. Generally, the most affordable bottlings are simple wines with light honey, almond, and peach flavors; any over $20 should pack more flavor into a richer texture.

The most esteemed (and the most expensive, beginning at $35 and soaring far higher) white Rhône wines are the few whites produced from the steep, stony slopes of Hermitage. These can be monumental white wines, with their rich, weighty textures and intense flavors more fitting for chicken, veal, or even a decade in the cellar than a simple fish dinner.

Winespeak

When a wine is **dumb**, it isn't expressing much scent or flavor. Most wines go through a dumb state soon after bottling; a few types of wine, like white Rhône wines, go through this state when they are a few years old, as if they hit growing pains, before emerging in glorious maturity.

A strange thing happens with these wines, though; as they age, they tend to go through a *dumb* phase at two to five years where they'll taste bland, oily, and unimpressive, before emerging sheathed in golden flavors of fruit, nuts, and spice. So if you splurge on a bottle of white Hermitage, drink it now or wait seven or eight years. Otherwise, you might wonder what the excitement and price are about.

Off the Vine

Thomas Jefferson, an avid wine lover, collector, and Francophile, described white Hermitage wines as "the world's finest white wine" back in 1787. It's about time we rediscover the Rhône's great whites; they are still in the running.

Rhône Whites Away from Home

As with Viognier, the unique flavors of Marsanne and Roussanne have caught on with wine lovers in the last few decades, and vintners around the world have tried their hand at them. In particular, look to:

- ◆ Santa Barbara, California
- ◆ Washington State
- ◆ Victoria, Australia

In general, New World Marsanne and Roussanne tend to taste fruitier and less mineral than the Rhône's examples. In warm regions and years, the wines can become ponderous with fruit and alcohol, losing the little acidity that keeps good examples vivacious and lively despite their hefty size. Still, when they are good, they are heavenly.

Outside of France, you'll typically find Marsanne and Roussanne bottled separately, an indication of both the New World's preference of labeling wines varietally as well as the newness of the grapes to these countries. Here's what you can expect from each grape on its own:

♦ Marsanne: bottled on its own, Marsanne tends to be smooth and rich-feeling but with very light flavors—raw almonds, minerals, green grapes. Since the majority of people don't cellar wines for years before drinking them, many winemakers put Marsanne into oak barrels to give the wine more immediate flavor. For a more traditional style, vintners will go very light on the oak in the hope that the wine buyer will let time instead work its magic, and add flavors as it ages in the cellar. Examples run from $10 to $15 for easy-drinking versions and up to $30 for richer wines that can be aged.

♦ Roussanne: harder to grow, Roussanne is harder to find, but when you do, expect it to be worth its hefty price tag ($22 to $40, with a couple reaching higher) in weight of honey, spice, apricot, and mineral flavors. It also has higher acidity than Marsanne, which brings nerve to a blend. It typically gets richer and more golden as it ages.

Increasingly, New World vintners are also taking a cue from the Rhône Valley and blending these grapes. Blends range from light and affordable $10 to lush, floral, apricot-scented beauties that aim for Hermitage in style and price. Either way, check them out; they can be terrific alternatives to Chardonnay when you're looking for rich white wines.

Southern Rhône Whites

Continuing south along the Rhône River, the river valley widens out, letting more light into the valley, and the sun seems to shine warmer and brighter.

Taste the white wines as you go, and you'll notice a difference; instead of the burly winter whites of the Northern Rhône, the wines south of Valence are lighter, brighter, more summery. A happy fray of obscure white grapes with whimsical-sounding names like Bourboulenc, Clairette, Grenache Blanc, and Picpoul come to lighten up Marsanne and Roussanne along the way.

Again, these grapes won't appear on a wine label; they'll just be part of a mix labeled by the region from which it came. Most are labeled simply "Côtes du Rhône," which indicates wines made from grapes grown anyplace between Vienne in the north and Avignon in the south.

For more flavor and body (at least in theory), try wines marked Côtes du Rhône-Villages. The "Villages" appended to the appellation indicates that a wine came from a specific range of vineyards and that the grapes met more strict requirements for ripeness and quality than those that go into straight Côtes du Rhône wines. Or look for wines from specific appellations within the southern Rhône. Some of the most popular appellations are:

- Châteauneuf-du-Pape (sha-toe-*newf*-dew-pahp)

- Coteaux du Tricastin (co-*toe* dew tree-kahs-*tan*)

- Côtes du Lubéron (coat dew loo-bear-*ohn*)

- Côtes de Ventoux (coat de vahn-*too*)

With eight different white wine grapes available over 104,000 acres of vineyards, it's tough to generalize about what you'll find in a bottle of white wine from the southern Rhône, but typically whatever the blend, at $8 or less it'll taste light and wet; at $10 to $15 it'll have a little more fruit flavor and some mineral character. These aren't fruity wines, though. They are more near-weightless summertime drinks with vague, savory fruit and stone flavors.

The exception is Châteauneuf-du-Pape, a 7,500-acre appellation set apart by the smooth, racquetball-size stones, or *galets*, that cover the vineyards. The stones not only make walking very difficult, but they also reflect warmth up to the grapes, making for riper, richer fruit. Variable blends of Roussanne, Bourboulenc, Clairette, Grenache Blanc, Picardin, and Picpoul, the teeny bit of Châteauneuf-du-Pape Blanc made tends to be fairly full-bodied with light stone fruit flavors and herbal notes. Like Hermitage, drink it young or drink it old. It will disappoint in middle age and reward patience with savory, sophisticated nutty mineral flavors. It will also set you back a good $30 to $60, with some reaching over $100.

Off the Vine

About 95 percent of the entire Rhône Valley's wine production comes from the southern Rhône.

Off the Vine _____

Châteauneuf-du-Pape wines can be blended from 13 different red and white grape varieties. The allowed varieties are (in order of importance) Grenache, Syrah, Mourvèdre, Cinsault, Counoise, Vaccarèse, Terret Noir, Muscardin, Clairette, Bourboulenc, Roussanne, Picpoul, and Picardin.

Pay Dirt in Vin de Pays?

Vin de Pays (van de pay-*yee*) is a designation reserved for wines that come from a particular area but do not meet the requirements for the more specific appellation designation (AOC). It used to be an almost derogatory designation, implying that a wine wasn't good enough to earn the more specific designation. But today vintners who want to experiment with grapes not explicitly allowed in an AOC wine will use a Vin de Pays designation instead, and those wines can be impressive.

The Rhône Valley offers a few Vin de Pays wines, all of which state the grape on the label. The most frequently seen Rhône Vin de Pays is Vin de Pays de l'Ardèche, a good source for affordable, varietally labeled Chardonnay and Viognier.

While looking for wines from any of these places, you'll probably find more reds than whites, so let's cover those while we're at it.

Off the Vine _____

Vin de Pays is a designation used for wines made within a specific region that do not meet the requirements of the more specific controlled appellation (AOC). There are well over 100 Vin de Pays regions in France; all wines from Vin de Pays areas will list the region as well as the grape variety on the label.

Southern Rhône Reds

If you start at the northern end of the Rhône, in Côte Rôtie, the Syrah is staid and solid, with tons of tannin and plenty of acidity holding its roasted fruit flavors tightly. Move south into St-Joseph and Syrah gets softer, a reflection of its warmer, gentler growing conditions.

Slip south of Valence, where the Southern Rhône begins, and the grape practically goes on vacation, getting softer and fatter and partying it up with a host of other red wine grapes. The very first major red wine appellation here, in fact, allows 13 different grape varieties into its wines.

Some grapes play bigger roles than others, though, so we'll skip most of the 13 and concentrate on the powerhouses Grenache, Syrah, and Mourvèdre.

Grenache, Mourvèdre, and Syrah

If three grapes were most responsible for the character of Southern Rhône reds, it would be Grenache, Mourvèdre, and Syrah. The trio, alone and in combination with many lesser-known varieties, makes spicy, meaty reds for which the Southern Rhône is known.

> **Quick Sips**
>
> Grenache, Mourvèdre, and Syrah are the three most important grapes in Southern Rhône reds: Grenache for ripe, sweet, juicy cherry flavors; Mourvèdre for underlying meaty, black fruit flavors and tannin; and Syrah for body, color, structure, fragrance, and peppery flavor.

Though you'll rarely find a Southern Rhône wine made from just one of this trio, it often helps to have an idea of what each one contributes to have an idea of what to expect from them in tandem:

- **Grenache** (greh-*nahsh*): the hallmark grape of Côtes du Rhône reds, Grenache provides charming, juicy red cherry flavors. High in alcohol and low in acidity, Grenache typically makes short-lived but easy-drinking wines unless it gets help from more tannic and acidic varieties.

- **Mourvèdre** (moor-*ved*-dra): this dark grape is less obvious in blends than the other two but just as important, its meaty, more tannic, black fruit flavors laying down a bass line for the lighter Grenache to play on.

- **Syrah** (syr-*ah*): as in the Northern Rhône, Syrah offers a full complement of spicy, plummy fruit with considerable tannin and acidity.

Other grapes are important in their own ways for the blends common to this region. Counoise, for instance, adds a plump blueberry flavor that's appreciated against the tannins of grapes like Syrah, whereas Cinsault adds acidity and bright color. To taste how seamlessly these Southern Rhône grapes blend, look for wines labeled …

- Côtes du Rhône.
- Côtes du Rhône-Villages.
- Gigondas (zhe-goan-*dahs*).
- Lirac (lyr-*ahk*).
- Tavel (tah-*vel*).
- Vacqueyras (vah-kair-*ahs*).

All these appellations (except for Tavel, which makes only pink wines) make spicy red wines with lots of ripe, warm fruit flavor. Each appellation, however, was defined to show off the unique character of its wines. It may take some practice to determine a Gigondas from a Vacqueyras, but in case you want to try, here's a brief breakdown of what sets each apart from the next:

♦ Côtes du Rhône reds, as with whites, can be made from grapes picked from anywhere between Vienne and Avignon. Typically, these are light, everyday reds pulled from high-yielding vineyards in the south of the region. The few that reach $20 should be richer in color and flavor.

♦ Côtes du Rhône-Villages wines come from vineyards that are considered better than most but not as good as village wines, like Lirac or Gigondas (see below). They vary wildly in composition and quality, but Rasteau, Beaumes-de-Venise, and Cairanne are three that offer good value.

♦ Tavel is by law rosé. Made mostly from Grenache and Cinsault with possible small portions of darker, more tannic grapes, these pale pink wines are always completely dry, with savory cherry and mineral flavors. As one of the few rosé wines that's been historically highly esteemed, Tavel rosés can be expensive, at $20 to $30.

♦ Lirac depends most heavily on the juicy cherry charms of Grenache and tends to make wines as lyrical as the name suggests, soft and plump. Lesser known, its wines can be a steal at $10 to $20.

♦ Gigondas' vineyards climb the foot of the jagged Dentelles de Montmirail, a small but imposing rocky outcrop that's home mainly to Grenache, Syrah, and Mourvèdre. The wines can also be the most imposing of the Southern Rhône, with meaty, spicy fruit flavors barbed with strong tannins. You'll pay for that heft, with prices ranging from $15 to $40.

♦ Vacqueyras is right next door, but without the jagged peaks looming over the vineyard, the wines tend to be gentler, sleeker, and a little cheaper.

Rhône Reds Around the World

With warm flavors of sun, spice, and fruit, Rhône grapes now circle the globe. Grenache and Mourvèdre actually originated in Spain, where they go by the names

Garnacha and Mataro or Monastrell. Garnacha is most famous there for the lip-smacking, cherry-flavored reds of Priorat while Mataro plays a large part in the wines of Spain's eastern regions such as Alicante, Jumilla, Valencia, and Yecla (see Chapter 15).

From Spain, Garnacha makes its way across the Mediterranean to Sardinia, where it makes lush, soupy reds under the local name Cannonnau. But the most famous examples of this grape outside of France are in Australia.

Rhône Down Under

Though Shiraz makes most of the buzz when it comes to Australian wines, the Rhône-loving settlers who brought the vines down also packed in Grenache and Mourvèdre. Some of these original vines still exist; others have been replanted since these Rhône varieties thrive in South Australia's climate.

As with Shiraz, vintners often bottle Grenache and Mourvèdre separately, and they always put the name of the grape on the label. This makes it easy to check out each grape variety on its own.

More importantly, Australian Grenache and Mourvèdre can make some of the country's most delicious wines. However, don't expect the wines to taste much like France's Rhône-grown versions. Whether it's sun and warmth or the outgoing Australian personality, Australian versions are far bigger, louder, and juicier than anything France typically produces.

The range of Australian Grenache is large, from simple, cherry lollipop-like pours to reds as dense and concentrated as a cherry pie. Price will give a good indication of the sort of wine it is: simple versions sell for $8 to $16; more concentrated versions average $20 to $30; and a few reach $65.

Much of Australia's Mourvèdre was ripped up to make way for Shiraz and Chardonnay, so the little that remains today tends to be fairly expensive ($20 to $30) and very good, with dark licorice- and plumlike flavors supported with tannin.

Rhône in the States

While the Rhône Rangers of the 1980s concentrated most intensely on cultivating Syrah, they paid some attention to Grenache and Mourvèdre, too. In fact, Mourvèdre turned out to be a bonus as it was already planted all over the state as Mataro, a grape brought to California by Spanish settlers.

However, Mataro had been valued for quantity, not quality, and much of it was pulled up to make way for grapes with better reputations. Today, only about 400 to 600 acres of Mourvèdre remain, less even than Grenache's at only 11,000. Because of lingering negative connotations, American Mataro is almost always labeled under the sexier-sounding Mourvèdre.

Some of the best California Grenache and Mourvèdre come from Contra Costa County, a sandy, warm area east of San Francisco Bay once populated by many Spanish, Portuguese, and Italian grape growers.

Quick Sips

More than 20 Rhône grape varieties are grown in the United States. To find out what they are, who grows them, and when you next might be able to sample them at a Rhône Rangers tasting, go to www.rhonerangers.org.

The Least You Need to Know

◆ Blends of grapes are not better or worse than single variety wines, just different.

◆ Except for the Viognier-centric regions of Condrieu and Château-Grillet, white wines from the Rhône Valley rely on Marsanne and Roussanne, together and in combination with other white wine grapes.

◆ Most red wines from the southern half of the Rhône Valley depend on Grenache, Syrah, and Mourvèdre, along with bits of many other grapes.

◆ Some of the best red wine values in the Southern Rhône are wines from Gigondas, Vacqueyras, Lirac, and Côtes du Rhône-Villages.

◆ To find examples of Rhône grapes grown outside of France, look to California, Washington State, and Australia.

◆ In California, Mourvèdre is sometimes called by a Spanish name, Mataro, though in Spain, it's often called Monastrell.

Chapter **15**

Incredible Iberians

In This Chapter

- Iberian whites for seafood
- Tempranillo temptations
- Garnacha or liquid rubies
- Monastrell and more
- Portugal's varied regions

The Spanish wine scene has exploded in the last 30 years. First came the fall of the Franco regime in 1976; then came Spain's entry into the EU, spurring innovation in every sector as the country learned to compete in the global market.

The result has been a ferment of creative work that's come to a head in the twenty-first century, from architecture (think Bilbao) to cutting-edge cuisine (think Ferrán Adrià and his cohorts) and the wines to go with it.

Those wines are now everywhere, from hip tapas bars to mainstream American restaurants, and Portugal's restaurants are beginning to join them, too. Why? Not only are these Iberian wines good, but they also aren't like any others. Most of the grapes grown in Spain and Portugal don't excel anywhere else. So when you're looking for something different, something that sounds and tastes like it comes from a specific place, Spain's a terrific place to look. Here's a guide to the best it has to offer.

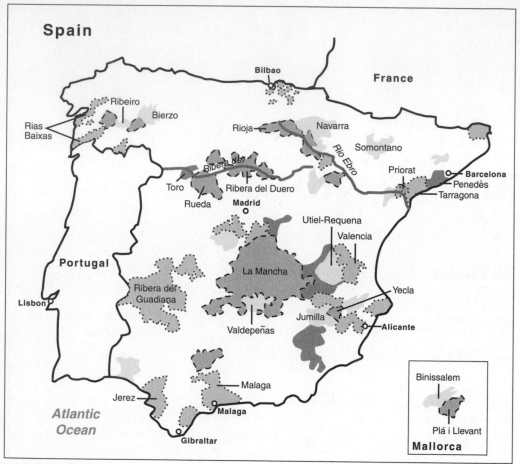

Spain's major wine regions.

Albariño/Alvarinho

Lobsters, clams, mussels, squid, snapper—the list of succulent seafood pulled from the cold waters off Portugal and Galicia in the north of Spain goes on. What do they drink with it all? Not red Rioja! They drink crisp, light white wine, especially those made from the Albariño (al-bar-*een*-yo) grape.

Albariño is the Spanish name; Alvarinho (al-vahr-*een*-yo) is the same grape in Portuguese. It grows in the northwest end of the peninsula, along the Minho (or Miño, depending on your point of view) river, which forms the border between Spain and Portugal. There's not much difference between the two sides save for language, and yet the wines produced taste as different as any from different countries.

En Español

Spanish Albariño has made it to the big time, showing up on wine lists everywhere, and it's easy to taste why. The grape makes wines that are fresh, bright, and lemony with a rich, almost oily texture, giving them the weight of a rich Chardonnay without the heavy flavors. They can be palate-whetting aperitifs as well as worthy companions to a main course, particularly if grilled fish or seafood paella is on the menu.

Quick Sips

Albariño at a glance: bright, fresh, lemon and pear flavors on a rich, almost oily texture; high acidity.

The best Albariño, and the majority, come from the cool climes of Rìas Biaxas (*ree*-ahs *bye*-schuss) in Galicia, in far northwest Spain. Some producers blend in small amounts of other local grapes (Treixadura and Loureiro most notably), but most are made entirely from Albariño and say so proudly on their label. A few examples still run $10, but the wine's popularity has pushed prices up so that most cost about $15 to $20 now.

Some terrific Albariños/Alvarinhos to try are Adega de Monçao, Aveleda, Quinta do Feital, and Palacio de Brejoeira (from Portugal); As Laxas, Fillaboa, Martin Codax, and Pazo de Senorans (from Spain).

Off the Vine

Albariño is Spain's most popular white wine here in the United States, but it's not the most planted grape. That award goes to Airen—and although you'll never see *Airen* on a wine label, it's responsible for the sea of simple white wine drunk in Spanish cafés.

En Portugues

Cross the Miño River into Portugal, where it becomes the Minho, and the vines will look pretty much the same. But here, in Portugal's lushly green Costa Verde, *Alvarinho* takes a Portuguese accent in pronunciation and taste. It's typically lighter, crisper, and sharper, and sometimes a little spritzy on first taste.

Alvarinho's stronghold is Vinho Verde, a lush expanse of damp, green land kept cool by Atlantic breezes. The wines retain this chill in their crisp, bright flavor, as bracing as a squeeze of lime. Most Vinho Verde blend local grapes, such as Trajadura

Quick Sips _____

Alvarinho at a glance: pale, almost green color; light, crisp, citric flavors; high acid.

(the same as Spain's Treixadura) and Loureiro with Alvarinho, and won't list any grapes on the label. These tend to be very light, bright, and crisp wines that, at $6 to $10, are excellent for summer sipping.

If you want a Vinho Verde with a little more substance, look for those labeled Alvarinho, and be ready to pay another $5. Some of these wines can even benefit from a few years of aging, though the vast majority are best drunk immediately.

Verdejo

Move inland from Alvariño's stronghold of Galicia, and you'll be in Castilla y León. Far from the sea and surrounded by mountains, it's a hardy region long known more for thick, heavy reds than any whites.

Rueda is the exception. In Rueda (rue-*ay*-da), a white wine appellation that follows the Duero River, Verdejo (ver-*day*-ho) thrives, making light whites with bright, lemony, herbaceous flavor. It can be reminiscent of Sauvignon Blanc; in fact, today it's often blended with Sauvignon Blanc, a recent import to the region.

To find these wines, look for those labeled Rueda; rarely will they list Verdejo on the label. Most run $8 to $15 and are refreshing hot-weather pours, especially with light fish and vegetable dishes. Basa, Las Brisas, Martínsancho, and Naia are a few common examples.

Sour Grapes _____

Every once in a while you may spot a wine from Australia labeled Verdelho. While delicious in its snappy lime flavors, Verdelho has nothing to do with Verdejo. Originally from Madeira, Verdelho made its way to Australia in the 1800s with vintners who planned to use it to make fortified wines; today, it mostly appears in dry whites. Nonetheless, Verdelho and Verdejo are both worth checking out.

Rioja Blanco

It's hard to be a white wine in a red wine appellation since it's so easy to get overlooked. That's too bad for white Rioja (ree-*oh*-ha) because the white version can be as fascinating and long-lived as the more famous and sought-after red version.

Named for the region in which it's grown, most white Rioja is nothing to write home about; it's either light and barely even lemony, more like bottled water than wine, or blanketed with the vanilla tones of American oak. At least it's cheap at $8 or so.

Outstanding white Rioja is far harder to find, and it'll cost two or three times the price. Thirty dollars isn't bad, though, for a white wine with a texture like satin that offers everything from toasted almond notes to ripe pears, honey, spice, butterscotch, even fresh mushrooms, and gets more interesting every year it ages.

The main grape used to make white Rioja is Viura (also known as Macabeo), a variety used more for its indestructibleness than its flavor integrity. Better Riojas incorporate at least a little Malvasia, a grape with sweet stone fruit flavors and floral characteristics as graceful as its name sounds.

Quick Sips

To find light, nonoaked white Rioja, look for wines that say *Joven*. Richer wines will say *Crianza*, *Reserva*, or *Gran Reserva*, each of which require longer aging in oak barrels. The older the wine, the deeper the color and the flavors will be.

Some Riojas spend time in oak barrels, where they take on vanilla and nut flavors that add weight and substance. True old-style Rioja is made in this way but is not released for several years, by which time it will have turned golden and spicy and added more flavor. This style of Rioja is sophisticated and detailed enough to warrant white-tablecloth treatment, particularly with scallops in brown butter or other rich, buttery seafood. R. Lopez de Heredia is the custodian of this style; its golden, aged versions cost about $40 and are worth every penny.

Chalky Txacoli and Other Noteworthy Iberians

Txacoli (*cha*-ko-lee) whites are some of the most refreshing on the planet. Made from a local grape called Hondarribi Zuri grown on the coast near Bilbao, these white wines tend to be searingly dry and acidic, with chalky lemon flavors and low alcohol, about 9 to 11 percent. Many are a touch spritzy when first poured, adding to their refreshing personality.

Over on the Costa Brava, near Barcelona, is Penedès, most famous for its sparkling wines (see Cava in Chapter 17) but also home to versions of the local white wine grapes Xarel-lo, Parellada, and Macabeo as well as Chardonnay. There's also the tiny appellation of Alella, which pulls from the same array of varieties.

In Portugal, white wines are labeled *vinho branco* (white wine). Outside of Vinho Verde, white wines aren't nearly as popular as reds, but those made from Arinto are worth searching out for their crisp, lemon–orange flavors. Most come from Bucelas, just north of Lisbon. Farther north in Beiras, forward-thinking vintners such as Luis Pato are making spicy, fuller-bodied wines with the local Bical and Maria Gomez grapes. And in the red wine stronghold of the Douro, vintners such as Niepoort and Quinta do Vallado are producing some super-rich, satin-textured whites from local grapes.

Quick Sips

Txacoli wines are labeled Bizkaiko Txakolina, Getariako Txakolina, or Arabako Txakolina (Chacolí de Vizcaya, Chacolí de Guetaria, and Chacolí de Alava in Castillian Spanish), after the areas in Basque country from which they come.

These are just some of the most exciting white wines coming out of the Iberian peninsula; if you find others, give them a try; few ask more than $20.

Tempting Tempranillo

When it comes to Iberian red wines, Tempranillo (temp-ra-*nee*-yo) rules. It's the most planted grape in Spain and is widely found in Portugal as well, where it's known as Tinta Roriz.

The appeal is two-fold: tempranillo deals well with warm summers and harsh winters, and since it tends to ripen early (*temprano*, as the name suggests), it mostly escapes the brunt of rainy autumns in higher altitudes where it thrives.

Quick Sips

Tempranillo at a glance: light red cherry to dark dried cherry flavors; spice, vanilla, and coconut notes from oak; soft tannin and relatively low acidity.

It also tastes great, with smooth, ripe strawberry or red cherry flavors with a spicy flair. Add the toasty, vanilla-toned flavors of American oak, which is widely favored in Spain, and it's awfully hard to hate. You'll find Tempranillo all over the Iberian peninsula, but the best place to get acquainted with it is Rioja.

Rioja

Rioja has been producing wines since Roman times. The region takes its name from the Rio Oja, which courses through the center of the appellation, or *Denominacion d'Origen Calificada (DOC)* in Spain. While it's close enough to the Bay of Biscay that the higher elevations can catch refreshing Atlantic breezes, for the most part, the Sierra Cantabria Mountains protect the area from the Atlantic's cold, wet blasts.

Tempranillo rules throughout the region, excelling particularly in the higher parts of Rioja, such as Rioja Alta and Rioja Alavesa. Everywhere, and particularly in the lower altitudes (Rioja Baja), Tempranillo is often joined by Mazuelo, Garnacha, and Graciano (also known as Carignan).

Off the Vine

As in many parts of the Old World, some Rioja vintners are chafing at the restrictions set forth by their appellations and making wines outside of their terms. The result has been a rash of Rioja unofficially termed Alta Expresión. These wines are as high quality as any Gran Reserva Rioja but may forgo the long barrel aging for a fresher flavor. Some are single-vineyard wines, unusual in a region that has long relied on blending wines from different areas. Some might include nontraditional grapes. Though labeled simply Rioja or even *vino de la tierra*, the higher price tags give them away as more ambitious than the classification lets on.

Regardless the mix, the region's warm temperatures pretty much guarantee wines with ripe, red cherry flavors. Beyond that, the flavor of Rioja wines largely depends on how they are made. Most Rioja is light and unoaked and designed for immediate drinking, so much so that few make it out of the country. Most of the Rioja we see in the States has spent at least a year in American oak barrels, which often adds vanilla, spice, and even coconut flavors to the wines.

Quick Sips

Rioja also makes some wonderful *rosados*. These pink wines tend to be bright, fresh, and full of succulent dry cherry flavor.

How long the wines stay in the barrel contributes to how they'll taste. Generally, Riojas fall into four categories:

- ◆ Joven means "young," and these wines are designed to drink young. They are typically made in stainless steel or other nonreactive vessels and released the year after their vintage date to keep them fruity, lively, and fresh. Most sell for about $8.

- ◆ Crianza wines must be at least two years old when they are released, and one of those years must have been spent in barrels.

- Reserva wines are required to spend three years in the cellar before release, one of those years in barrels.

- Gran Reserva wines are made only in exceptional vintages and arc required to spend two years in oak and three years in the bottle.

Winespeak

Oxidation is what happens when wine comes in contact with air. Excess oxygen robs a wine of its freshness, turning it brownish and making the flavors nutty, but when controlled, it can add flavors that make the wine taste more complex.

You might think that the wines that spent the longest time in oak barrels would taste the oakiest, but that's not necessarily the case in Gran Reserva Rioja. All that time spent in barrels mellows the wine out; plus, barrels allow a little bit of oxygen to come in contact with the wine. The flavors created by *oxidation*—nuts, dried fruit, spice, mushrooms—add to the wine's complexity. So a Gran Reserva Rioja should taste not just like cherries and vanilla, as many Crianza deliciously do, but like cherries and vanilla and spice and nuts and more.

Gran Reserva Rioja is also only made in very good vintages, and so most Gran Reservas are expected to last for years in the bottle. Compared to the $10 to $20 most Crianzas ask, they are pricey at $30 to $60, or even more, but they hold their own next to the best red wines in the world.

Ribera del Duero

Farther south in Castilla y Léon, the locals call Tempranillo *Tinto Fino* (fine red) or *Tinto del País* (country red), each name describing in itself just how important it is to the wines of the region. It stars particularly in the wines of Ribera del Duero, named for the Duero river.

At its high altitude, about 3,000 feet, Ribera del Duero is one of the coolest wine regions in Spain. The warm summer days are countered by downright chilly nights, which stretches out the growing season. This allows the grapes to ripen slowly, packing on flavor without loosing vibrancy. The resulting wines tend to feel richer and more intense than Rioja's, especially when they are bolstered by a splash of Cabernet Sauvignon (for bass notes of black currants and tannin) or Merlot (for flesh—and flash). Vega Sicilia is the region's most famous winery; Abadia Retuerta, Alion, Arzuaga, Condado de Haza, Emilio Moro, and Pesquera are just a few outstanding names to look for. But be prepared to pay; Ribera's wines start at $20 and can rise over $300.

Toro

Toro used to be known more for the grains it produced than the wines, but when Ribera del Duero became so hot that land prices shot up, many vintners looking for the next big thing found their way here. Another high valley along the Duero, west of Rueda, Toro is similar to Ribera del Duero but drier and warmer, aspects that show up in the region's very ripe wines.

Most of the region is planted in Tempranillo, which the locals call *Tinto del Toro* (red of Toro, which shows how emblematic it is). The torrid daytime temperatures and dry climate can make for very ripe, rustic wines as full of jammy cherry flavors as they are with alcohol—16 percent isn't uncommon—but the best combine that power with structure and grace. Campo Elisio, Lurton El Albar, Numanthia-Termes, and Rejadorada are names to look for.

Portugal's Tempranillo

Follow the Duero River through Spain and into Portugal, and it becomes the Douro, the region that's responsible for the famous fortified wine Port (see Chapter 20). The region also produces dry wines bottled under the name of the region (Douro). Among the hundreds of red wine grapes grown here, Tempranillo (here known as *Tinta Roriz*) plays an important part.

Some vintners bottle Tinta Roriz on its own, and they'll tell you so on the label; many, however, blend varieties and don't list any of them. Either way, to guess what the dry wines are going to taste like, all you need to do is think about the region and its most famous wine: it's hot, and Port is ripe and thick with rich fruit flavors. The dry Tempranillo and Tempranillo-blend wines are likewise rich and dark, but dry as stone, with considerable tannin and acidity. These are about as far as you can get from a simple Rioja, and they are meant more for sipping over roast boar than slugging back on a hot day.

Far to the south, Tempranillo shows up in Alentejo, where it's called Aragonez, and is typically blended with other local grapes. The results are all over the board, from rustic reds with spicy baked berry flavors to the powerful, rich reds of leading producers, such as João Portugal Ramos.

Whether Douro, Alentejo, or anywhere in between, Portugal offers excellent values; most wines cost less than $20, and a few exceptional bottles reach $75.

There's More ...

Also look for Tempranillo in wines from ...

♦ Valdepeñas and La Mancha (where it's known as Cencibel).

♦ Penedès (where it's known as Ojo del Liebre).

Both places label their Tempranillo wines by region, not grape, and they'll tend to be soft and ripe.

Lately, North American wineries have become interested in planting Tempranillo. While acreage is still small, thirty-plus wineries have joined together to form TAPAS, the Tempranillo Advocates, Producers, and Amigos Society. Keep an eye on Argentina, too, where José Zuccardi at Santa Julia is making some headway in recent bottlings. A few Australian vintners are making noise about the variety, too, citing similarities between the climate of Ribera del Duero and parts of South Australia, like the Eden Valley and Adelaide Hills, where Nepenthe has already started bottling some. But don't stop at Tempranillo; Spain uses a bevy of other great grapes for its wines, such as Garnacha.

Garnacha

Garnacha—the name always reminds me of garnets, which is fitting since it looks like liquid garnets when poured into a glass. Known in France as Grenache (see Chapter 14) and in Italy as Cannonau, Garnacha is a firmly Mediterranean grape both in habit and in personality. Its bright red cherry flavors can get as sweet as a lollipop if not controlled. Lush, languid, and filled with sunny summery flavors, it's a favorite for blending with the leaner Tempranillo in Rioja and for making cherry-scented rosés in Navarra, where it makes up most of the plantings.

Quick Sips

Garnacha at a glance: ruby color, juicy, red cherry flavor, medium acidity.

Garnacha can make some really good, juicy reds and brisk, fruity pink wines in Navarra, and occasionally you'll find a Garnacha from elsewhere in Spain, but otherwise, when you're looking for good Spanish Garnacha, head straight to Priorat.

Priorat

Far up in the northeast corner of Spain, just inland from where the country falls into the sea, a series of jagged, rocky hills are impossibly covered in vines. Why anyone would be crazy enough to plant wines in this hot, steep region is beyond imagination until you taste the wines, simply labeled Priorat (*pree*-or-at).

Priorat's wines are usually blends that can include local varieties, such as Cariñena, as well as international varieties Cabernet Sauvignon and Syrah, but most all rely on Garnacha. In the warm Mediterranean climate, Garnacha gets extremely ripe, packing the wines with a wallop of cherry fruit, spice and, often, alcohol—up to 16 percent. These aren't reds for the faint-of-heart; rather, some require a day of manual labor followed by a pig roast to really appreciate. But they are beautiful, their garnet hue as vibrant as their flavor.

Quick Sips

For Priorat-like wines at a fraction of the price, look to Montsant, a region that hugs Priorat. The wines here rely on a similar mix of grapes as Priorat, with an accent on Garnacha. Different soils and generally lower altitudes make for wines that are similar to Priorat but softer and more approachable—and less costly.

The deepest, darkest Priorat wines come from vines as old as a century, but there aren't many of those left, and the current vogue for bodacious reds has inspired many new plantings. Wines from newer vines tend to be lighter than those from low-yielding old vines, so a range of intensity is available. However, there's no way to tell from the label whether you're getting something from young vines. Price may offer a key; the top Priorats go for $30 to $70 or more. Key names to know: Buil & Gine, Capafons-Osso, Cims de Porrera, Clos de l'Obac, Clos Mogador, Finca Dofi, and Vall Llach.

Off the Vine

Rare but delicious, white Priorat wines are made mostly from the white version of Garnacha, Garnacha Blanca, and offer big, full flavors of pineapple, vanilla, and honey.

Navarra and Environs

Garnacha's domain extends as far west as Rioja, where it's typically blended with Tempranillo, although some winemakers make Rioja entirely from Garnacha, and label them as such.

Nearby Navarra made its name on fresh, bright pink rosés made from Garnacha. Tempranillo has usurped some of Garnacha's territory, but the region's old Garnacha vines are responsible for some of its most impressive wines, giving generously fruity flavors and plush textures.

And just south of Navarra is Campo de Borja, a treasure chest of old-vine Garnacha. The wines may be simple in general—ripe with spicy strawberry flavors—but they also tend to be wonderfully affordable. Good examples can be had for $10 to $20.

Quick Sips _____

Spain offers many more wines than are covered here. Get a basic overview from www.winefromspain.com, or delve deep with CataVino.net, an informative blog run by two Americans in Barcelona. Also check in at www.spanishtable.com; not only is this store's newsletter informative, but the retail store can supply everything you need for your next Iberian feast, from enormous paella pans to saffron and jamón Serrano.

Monastrell, Spain's Mourvèdre

Some of the most exciting developments in Spanish wine have been in areas that depend on Monastrell, the same grape that provides earthy, black fruit flavors to many wines in southern France, where it's called Mourvèdre. In Spain, Monastrell's lair is the Levante, a swath of Mediterranean coast that covers Murcia and Valencia. Until recently, these areas were known more for their beaches than their wines, but that's changing.

At the forefront is Jumilla, a dry, hot area inland from Alicante. Wineries such as Agapito Rico, Bleda, Finca Luzón, Juan Gil, and Julia Roch y Hijos, are turning out red wines with black, figgy flavors, tannic textures, and earthy complexity. Best of all, most run $8 to $15.

Jumilla's neighboring regions of Bullas, Alicante, and Yecla also boast lots of old-vine Monastrell from which they are producing everything from the usual teeth-staining, palate-filling basic quaffs to some unusually elegant, if tannic, examples. Lesser known, these regions can offer super value.

Touriga and Portuguese Varieties

Portugal is a repository of ancient grape varieties, many of which show up nowhere else. There are so many, and they go by so many different names, that it would be futile to try to recount them all here. Besides, most of Portugal's red wines are blends of different varieties. So instead, I give brief overviews of the major wine-growing regions so you'll have an idea of what to expect when you encounter a Portuguese red.

Portugal's Douro major wine regions.

Douro and Dão

The Douro is arguably Portugal's most important region, mostly because of the fame of its fortified Port wines (sec Chapter 20), though more recently due to the excellent dry wines vintners are producing from Tinta Roriz and any of the 50-odd other grapes that flourish on the steep banks of this dramatic valley. The multitude of grapes and winemaking styles make for a variety of wines, but in general, you can expect dry Douro reds to be juicy yet tannic, with a slightly herbal note adding brightness to their earthy, black fruit. Some new-style wines spend considerable time in new oak barrels, too, which adds a vanilla softness around their tannic core. The best can age for years and cost $50 or more.

South of the Douro, in the hilly valleys along the Mondego River, lies Dão, where the Touriga Nacional grape (along with nine others) flourishes in the summer warmth. Dão wines tend to be more delicate Douro than Douro reds, more fine than robust.

Bairrada

Bairrada is a smaller region between Dão and the Atlantic Ocean. On this relatively flat plain, the fiercely tannic, black Baga takes up most of the acreage. Its wines are typically rustic, black, and barbed with enough tannin to make very short work of a steak. Some producers blend other grapes with Baga to make it softer and more approachable, though whether that's necessary is debatable. A few vintners—most notably Luis Pato—believe its potential is yet to be uncovered, and with care and kid gloves, they are making kinder, gentler Baga—though it still shows best next to a steak.

> **Off the Vine**
>
> Some producers in Bairrada prefer to use the more generic appellation of Beiras on their labels to protest the limiting Bairrada wine regulations.

Alentejo

East of Lisbon, Alentejo is a broad, rolling plain known as the breadbasket and cork capital of Portugal. A few subregions specialize in wine—Borba, Redondo, and Reguengos to name three. However, most of the region's wines come labeled simply Alentejo. Most of these tend to be good, hearty country wines, with ripe, earthy flavors, though a few wineries, like Cortes de Cima, Esporào, J.P. Ramos, and Quinta do Carmo, put out more modern, fruity yet structured wines.

The Least You Need to Know

◆ Albariño/Alvarinho, whether in Spain or Portugal, make some of the Iberian peninsula's greatest white wines.

◆ For the lightest, most refreshing Iberian whites, look to Vinho Verde in Portugal and Txacoli in Spain.

◆ For slightly richer Spanish whites, look to Rueda, Rioja and Penedès.

◆ Tempranillo stars in Rioja, Ribera del Duero, Toro, and Portugal's Douro.

◆ Monastrell, Spain's version of France's Mourvèdre, is responsible for some of Spain's best deals; look for it in wines from Jumilla, Bullas, Yecla, and Alicante.

◆ Most of Portugal's wine regions blend many grapes together for their signature wines, so don't sweat the grape names.

Chapter **16**

Italy's Originals

In This Chapter

◆ Beyond Pinot Grigio: Italy's other white wines

◆ Sangiovese from Tuscany and beyond

◆ Vinous truffles from Piedmont

◆ Wines from the toe of the boot

With 20 regions and an estimated 1,000-plus grape varieties, Italy boasts enough options to keep the most dedicated wine lover interested and happy for a lifetime.

The only downfall of such abundance is that Italy can make even a seasoned connoisseur feel like a complete idiot from time to time as new wines and unheard-of grapes come up. But not even the Italians know everything about Italian wine. So don't worry about it; just explore and enjoy.

A Few Caveats First

Before we dive into Italy's major grape varieties and the wines they make, consider a couple caveats. The first is that I don't even try to cover them all. Many of Italy's regions claim grapes that have rarely if ever left the region's borders in vine or bottle. I hit the major varieties, but know many more are worth seeking out (see Appendix C).

Italy's wine regions.

The other caveat is Italy's classification scheme. Like most of the rest of the world, Italy classifies wines by the place they were made and attempts to classify by quality as well. However, as everywhere, but perhaps in Italy a little more so, some classifications were made with politics in mind more than quality. This rundown of Italy's classifications scheme explains what the letters or words on the label mean, but don't let them rule your choices:

- *Vino da tavola:* table wine, as in all EU countries, can come from anywhere and any grape; it makes no guarantee as to quality.

- **IGT:** *indicazione geografica tipica* is a relatively new classification developed in response to the very good, very expensive wines, such as Super Tuscans, being made from untraditional grapes that had to be classified *vino da tavola* for lack of a more fitting category.

- **DOC:** *denominazione di origine* wines must be grown within a delimited area and to set standards of varieties used and, sometimes, winemaking.

- **DOCG:** *denominazione di origine garantita* wines are made to stricter standards than DOC wines.

Also, unlike in the New World, where Reserve has no legal meaning, *Riserva* is a legal designation in most Italian regions, usually signifying a wine that has had longer aging than non-Riserva wines.

Armed with this knowledge and this handy map, you're ready to proceed.

Italy's Belle Bianchi

Italian white wines get far more interesting than the ubiquitous Pinot Grigio (see Chapter 7). Every region boasts some sort of white wine, from light delicacies to forceful, heady brews. So let's start in the north and head south, highlighting the best whites Italy has to offer.

Piedmont's White Alternatives

Piedmont is famous for its red wines—tannic Barolo, boisterous Barbera, and charming Dolcetto. However, even the Piedmontese don't live on red alone. Check out the local whites made from Arneis and Cortese.

Arneis

Arneis (ahr-*nays*) was largely ignored until the 1970s, when technological advances such as refrigerated stainless-steel tanks made it easier to make high-quality white wines. Today, the wines are so good they've been awarded DOCG status and are bottled as *Roero Arneis* or *Arneis di Roero*. Their savory almond, pear, and herb flavors make a terrific companion to fish and vegetable dishes or even a plate of salumi. Good versions tend to be a little pricey, at $12 to $23. Recommended producers are Ceretto, Fontanafredda, Giacosa, Roagna, and Vietti.

Cortese

Cortese (core-*tay*-zay) is rarely talked about by name, but it's the grape behind the popular Gavi di Gavi. Named for the town in southeast Piedmont near where it grows, Gavi is the consummate summer vacation wine. A very few versions reach for complexity, adding some mineral notes to their light, dry, citrusy flavors, but for the most part, it's simple, refreshing stuff to drink cold and young.

Because Gavi di Gavi enjoys a certain chic, it can get ridiculously expensive, reaching $45. It's worth looking for wines labeled Cortese di Alto Monferrato, which are made from Cortese grown close to, but not in, Gavi. Trustworthy names are Banfi, Pio Cesare, Fontanafredda, and La Scolca.

Northern Stars Ribolla Gialla, Tocai Friulano

If you think of Italian whites as lots of Pinot Blah and other blasé whites, head straight for Friuli in Italy's far northeast, where Alpine breezes and altitude keep the vines cool and the grapes full of acidity. Not only do its Pinot Grigio and Pinot Bianco set the standard for the rest of Italy (see Chapter 7), but it also offers unique wines from grapes such as Ribolla Gialla (ree-*bowl*-a ghee-*al*-a) and Tocai Friulano (toe-*kai* free-oo-*la*-no).

Ribolla Gialla

Yellow Ribolla, as Ribolla Gialla translates, makes crisp, mineral-laden, pear-scented white wines in Friuli in northeastern Italy as well as over the border in Slovenia where it's labeled Rebula. Dry but full-flavored, it's sometimes lightly oaked to bring out its broad, almost buttery flavors. Examples are easy to recognize as they are clearly labeled with the variety. Names to look for are Dorigo, Filliputti, and Movia (Slovenia).

Tocai Friulano

The name of the grape makes it clear where it excels: all over Friuli. Its spread makes for an equal spread of styles, from light and undistinguished to tangy with citrusy acidity, juicy with pear and apple flavors, fragrant with flowers, and savory with nut, spice, and mineral flavors. Most run $15 to $30. Some names to check out are Bastianich, Scarbolo, and Schiopetto.

Trebbiano's Reach

Trebbiano takes up more room than any other white wine grape in all of Italy. Light and vaguely fruity, its most remarkable trait may be that it grows all over the place, but it forms the basis for many of Italy's best-known white wines, such as:

◆ **Orvieto** is the wine that put Umbria on the wine map. Light, soft, and simple, it seems designed for pasta salads and summertime picnics. Antinori's versions pretty much define the region's style and run $10 to $15.

◆ **Frascati** fuels Roman trattorias with its crisp, light whites, grown near the eponymous town about 12 miles outside Rome. They might not be much to write home about, but with a slice of white pizza on a hot summer day, they can be perfect, especially at the $12 or so they ask. Fontana Candida Frascati is widely available; Castel de Paolis is worth seeking out.

◆ **Trebbiano d'Abruzzo** is rarely exciting, producing a lot of light, easy whites in Abruzzo, but in rare cases (namely, Eduardo Valentini) turns out long-lived golden wines. In fact, it may be made from a different grape, Bombino Bianco, but never mind; if someone offers you a glass of Valentini Trebbiano, take it. Other producers of note are Cataldi Madonna, Nicodemi, and Zaccagnini.

◆ **Galestro** is what some Tuscan producers make with Trebbiano, now that quality concerns discourage them from adding many white wine grapes to their Chianti as was custom a few decades back. Named for the local soils, Galestro can be a pleasant, lightly fruity aperitif. Many Tuscan producers now opt to add international grapes to the mix and bottle their Trebbiano blends under the simple name Toscana IGT.

◆ **Est! Est!! Est!!! di Montefiascone** is as light-hearted as its name, which supposedly descended from some twelfth-century graffiti. Grown near Lake Bolsena in Lazio, good versions of the wine are bright, clean, savory, and refreshing, and usually run $10 or less.

Garganega

Rarely does Garganega appear on a label, but if you've had Soave, you've tasted it. Its starring role is in this white wine from the Veneto in northeastern Italy, the best of which are creamy with marzipan flavors. It's worth paying extra for better examples; try Soave Classicos from Gini, Inama, Pieropan, and Prà which should run $30 or far less.

Falanghina, Fiano, and Greco: Campania's Ancient Trio

Campania's wines were some of the most revered in the ancient world; wines such as Falernum kept Pliny and company refreshed. Lost to history for centuries, Campania's ancient grapes are undergoing a renaissance. With the vogue for southern Italian food, these grapes are even appearing with regularity on wine lists. Here's what to expect.

◆ **Falanghina** is thought to be the grape on which the ancients based the brew they called Falernum. Falanghina makes unusual, almost otherworldly, white wines full of smoky, nutty flavors kept refreshed by lemony acidity. Many examples are labeled by the name of the grape, but you can find others under the DOC Falerno di Massica. Falanghina also stars in Lacryma Christi del Vesuvio, a smooth white that smells as smoky as you might imagine a wine grown on the side of a volcano.

◆ **Fiano** makes light, dry whites fragrant with smoky, woodsy lemon pith and mineral notes. Its most esteemed version is Fiano di Avellino, grown in the hilly region of Avellino about 20 miles outside of Naples.

◆ **Greco** grows all over southern Italy, but its best version is Greco di Tufo, a crisp, lemon-scented wine with a lot of savory minerality made in Avellino. Dry and refreshing, it makes a great match to fried fish and other richer fish dishes.

Quick Sips

For great Campanian whites, look particularly to Feudi di San Gregorio, Mastroberardino, Terredora, and Villa Mathide, producers who have led Campania's winemaking renaissance. All tend to run $15 to $30.

The Three V's: Verdicchio, Vernaccia, Vermentino

None of these grapes has anything to do with the others besides its first letter. But what other country can boast three grapes beginning with V? All are found labeled by their variety, too.

Vernaccia

There are several types of Vernaccia, but the most common wine from the grape is Vernaccia di San Gimignano, a sturdy, savory white wine made from Vernaccia grown around the hill town of San Gimignano in Tuscany. Light, acidic, and full of minerality, Vernaccia makes an excellent summertime quaff on its own or with delicate fish. Wines from producers like Ca'del Vispo, Le Calcinaie, and Teruzzi & Puthod run less than $18.

Verdicchio

Verdicchio's claim to fame is its tall, curvaceous bottle, a ploy to bring some extra attention to this light, anise-scented, nutty wine. It can be better than the bottle suggests, though, with deeply nutty flavors and an acidity that can help it age well for a few years. The most notable Verdicchio grows not too far from the ocean in Le Marche, in a DOC called Verdicchio di Castelli di Jesi, and seems made for the region's abundant fish. Bucci and Fazi Battaglia make good examples at $10 to $20.

Vermentino

Vermentino comes in two very different styles: light and piercingly crisp from far up north off the chilly, jagged coast of Liguria, and rich and honeyed yet vibrant with acidity from far south, on the warm, sunny island of Sardinia. Antinori makes a version in Tuscany, too, which tends toward Sardinian fullness and incorporates oak for Tuscan flair and an expensive-tasting vanilla note. For Ligurian style, look to Bisson; for Sardinian style, try Argiolas or Santadi. Plan to spend $12 to $20.

Vini Rossi

Italy lays claim to even more red wines than whites, but the country's reputation for fine wine stands on the backs of just two: Sangiovese, the grape of Chianti, and

Nebbiolo, the key ingredient in Barolo. I include a few others, though, which deserve attention if not equal standing—and often come in at a fraction of the price.

Sangiovese

Heard of Chianti? Then you already know about Sangiovese. It's the grape that plays the biggest part in the cherry-scented, earthy red wines of Chianti, Tuscany's most famous wine and wine region. There's more to Sangiovese than Chianti, though. It's also found throughout Tuscany, starring in the wines of …

◆ Carmignano.

◆ Rosso and Brunello di Montalcino.

◆ Vino Nobile di Montepulciano.

◆ Morellino di Scansano.

Here's a rundown of the grape's most famous Tuscan interpretations.

Chianti

Some people mock Chianti for being so popular with tourists, but what's not to like? It's gorgeous country, green hills carpeted with vines, a forest here, an olive grove there, and old farmhouses dotting the landscape. The food matches the scenery, rustic and soulful, and the wine, a juicy, high-acid red smelling of cherries and herbs that recall the surrounding forests, couldn't be more fitting.

There's also a version of Chianti for every occasion and every pocketbook since it comes in many styles. The guidelines a vintner needs to follow in order to classify his wine as Chianti are pretty lenient: it needs to be made from a majority of Sangiovese, but it can include other local grapes, such as Canaiolo and Colorino, and up to 15 percent of Cabernet Sauvignon, Merlot, and Syrah.

So the vintner can make very traditional Chianti—light and cherry-scented with palate-whetting acidity and no noticeable oak—or very modern Chianti, with dark fruit flavors, tongue-tingling tannin, and a full complement of toasty, vanilla-like oak flavors. It's tough to tell what's in a particular bottle without knowing the philosophy of the vintner, but there are some regulations that help. Here's the scoop:

- **Chianti** can come from anyplace within the sprawling Chianti zone. Most are light, easy reds with lots of juicy fruit flavor, little noticeable tannin, and a modest price tag.

- **Chianti Classico** must be made from grapes grown within this demarcated region, the historic center of Chianti production. The hillier terrain and stricter yield controls than those of straight Chianti tend to make for more concentrated wines, and these wines are required to age one year before they are sold. Still, prices and styles range drastically, from light and acidic to dark and full-bodied and from $10 to $25.

- **Riservas** are typically the most concentrated Chiantis. They must age for at least two years before being released. Age causes the wine to trade youthful power for the quieter charms of earthy, spicy, mature flavors.

Off the Vine

In addition to Chianti Classico, Chianti has seven other subregions. More concentrated than most Chianti and less famous than Chianti Classico, wines from these areas can be good deals. Look for:

Chianti Colli Arentini   Chianti Colli Pisane

Chianti Colli Fiorentini   Chianti Colli Rúfina

Chianti Colli Montalbano   Chianti Colli Senesi

Chianti Colli Montespertoli

Carmignano

Just outside of Chianti, west of Florence, lies this little DOCG where Sangiovese is required to be mixed with 15 percent of Cabernet Sauvignon. The resulting wines tend to have a little more grip and *grrrrr* to their dark cherry flavors than most Chianti. Wines labeled Barco Reale di Carmignano come from the same area but tend to be lighter and cheaper, around $12 instead of $25 or so. Look for Ambra, Cappezzana, and Pratesi.

Rosso and Brunello di Montalcino

Brunello is a clone, or variety, of Sangiovese; Montalcino is a relatively warm, hilly region just south of Siena. The region's wines come in two styles: *Rosso di Montalcino,* which tend to be as simple as red of Montalcino sounds; and *Brunello di Montalcino,* which are among the burliest red wines in Tuscany. The warmer area, particular clone, and soils give both versions darker, riper fruit flavors and more tannin than most Chiantis offer. Rossos can be bargains at $12 to $20; Brunello is comparatively expensive at double that or much more, but good examples can age for decades. Banfi and Biondi-Santi are the most famous; Barbi, Col d'Orcia, Il Poggione, and La Poderina are also worth checking out.

Quick Sips

Between the immense array of wine and the ever-shifting rules and regulations, Italian wine can be hard to get a handle on. The Italian Trade Commission's site on food and wine, www.Italianmade.com, is a boon to the Italophile; also sign up for the free newsletter at www.italianwinemerchant.com, an all-Italian wine store in New York City.

Vino Nobile di Montepulciano

Made from a majority of Sangiovese and a smattering of strictly local grapes grown around the town of Montepulciano southwest of Siena, Vino Nobile show a more delicate side of Tuscan wine, with fragrant scents and flavors of violets, earth, and spice accompanied by lightly tannic dried cherry flavors. They've fallen out of fashion since they were given the noble moniker in the seventeenth century, so they can be great buys at $15 to $30. Avignonesi, Dei, and Poliziano all fall in that range.

Morellino di Scansano

Morellino is another clone of Sangiovese, this one common to the far southwest corner of Tuscany. In this warmer climate, the grape becomes riper, rounder, and softer than most any other Sangiovese in the region. Most examples run about $10 to $30. Moris Farms and Le Pupille are leading names.

Nebbiolo, Piedmont's Liquid Truffle

Nebbiolo is to some wine lovers what Pinot Noir is to Burgundy addicts: frustrating, expensive, and irresistibly sexy and delicious. It thrives in even fewer places than the finicky Pinot Noir, preferring the cool hills of Piedmont in Italy's far northwest. And with lots of acidity and tannins yet light fruit flavors, traditional styles can take years to become actually pleasurable to drink. Still, a good version can be as fragrant as a truffle shaved over hot pasta: earthy, fruity, spicy, exotic. To find such pleasures, look to:

- **Barolo** is the apotheosis of Nebbiolo, producing wines with as many heady, delicate scents of earth, violets, roses, and dried cherries as they have tannin and acid. Even though basic Barolos are aged three years before release and Riservas are aged for at least four, most need to be cellared for a decade or more before they reach their peak. If you're looking for one to drink sooner, look for the oldest vintage you can find, or buy a less-expensive bottling (around $30 instead of $75 or more).

Quick Sips _____

Nebbiolo at a glance: high acid, very tannic, with scents of rose, licorice, truffles, and earth and dark cherry flavors. The best age for decades. Great producers: Ceretto, Conterno, Giacosa, Marcarini, Marchesi di Barolo, Mascarello, and Pio Cesare.

- **Barbaresco** grows on the other side of Alba from Barolo and tends to be a little less severe yet still plenty burly. Prices are right up there with those of Barolo.

- **Langhe** is the region that boasts Barolo and Barbaresco; wines labeled Langhe can be made from grapes grown anywhere within its borders. Most do not have the power of Barolo or Barbaresco but will offer Nebbiolo's hallmark truffle-and-rose fragrance and dried cherry flavors at a fraction of the price.

Quick Sips _____

Can't afford Barolo? Check out Nebbiolos labeled simply Langhe or from less esteemed areas such as Alba, Gattinara, and Ghemme. They may not be as age-worthy as Barolo, but they will give you a taste of this fragrant grape.

Barbera and Dolcetto

As if to offer some consolation to those who can't wait for their Nebbioli to age into pleasant palatability, Piedmont also offers two of Italy's friendliest grapes, Barbera and Dolcetto. Barbera is the heartier of the two, with shockingly bright acidity and ripe red fruit. It produces anything from $12 gems brimming with ripe cherry flavor, like basic bottlings from Batasiolo, Chiarlo, and La Sera, to brawnier reds with similar flavors but meatier tannin. The heartiest and most expensive can rival Barbaresco in stature and in price, such as single-vineyard bottlings by Conterno, Prunotto, Vajra, Vietti, and Voerzio). Some of the best-regarded Barbera wines come from the DOC Barbera d'Alba; those from Asti are also esteemed and tend to be a little lighter.

Dolcetto means, loosely, "little sweet one," a reference to its charming, plump fruit flavors. Dolcetto that runs $8 to $15 tends to be for casual quaffing; bottlings from Asti and Alba (noted on the label) tend to run a little deeper in flavor—perfect for first course of meat-filled agnolotti—and higher in price. Einaudi, Poderi Colla, and Conterno Fantino are some trusted names.

Friuli's Freaky Reds and Trentino's Teroldego

Friuli's cool climes are most famous for white wines, but anyone who likes high-acid reds should search out this region's reds. Start with Refosco, which has tart blueberry flavors edged with earthy tannin—delicious with rich ravioli stuffed with meaty porcini mushrooms. Then there's Schioppettino, with peppery notes on its dark plum flavors that some compare to France's Syrah. Pignolo is lighter, with piquant red berry flavors, and Tazzelenghe can live up to its name, tongue-cutter, with acidity that tears through its dark blackberry flavor. Examples are hard to find Stateside; scoop up whatever you can find.

Next door, in Trentino, Teroldego Rotaliano is the starring red wine grape, producing deep purple wines with spicy, herbal black fruit flavor and lots of enlivening acidity. Foradori is the model; it runs about $25. And in Alto Adige, look for wines made from Lagrein (Colterenzio, Elena Walch, Hofstatter, Lageder) for juicy blueberry flavor.

Corvina, Valpolicella's Star

Corvina is rarely spoken by name but widely known by taste. It's the main component in Valpolicella, a wine grown not far from Verona in the Veneto. The basic version is one of the easiest-going wines on the planet: bright purple, brimming with simple, juicy plum and cherry flavor, and costing about $10, what's not to love?

Valpolicella also comes in two more substantial versions:

◆ **Valpolicella Ripasso:** Traditionally, Valpolicella makers would "re-pass" their fermented wine over the grape skins left over from making Amarone, a last-ditch effort to give the wines more flavor. Today, many vintners use grapes that haven't already been used, so the wines pick up more sweet grape flavors. The end result falls someplace between Valpolicella and Amarone in flavor, but most cost only a few dollars more than straight Valpolicella.

◆ **Amarone di Valpolicella:** Amarone is Valpolicella made with grapes that have been partially dried to concentrate their flavor. Almost as intense in fruity purple flavor as Port, yet dry, with notes of bitter chocolate and spice, it's a wine for drinking with rich dishes like *osso buco*, or with a cheese course. Often overlooked, good deals can be had for $20, though Amarone can cost $100 or so, too.

Quick Sips

Many Valpolicella producers make straight Valpolicella as well as Amarone and Ripasso styles; buy one of each and taste them side by side to compare. Allegrini, Masi, and Quintarelli are three leaders in the region.

Southern Specials

Long isolated from the more industrial northern regions and slow to pick up technological advances in the wine world, Southern Italy was largely ignored as a source of good wine until very recently. That means there are great deals available at every turn, so look for these wines.

Montepulciano

Montepulciano might not make distinguished wines, but it sure makes hard-working reds, full of lusty red fruit flavors ready to take on a sausage-and-pepper sandwich. Most are from Abruzzo and labeled Montepulciano d'Abruzzo; some finer examples, like those of Cocci Grifoni and Umani Ronchi, come from Rosso Conero and Rosso Piceno in the Marches. Prices range from $6 for the former to $20 for the latter.

Sour Grapes _____

Here's a confusing fact: Montepulciano the grape has nothing to do with Montepulciano the place. The grape is a hearty red-wine grape that grows all over Abruzzo and the Marches; the place is in Tuscany and makes its wines from Sangiovese (see "Vino Nobile di Montepulciano" earlier in this chapter).

Aglianico

Aglianico (ah-ghlee-*an*-ee-ko) rules the tongue of the boot, from Campania through Basilicata. With plenty of dark fruit flavors fully supported with tannin and acidity, Aglianico can make some of the South's most sophisticated reds. To taste them, look for wines labeled *Aglianico del Vulture*, named for the volcanic slopes of Mount Vulture in Basilicata where the grape picks up as much mineral flavor as it does ripeness; and *Taurasi* or *Falerno del Massico*, regions in Campania where the grape excels. Bottles run from $8 for simple stuff to $40 for ambitious reserve bottlings from Mastroberardino and Paternoster.

Negroamaro

Primitivo may enjoy the most notoriety in Apulia these days, now that we know it's Zinfandel in Italian form (see Chapter 12), but Negroamaro deserves a look, too. The grape's name, Black-bitter, comes from its dark color and the bitter note that often helps cut through its superripe, black fruit flavors. Many of the best examples hail from Salice Salentino in Salento. Try Apollonio, Feudi Monaci, or Taurino; most run $10.

Nero d'Avola

Nero d'Avola wines are a bit like Sicily's mountainous terrain: warm, sunny, and a bit wild. The best take on rich, chocolaty-plum flavors, often with impressive amounts of tannin that make them terrific matches to the island's lamb and sheep's cheeses. COS, Donafugata, Morgante, Regaleali, Rapitalà, and Santa Anastasia are just a few wineries making good examples today; expect to pay $15 to $20.

The Least You Need to Know

♦ Most of Italy's wines are labeled by region or by grape and region.

♦ Designations like IGT, DOC, and DOCG can mean very little quality-wise with Italian wine; it's better to get to know each region's wines and the producers.

♦ Riserva usually indicates a wine that has been aged a few years before it's released, so it will have more mature flavors than non-Riserva wines—important to know if you prefer fruity, fresh wines.

♦ When you're bored with Pinot Grigio, try Arneis, Fiano di Avellino, Falanghina, Greco di Tufo, Ribolla Gialla, or Tocai Friulano.

♦ If you like Chianti, also try wines such as Carmignano, Morellino di Scansano, Rosso di Montalcino, and Vino Nobile di Montepulciano, all made in Tuscany.

♦ If you want wines with lots of flavor at little cost, Southern Italy is a gold mine.

Chapter 17

Awesome Unsung Varieties

In This Chapter

- ◆ Scheurebe, Germany's hidden treasure
- ◆ Austria's awesome Grüner Veltliner
- ◆ Melon, the grape behind Muscadet
- ◆ Tannic Tannat and plush Malbec
- ◆ France's Languedoc offerings
- ◆ Provence's best reds
- ◆ Gamay in Beaujolais
- ◆ Greece's ancient grapes

We've covered all the major grapes you'll see on a label and a whole bunch that rarely appear in word but frequently do in flavor, yet there are still great grapes and great wines we haven't even begun to discuss.

So I've filled this chapter with some of the greatest obscurities of the wine world. Often, they will be harder to find and harder to pronounce, but their unique flavors will make up for the hunt. Just keep it quiet, okay? If more people find out about these wines, prices will go up, and they'll no longer be such good finds.

A Trio of Obscure Whites

When you're sick of Chardonnay, bored with Pinot Grigio, confused by Riesling, and Sauvignon Blanc just doesn't fit, where do you turn? You have plenty of options, but these three are some of the most interesting and versatile.

Grüner Veltliner

Grüner Veltliner (*grew*-nair *velt*-leen-er) seemingly came out of nowhere in the late 1990s to steal the hearts of cork dorks across the United States. Once mainly appreciated by Austrians who slugged down enormous draughts of it in the casual wine bars that dot the countryside, now the American wine cognoscenti drink it up, loving it for its unique flavors. Grüner Veltliner's flavors span the range of green (*grüner* means green, after all), from bright lime zest through sweet honeydew to earthy pea and lentil. Sounds strange, I know, but with its bright acidity and strong mineral notes, Grüner Veltliner has the delicacy to complement fish dishes as well as the personality to stand up to tandoori chicken, not to mention wiener schnitzel, a breaded, fried veal cutlet that is a staple of Viennese cuisine.

Quick Sips

Grüner Veltliner at a glance: *grüner* (green) flavors from lime to lentils; high acidity and minerality. It excels in Austria and is labeled by grape name.

Grüner Veltliner ranges widely in price, from $10 to $15 for light, easy versions for casual aperitifs to $40 or more for powerful, mineral-laden versions that will last years in the cellar. A few great names are Bründlmayer, Gobelsburg, Hirsch, Nigl, Pichler, and Prager.

Scheurebe

Scheurebe (*shoy*-reb-bah), thankfully called Shoy for short, is an entirely German construction, a cross between delicate Riesling and heartier Sylvaner performed by a Dr. Georg Scheu in 1916. The result is far richer and wilder than either of those grapes on its own, an exotic mix of sweet-tart pink grapefruit, smooth honey, sharp herb, and exotic tropical fruit and cassis notes. It excels in Germany's Pfalz region, where it makes wild, mouth-filling dry white wines as well as rich sweet wines marked TBA or Eiswein (see Chapter 6). Wines made from Scheurebe always say

Quick Sips

Scheurebe at a glance: cassis, pink grapefruit, honey, herb, and tropical fruit flavors; full-bodied, medium to high acidity.

so on the label; most dry versions run $20 to $35. Some Scheurebe stars are Darting, Kruger-Rumpf, Lingenfelder, Theo Minges, and Müller-Catoir.

Off the Vine _____

How to pronounce Scheurebe? The answer is so far-ranging (and funny) that vintner Rainer Lingenfelder has compiled recordings from people around the world at www.lingenfelder.com.

Melon

If you're looking for an affordable white wine for summertime sipping, look to Melon, though you'll rarely find it marked on any label. Instead, look for Muscadet, the name of the French region in which it thrives. Grown near where the Loire meets the Atlantic Ocean and made without oak, Muscadets are as light, crisp, and fresh as the region's cold, salty air. They come cheap, too; $8 can buy decent casual sipping while $25 buys Muscadet that has the elegance to stand up to any white-tablecloth meal and can age well for years. Look especially for Guy Bossard, Luneau-Papin, and Sauvion.

Adventurous French Reds

It's easy to impress wine connoisseurs by buying a well-known wine. It's even more impressive when you pull out something they've never heard of that blows their socks off. After all, part of what makes wine interesting is the never-ending choices. These places and wines should give you plenty of fodder next time you're looking for a great, lesser-known red.

Languedoc-Roussillon Reds

The Languedoc and the Roussillon of Southern France, two regions typically referred to as one, burgeon with under-discovered red wines. The area forms a chain of vineyards from just west of Avignon, around the curve of the Mediterranean to the Pyrenees.

Warm, sunny, and affordable compared to other French regions, this area has become home to acres of international grapes such as Chardonnay and Merlot. and international companies—for instance, Gallo is here with Red Bicyclette. Most wines are varietally labeled and aspire to be no more than tasty, affordable buys at around $10, such as Jaja de Jau, Lurton, Tortoise Creek. A few fancy bottlings reach into the $40s.

Far more interesting are wines from local grapes. Most are based on a combination of Carignan, a Spanish grape with dark red fruit flavors, plus Grenache, Syrah, and Mourvèdre, and other more obscure local varieties. Many are rustic, the sort of rough-edged, dark-fruited wines that show best next to a burger and are priced accordingly, at $6 to $15. Others rank among the most sophisticated and delicious in France, with smooth, spicy, concentrated black fruit flavors and the structure to age for years. Some top producers are d'Aupilhac, d'Aussières, Daumas-Gassac, Donjon, l'Hortus, Peyre-Rose, and Sarda-Malet.

Quick Sips

Several places within Languedoc–Roussillon stand out for the quality of their wines and have been granted the right to appear on wine labels. Look particularly for:

- La Clape
- Collioure (koal-*yur*)
- Corbières (core-bee-*aire*)
- Faugères (foh-*zhaire*)

- Fitou (fee-*too*)
- Minervois (min-er-*vwah*)
- Pic-St-Loup (*peak* sahn *loop*)
- St-Chinian (sahn shin-ee-*ahn*)

Provence's Pleasures

On the other side of Avignon, the grapes Carignan, Grenache, Syrah, and Mourvèdre continue the trail they started down in Roussillon and stretch east along the Mediterranean almost up to Nice. The climate is similarly warm and sunny; the difference is that tourism has traditionally overshadowed winemaking.

Quick Sips

Some of the most sophisticated rosé in the world comes from Provence, particularly from appellations such as Bandol, Cassis, and Palette.

However, among all the pink plonk made for vacationers (and some very fine rosés, too), there are some hearty, structured, fascinating reds. Most of these will be labeled by region, not grape, so when you want to try one, look for wines that say ...

- Côtes de Provence (coat de proh-*vahnce*)
- Coteaux d'Aix en Provence (co-*toe* d'ex ahn pro-*vahnce*)

- Coteaux Varois (co-*toe* vair-*wah*)

- Bandol (ban-*dole*)

- Les Baux de Provence (lay bow de pro-*vahnce*)

The first three on this list are large and varied appellations where quality depends more on the individual estate than on any inherent local advantages. The much smaller Bandol appellation, where the black grape Mourvèdre rules, stands out for some of the most intense and delicious wines in all of Provence; the best are tannic and structured enough to age well more than a decade. The small appellation of Les Baux de Provence, just east of Arles, is also a hotbed of excellent reds based on the traditional Grenache-Syrah-Mourvèdre trio plus smatterings of local grapes.

Prices range all over the board, from about $15 for good, casual rosé and red pours, to well over $50 for exalted rosés and reds, particularly from Bandol. Look especially for Commanderie de la Bargemone, Mas de la Dame, Mas de Gourgonnier, Pibarnon, Pradeaux, Tempier, and Trevallon.

Gamay

There's far more to Beaujolais than the light, young, bubblegummy wine that's jetted over from France with great fanfare every third Thursday of November.

That stuff is Beaujolais Nouveau, the first wine of the harvest. But Gamay, the grape that makes Beaujolais, can do better. In Beaujolais, France—a region considered geographically, if not philosophically, connected to Burgundy—Gamay can make wines with robust berry flavors and even a bit of tannin.

Quick Sips _____

Gamay at a glance: light, juicy, simple, cherry-berry flavors at low prices.

Mostly, though, Beaujolais is an easy, cheery wine, filled with cherry flavors and kept light and brisk by plenty of acidity. It's the perfect sort of wine for picnics, suppers, bistros, and casual sipping.

To find good Beaujolais, look for bottles that say Beaujolais-Villages, indicating that the grapes that went into them came from select vineyards. For Beaujolais with yet more substance, look for Beaujolais that don't say Beaujolais, but instead list the name of one of the 10 villages selected as exceptional. They are Brouilly, Chénas, Chiroubles, Côte de Brouilly, Fleurie, Juliénas, Morgon, Moulin-à-Vent, Régnié, and St-Amour.

Brouilly, Morgon, and Moulin-à-Vent in particular offer Beaujolais dark and rich enough to stand up to steak.

Besides the ubiquitous examples from Georges Dubouef, look also to small producers like Dupeuble, Janodet, and Thivin. Most cost $12 to $25.

Tannic Tannat

Tannat is just what it sounds like—tannic as all get-out. Its stronghold is south-west France, where it defines the black wines of Madiran as well as Irouleguy, in the rugged foothills of the Pyrenees. Though there is a trend toward making these wines softer and more approachable when young, most require years of age, as well as roast goose, duck confit, or other rich, hearty foods for maximum enjoyment.

So cellar some now; it'll cost you only about $8 to $20, maybe $40 for some special bottlings—not bad for wines that can last decades. Trustworthy names are Bouscassé, Montus, and Plaimont.

Quick Sips

Tannat at a glance: found in wines labeled Madiran and Irouleguy from France, and by variety from Uruguay. Its black flavors are as tough as nails, with lots of mouth-drying tannin.

Tannat also grows in Uruguay, South America, courtesy of a nineteenth-century Frenchman who imported it. It makes tannic, earthy black wines here, too, which have been getting better in recent years as Uruguayan winemakers have become more quality-oriented. The few available in the States run about $11 to $20, with a couple touching $50. Look especially for Los Cerros de San Juan, Pisano, and Carlos Pizzorno.

Off the Vine

As a friend put it, "Why aren't the streets of southwest France littered with dead Gascons?" He was referring to their penchant for duck confit, fattened goose livers (*foie gras*), and wine. According to doctors who've studied the French Paradox, the ability of the French to eat high-fat foods and drink wine yet remain enviously slim and healthy, it's the wine—especially those with high levels of procyanidins, antioxidants that improve blood vessel function, such as Madiran.

Argentina's Best Red, Malbec

Look at what people in different places eat, and you can often guess what they drink. In western Argentina, where cattle outnumber people, the Argentines drink red. And most of that red is made from Malbec.

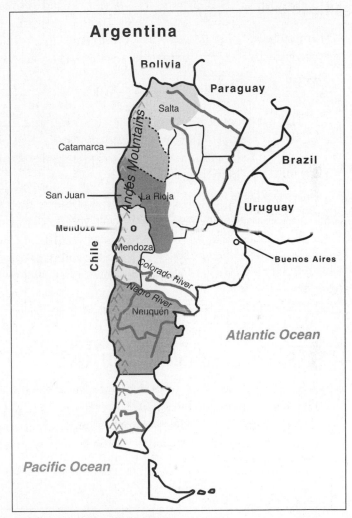

Argentina's winegrowing regions.

Quick Sips

Malbec at a glance: velvety black cherry, chocolate, and licorice flavors, smooth but firm tannin. Found in the wines of Cahors, France, and shines in Argentina, where the wines are varietally labeled.

Malbec came originally from Bordeaux, where it had trouble ripening in the cool, damp, maritime climate, and so most of the Malbec vines have been torn out.

The vine does better in Cahors, a warmer region in southwest France, where it ripens to an impressive blackness and yet retains intense tannin. Traditional Cahors wines often need years of age before they are truly enjoyable—and even then, they benefit from a dish of local goose or other meat to relieve the tannin.

With Argentine Malbec, there's no waiting necessary. It thrives in warm, sunny Mendoza, a large region on the other side of the Andes from Chile's capital, Santiago, filling with lots of black plum, black currant, and black licorice flavors. A fair amount of tannin supports all that blackness, but here the tannins feel velvety instead of hard and drying as in Cahors wines. Next to a steak, Malbec shines.

Off the Vine

With their chocolate-cherry flavors, Argentina's Malbec wines are some of the few savory wines that go well with chocolate desserts.

Malbec also grows farther north, in the high altitudes of Salta, and farther south, in Patagonia. The cooler climates of these places make for slimmer, spicier Malbec. Whether from Mendoza or beyond, most good Argentine Malbecs run $12 to $25, with a few rich, dark luxury cuvées approaching $100. Names to know are Catena, Noemia, Terrazas de los Andes, Trapiche, and Weinert.

Greece's Awesome Antiquities

Greece offers some of the best bargains in the wine world today, and I'm not talking about Retsina, the pine resin–flavored wine. Spurred on by joining the EU and further charged by the 2004 Olympics, Greece is regaining the reputation it had during Plato's time, when Greek wine ruled the wine world. Here are some its best wines, red and white.

Off the Vine

Why would the Greeks put pine resin in a wine? For the same reason the French put herbs in Vermouth: they like the taste. However, there's also a historical precedent. Before bottles, people needed to seal the earthenware casks in which they stored wine. Pine resin provided a watertight seal. This technique was used across the Mediterranean; today, Greece's Retsina is the only trace we have of this ancient tradition.

Assyrtiko

On the remnants of the volcano that is now the island of Santorini, Assyrtiko (ah-sir-tee-*ko*) holds on for its life, with strong winds, beating heat, and encroaching hotels threatening to take it away. There's a fair amount of support for the grape, though, as it makes arguably the best white wine in the country. Good examples are crisp and savory; great examples can recall white Burgundy in structure and minerality. All are bottled under the name of the island instead of the grape variety. Plan to spend $15 to $25 for a good example; Argyros, Hatzidakis, and Sigalas are the leaders.

Quick Sips

Greece offers far more great grapes than the three covered here. Don't forget fragrant Moschofilero, covered in Chapter 13, and check out www.allaboutgreekwine.com to find out about others.

Agiorgitiko

Agiorgitiko (ah-ghee-or-*gee*-tee-ko) is Greece's own Zinfandel, a red-wine grape that can make everything from gutsy pink pours to jammy barbecue wines to massive, brooding, long-lived reds. It grows mainly in Pan's former playground in the northeast Peloponnese; some list the grape on the label, but those grown within the designated area of Nemea (the majority) are bottled with only Nemea on the label. Prices range from $12 for an easy-drinking, soft, and fruity example, to bottles as sophisticated as their $35 price. Gaia, Papantonis, Pape Johannou, and Skouras make some of the best.

Xinomavro

Do you love Barolo but can't afford it? Xinomavro's your wine. Like Nebbiolo, the grape for Barolo, Xinomavro (ksi-*no*-mahv-ro) prefers it cool and damp; its home is Naoussa (*nah*-oos-sa), in part of Northern Greece where it actually snows. Also like Nebbiolo, the grape has intense acidity and tannins against light fruit fragrant with scents of dried cherries, spice, and truffles. Most is labeled simply Naoussa, though some carry the grape name. The best examples run $16 to $30—more expensive than most Greek wines, but affordable compared to Barolo. Look especially for Boutari and Kir Yianni.

The Least You Need to Know

◆ The best place to look for abundant good deals is in the places that most others ignore.

◆ When you're looking for an unusual white wine, try Austrian Grüner Veltliner or German Scheurebe.

◆ The south of France is full of good values, especially in traditional blends.

◆ Forget Beaujolais Nouveau; try Beaujolais from specific villages for Gamay-based reds with substance.

◆ For hearty winter reds, try the tannic, Tannat-based red wines of Madiran and Irouleguy from France, or Malbec wines from Cahors and Argentina.

◆ Look beyond Retsina for Greece's best wines, including white wines from Santorini and red wines labeled Nemea and Naoussa.

Part 4

Special Styles

Whew. We've covered a lot, but still we have barely touched on whole categories of wine. What about sparkling wines, dessert wines, and those strong, fortified wines like Port? They are all here in this part, a whirlwind tour of some of the most hedonistic styles of wine in the world.

Hedonistic, in my book, doesn't mean special occasion, so don't save this chapter for a rainy day. You can enjoy all the wines in this section as often as you want—and you won't need to break the bank to do so. So grab a glass—and by the way, Champagne flutes and little dessert wine glasses are nice, but a regular wine glass will do—and get tasting.

Chapter **18**

All That Sparkles

In This Chapter

- The difference between Champagne and other sparkling wines
- Getting the bubbles in the bottle
- Making those bubbles last
- Finding good, affordable bubbly

The idea of a wine that bubbles is as old as wine—after all, that's what wine does when it ferments. The discovery, however, of how to contain those fizzy, uplifting little bubbles in a bottle was a discovery that rivals the chocolate bar in terms of bringing pleasure to the world.

Bubbles are refreshing. They make a wine seem weightless and festive, and, by association, they enhance the event itself. Bubbles transform a wine into something more than a still wine with bubbles; without them, the remaining wine would be far less interesting. Bubbles—or the bead, the preferred word among connoisseurs—tickle the tongue, making it want more. They almost seem to scrub the mouth clean, leaving the tongue ready for another sip, another bite. It's surprising that we don't all drink sparkling wines every day.

However, it's no easy feat to get those bubbles into the bottle and to make them stay there. That's why prices for sparkling wine are generally higher than those for still wines. So let's look at the different methods of making sparkling wine and check out the major varieties.

Sour Grapes

All Champagnes are sparkling wines, but only sparkling wines from the region of France called Champagne are Champagnes. American wineries frequently used to "borrow" the name for their sparkling wines—and, embarrassingly, continue to do so, except for wines that are exported, though that practice is now banned.

Capturing Carbonation

Sparkling wine, at its most basic, is wine with bubbles in it. The wine had to ferment first, or it wouldn't be wine, so the bubbles have to be added later.

How do they get in there? There are a few methods, one that's traditional and some more recently developed shortcuts. All start with a wine that has gone through its first fermentation, and all result in a wine that foams upon opening, but the results are a little bit different depending on the technique. Here's the lowdown on how the sparkle gets in a sparkling wine.

Force It

The easiest way to get the bubbles into sparkling wine is to force them—literally. In what's referred to as the "bicycle pump method," the vintner simply injects carbon dioxide into the wine just before bottling and then bottles the wine under pressure, like a soft drink. The wine bubbles when opened—often violently—but those bubbles don't last long. To keep them longer, sparkling wines need a little more care, as they get in the "tank method."

Tank It

In the tank method (also called *Charmat*, after the Frenchman who invented the process in 1907, or *cuve close* in French), wine is put into a pressurized tank, and yeast and sugar are added to provoke a second fermentation, which makes the bubbles. The bubbling wine is then bottled under pressure.

This is the most popular way to make affordable sparkling wines, and the result can be pretty good, with relatively fine bubbles that last well. The finest, longest-lasting bubbles, though, are typically achieved by making sparkling wines the traditional way.

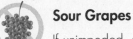

Sour Grapes

If unimpeded, a cork can leave a bottle of sparkling wine at as much as 40 miles per hour and go about 44 yards. Approach with caution!

Be Patient

The traditional method, or *méthode traditionelle*, is the one used in Champagne, the spiritual epicenter of sparkling wines. In this technique, after wine has been through its first, or primary, fermentation, the winemaker adds more yeast and sugar, just as in the tank method. Only in the traditional method, he now puts the wines into glass bottles and caps them with a crown cap, like the kind used on beer bottles. He then lays the bottles on their sides and lets them age for anywhere from 15 months to many years.

Now for the fun part: the bottles are traditionally placed horizontally in an Λ-shaped frame called a riddling rack. At regular intervals, a "riddler" comes by to turn the bottles a fraction of an inch, gradually and progressively moving them over time into a vertical position, so that they are nearly standing on their heads. The object of this painstaking task is to get all the lees, the residue left behind by fermentation, to repose in the neck of the bottle, where it can be easily removed. Today, gyropalettes, automated machines that mimic the riddler's art, take care of this job in most places, completing it in days rather than weeks.

Off the Vine

R.D. or L.D. on a sparkling wine label mean recently disgorged and late-disgorged. Both indicate the same thing—that the wine was left on its lees longer than usual (the bottle will often indicate how long) so as to pick up even more flavor from the lees.

Either way, in the end, he has a bottle standing on its head with a plug of muck at the mouth of it. To get it out, he takes each bottle and plunges its neck into a freezing solution, turns it over, opens it carefully, and lets the frozen plug fly.

Quickly, then, he adds a mixture of a little sugar and wine called a *dosage* to the bottle. The dosage makes up for lost volume as well as helps ensure a consistent house style by allowing the winemaker to sweeten the wine as he needs. Then he

Winespeak _____

Dosage is the mixture of sugar and wine that's put into a sparkling wine after the plug of lees has been disgorged. The amount and sweetness of the dosage affects the sweetness of the final wine.

corks the bottle and, for extra security, puts a wire cage over the cork to hold it tight and keep it from taking someone's eye out. Now the bottle will rest another several months or years before heading to the market.

Why take all this trouble when there are much simpler methods for getting bubbles into a bottle? Because the longer it takes, the more opportunity the wine has to pick up flavors from the lees and also from the different processes it goes through on its way to becoming a finished wine. A wine made by the traditional method tends to have finer, more complex flavors and finer bubbles.

Decoding the Sparkling Wine Label

A trip to the sparkling wine shelf of your local store will demonstrate just how many different styles of sparkling wine can be made. Do you want rosé Champagne, sweet Champagne, or half-sweet Champagne? The choices cover aperitifs through dessert.

Traditionally, sparkling wines are defined not only by the method by which they were made but also by what color the grapes were that went into them and the level of sweetness. So your choice will be made easier if you know how to parse the terms on a sparkling wine label.

A Matter of Color

In Champagne and most places that take Champagne as their model, sparkling wine is made from a combination of white and red grapes: Chardonnay, Pinot Noir, and Pinot Meunier. The skins are removed from the juice once the grapes are pressed so that the juice doesn't turn red. The flavor of the final wine depends in part on the mix of grapes used. Rather than listing the grapes on the label, however, the maker may use one of these terms:

◆ **Blanc de Blancs:** literally "white of whites," Blanc de Blancs (blahnk de blahnk) wines are made from white grapes, typically Chardonnay. They tend to be lean, even sharp, with the very white flavors of crisp Chardonnay and chalky minerals. A few sparkling wine producers forgo the French term and label their sparkling wine simply "Chardonnay."

◆ **Blanc de Noirs:** literally "white of blacks," Blanc de Noirs (blahnk de nwoir) wines are made from red grapes, traditionally Pinot Noir and a relative called Pinot Meunier. These wines are white because the vintner removes the pigment-rich grape skins from the juice directly after pressing. Blanc de Noirs wines often have a hint of red fruit flavor and a little deeper, darker flavor than Blanc de Blancs.

◆ **Rosé:** rosé sparkling wines are made by either letting the skins of red grapes soak in the juice long enough to lend it a little color or by adding some still red wine to the blend. The red fruit flavor ranges from a hint to a bold suggestion.

Off the Vine

There are red sparkling wines, too: Australia makes the most startling version: a heavy, dry, tannic, bubbly red traditionally made from Shiraz. Italy's Lambrusco is light and grapey—the dry versions are perfect with *salumi*—while Brachetto d'Acqui has sweet cherry flavors that make it a terrific complement to chocolate desserts.

Degrees of Dryness

Sparkling wine can also vary in sweetness from stone-dry to sticky sweet. Unfortunately, not all the terms are as intuitive as one might hope. From driest to sweetest, they are …

◆ Brut Nature (or Brut Zéro, Pas Dosé, or Sans Dosage)

◆ Extra Brut/Brut Extra

◆ Brut

◆ Extra Dry/Extra Sec

◆ Sec

◆ Demi-sec

Off the Vine

There are about 250 million bubbles in a bottle of sparkling wine, according to research by Champagne producer Moët et Chandon.

The first designation means no sugar is added to the wine at all. These are hard-core sparkling wines, for acid lovers and fatty foods only.

Sour Grapes _____

Confusingly, Sec (dry) and Demi-sec (half-dry) wines are actually sweet enough for dessert. When you're looking for a dry sparkling wine, look for those that say Brut.

Brut is the most common sweetness designation, though how sweet a Brut tastes depends on the style of the maker. All, however, are savory enough to have with dinner.

Sec and Demi-sec wines, counter to most of our understandings of "dry," are sweet wines, sweet enough to have for dessert.

Variations on Vintage

You have just one other decision to make before buying a sparkling wine: vintage or nonvintage? There's a difference, but it's not necessarily one of quality, as many people assume. It's style.

Nonvintage sparkling wine: most sparkling wine is nonvintage, or, more accurately, multivintage, as it contains the juice of grapes from different years' harvests. This tradition started in Champagne, a region of France where it's often too cold to get a decent harvest and the wines, therefore, benefit from additions of wines from other, riper harvests.

Quick Sips _____

Nonvintage sparkling wines are ready to drink as soon as they are sold. Many vintage Champagnes, on the other hand, taste better after a few years in your cellar.

Now the tradition is carried on around the world as the technique also allows winemakers to effectively create layers of flavors using wines of different ripeness levels and maturity. Some wineries, like Bollinger in France, have more than two decades' worth of stocks they can use to blend into their wines. The difference can be tasted in the richness and complexity of Bollinger's basic nonvintage Champagne. Nonvintage Champagnes are also ready to drink as soon as they are released to the market.

Vintage sparkling wine: sparkling wines bearing a vintage on the label must be made from the grapes of that year's harvest. In places like Champagne, only particularly good vintages are chosen to make these wines. Vintage wines are usually made in addition to the usual nonvintage wines, a snapshot of the vintage to have in a place where vintages worth recording are few. Because the wine is made from the grapes of only one harvest without the ameliorating effects of older wines, vintage sparkling wines often need years in the bottle to mellow out before they show their best. So if you're looking for a wine to drink now, stick with nonvintage sparklers.

Now that you know how to parse a sparkling wine label, let me tell you where to find the actual wines.

Pick a Country, Any Country

Just about every country that makes wine makes a sparkling version. After all, who wouldn't want to be able to bottle "stars," as Dom Pérignon, the eighteenth-century monk often credited with discovering Champagne, called the fine, bursting bubbles on his tongue. Some versions are more famous than others, but all are worth a try.

Champagne, France

France claims the most famous sparkling wine of them all: Champagne. The wine is made in the region of the same name, a large and cold area northeast of Paris. It's so cold here, actually, that Champagne is about the only wine the Champenois can make.

The grapes in Champagne rarely get ripe enough to make decent still wine; the juice, before it's made into sparkling wine, is mighty puckering. But sparkling wine needs lots of acidity to balance the extra sugar that goes into it to make it sparkle.

> **Off the Vine** _____
>
> Most Champagne is made by big firms that buy grapes from growers all over the region and blend them together to form wines that taste the same year after year. That's why, say, Veuve Clicquot Yellow Label tastes the same every time you buy it. Grower Champagnes are different. Denoted by RM (récoltant-manipulant) on the label, these wines are made by the person who grew the grapes. Small houses with limited production (in the thousands of cases instead of millions), they can offer unique views of the land and its wines—often at very good prices. Once rare, they are getting much easier to find in the United States, thanks to specialist importers such as Terry Theise Selections.

The end result is a bit like turning lemons into lemonade, except on a grander scale; it's Champagne, after all, the wine that set the formula for sparkling wines all around the world. And that formula is? Chardonnay on its own or in combination with red grapes Pinot Noir and Pinot Meunier (ratio left up to the winemaker), made according to the excruciatingly time- and energy-consuming tenets of the méthode traditionelle. Why? Because the end result will be at once bright and refreshing, fruity and toasty, mineral-studded and creamy with yeasty lees. Oh, and it will have the finest bubbles you'll ever feel.

Sometimes, you'll pay dearly for the pleasure. Top bottlings from big names like Veuve Clicquot, Bollinger, Moët et Chandon, and Salon run from $75 to well over $100. But there are some good buys for $40 to $50, too. Look for wines from Françoise Bedel, Chartogne-Taillet, Diebolt-Vallois, Nicolas Feuillatte, Marc Hébrart, and Leclaire-Gaspard, to name just a few.

Quick Sips

For extensive information on the Champagne region and its wines, look to www.champagne.us, put together by the trade association of Champagne growers and winemakers. Or for a more personal take, check out www.peterliem.com, where American wine writer and Champagne fanatic Peter Liem reports from a house among the vines.

France's Other Sparklers

Champagne isn't the only place in France that offers sparkling wine. Some delicious *crémants*, as the French call non-Champagne traditionally made sparkling wines, are made all over France and usually labeled *Crémant de* followed by the place they grew. Some of the best come from Alsace and the Loire; most run $12 to $25. A few sparkling wines even rise above this general designation and earn unique names. A few of these standouts:

Winespeak

Crémant indicates a non-Champagne sparkling wine made in the traditional method.

◆ **Vouvray Mousseux:** Mousseux (moos-*suhr*) means bubbly, and this is an effervescent version of the Loire white wine, Vouvray (see Chapter 13). Made from Chenin Blanc, Vouvray Mousseux is not your usual clean, light, apple-like sparkling wine but is instead a lush, savory wine filled with flavors of honey, pears, and chalky minerals. It's fascinating stuff, but prepare for a departure from the usual. Some cost around $10, but better quality comes in at $15 to $35.

◆ **Clairette de Die:** Clairette is the name of the grape; Die is the town south of Valence in the southern Rhône around which this grape grows. It makes a light, crisp, refreshing sparkling wine; better versions, labeled Clairette de Die Tradition, include Muscat grapes that give them a delicate floral scent. They are a steal when you can find them, most running less than $20.

♦ **Blanquette de Limoux:** a soft, fruity sparkler made in the high hills of Limoux where the Languedoc-Roussillon meets Southwest France. It's typically made from a local white wine grape called Mauzac; recently, inspired by Champagne, vintners have been planting more Chardonnay. They tend to run $10 to $20.

California

California's cooler valleys have attracted Champagne producers like Mumm (Mumm Napa Valley), Chandon (Domaine Chandon), Roederer (Roederer Estate), and Deutz (Maison Deutz, now Laetitia), joining Americans like Iron Horse, J Vineyards and Winery, and Schramsberg. The Spanish have also come over, with Gloria Ferrer and Codorníu (Artesa).

Most sparkling wine producers have gone to cool places like Sonoma's Green Valley, Anderson Valley, the bay-cooled reaches of Carneros and Monterey, and way up north to Mendocino. Here they grow crisp, tangy, acid-laden Chardonnay, Pinot Noir, and Pinot Meunier, like the Champenoise. The wines, however, taste a little bit different, a little fruitier, riper, and sunnier, perhaps. Most of the best examples run $18 to $35; the few that cost more than that can be exceptional.

It's also warm enough in these regions to ripen the grapes enough to make a still wine if desired. Many sparkling wine producers make still versions of Chardonnay, Pinot Noir, and Pinot Meunier in addition to their sparkling wines. It's fascinating to find these bottles and taste each component on its own and then taste their sparkling wines to see if you can pick out the different grapes.

Other American Bubblies

California doesn't have the corner on the sparkling wine market. Oregon and Washington make some good bubblies, too. Most are made from Pinot Noir and Chardonnay grown in cooler pockets of the states. The results strike a happy medium between California's richer bubbly and Champagne's crisp austerity. For Oregon examples, check out Argyle in particular; Chateau Ste. Michelle and Mount Dome make some of Washington's best. Most run $11 to $30.

New Mexico might seem like a strange place to grow grapes for sparkling wine, but in fact it was the similarities between its climate and that of Champagne that convinced the Gruets to plant vines there. Up at an elevation of 4,300 feet, the air is nearly as cool as it is in Champagne, so the Chardonnay and Pinot Noir they grow make Champagne-like wines of lean fruit and sparkling acidity. At $14 to $30, they are good bargains.

Spain's Cava

Cava is the sparkling wine lover's best friend. Spain's version of Champagne, it's affordable ($10 buys excellent examples; $20, extraordinary bottles); it's widely available; and it's delicious, so it's easy to keep some on hand for any time.

The Spanish have their own trinity of grapes from which they make Cava: Macabeo, Xarello, and Viura, though they make it in the same way that the Champenoise make Champagne (called *método tradicional*). The different grapes, however, give Cava a different flavor, one that recalls fresh apples and fresh-risen bread. It's rarely complex, but it's also rarely boring. In Barcelona, it's drunk all the time, as Americans would have a beer. Castillo Perrelada, Freixenet, and Segura Viudas are all great names to know.

Italy

Italy offers a variety of sparkling wines, from sweet little nothings to strident, lean, mineral-laden wines with bubbles like laser beams. The two main savory sparklers are …

- **Prosecco:** this grape makes soft, peach-scented sparkling wines in Italy's Veneto region, particularly in Conegliano di Valdiobbiadene. Most are fruity enough to feel a touch sweet, so they are best served chilled as aperitifs. Great examples like those from Nino Franco, Mionetto, and Zardetto cost only $10 to $20.

- **Franciacorta:** this area of Lombardy specializes in sparkling wines made in the French style, only it exchanges Champagne's Pinot Meunier for the related but distinctly more Italianate Pinot Grigio. The blend and the climate make for cold, crisp wines with high acidity and mineral flavors. Well-regarded brands, like Bellavista and Ca' del Bosco, are priced in line with Champagne.

Italy also makes Moscato d'Asti, a delightfully light, low in alcohol, sparkling dessert wine (see Chapter 19).

Tasmania and More

Tasmania's cool temperatures are excellent for sparkling wine-growing. Check out Taltarni's rose-hued Brut Taché or Jansz, which top out at $20. Most German Sekt is quickly produced, bulk wine for the bubble-loving domestic market, but a few producers, like Lingenfelder, Georg Breuer, and Reichsrat von Buhl, make crisp, lively versions from Riesling. Plan to spend $30 or more. In Austria, Schloss Gobelsburg and Willi Brundlmayer make terrific sparkling Rieslings that run $30 to $40.

Don't Point That Thing at Me!

A flying Champagne cork really can take out an eye. But if you follow these steps, no one will get hurt, and you won't lose any of your precious wine.

1. Chill the wine—about 40 degrees is perfect. If it's warm, the pressure will be higher, and the wine may foam out the top.

2. Hold the bottle with your thumb over the capsule, pointing it away from your body and away from everyone else.

3. Remove the foil covering the cork, removing your thumb briefly.

4. While holding the capsule down, untwist the wires holding the cage tight to the bottle. As soon as it's loose, the cork could fly, so hold on!

5. Slip the cage off the bottle. Or leave it on, if it's not getting in your way.

6. If the cork isn't trying to come out on its own accord, hold it firmly and turn the bottle, pulling it gently away from the cork until the pressure begins to push the cork out. Rather than letting the cork shoot off, let the air out slowly. When the cork comes out, it should make a soft sigh, not a loud pop. A pop sounds celebratory, but the fast exit of air will make the wine foam and use up its bubbles far faster than if it was opened slowly.

You're done! Now pour the wine—but again, do it slowly. If you pour it quickly, it'll foam up and spill over the side of the glass. Prime the glass instead by filling it one quarter full and letting the bubbles subside. Then finish filling the glass.

Off the Vine

Flutes, those tall, thin glasses, aren't absolutely necessary for sparkling wine, but they do have advantages: the long, narrow shape of the glass channels the bubbles so that they rise up in a steady stream and the reduced surface area allows the wines to bubble longer. Whatever you do, don't use the broad, shallow coupes that were once fashionable.

When to Serve Sparkling Wines

Most people think of sparkling wines as special-occasion pours, but as you can see from this chapter, some choices are affordable enough to drink every week. With high acidity and those scrubbing bubbles, sparkling wines also go with just about anything, except perhaps large cuts of red meat. Keep sparkling wine on hand to pour when friends drop by; pull it out to jazz up a bowl of potato chips; or drink it with dinner—you might be surprised how much sparkling wine can take. Whatever you do, don't limit the bubbly for special occasions. It's just wine, and it's meant to be enjoyed.

The Least You Need to Know

- If it's not from Champagne, France, it's not Champagne.

- For the best sparkling wines, look for those that say *méthode traditionelle* or traditional method on the label.

- Demi-sec sparkling wines are actually sweet; look for Brut when you want dry.

- Champagne is the most revered sparkling wine, but Cava, Prosecco, Sekt, and sparkling wines from the United States and Australia are terrific alternatives.

- You *can* take an eye out opening a bottle of sparkling wine, so remove the cork carefully and point it away from people, yourself included.

Chapter **19**

How Sweet It Is

In This Chapter

- What's meant by "dessert" wine
- The versatility of sweet wines
- Dessert wine's myriad styles
- Great examples of great dessert wines

Light as air and sweet like cotton candy or dark and rich as a chocolate-enrobed cherry, there's a sweet wine for every sweet-tooth and some for those who think they don't like sweet wines, too.

Like sparkling wines, dessert wines are often considered special-occasion pours, but like bubbly, you have no reason to wait. You don't even need to save them for dessert. Pour a lightly sweet sparkler before dinner: its combination of bubbles, sugar, and acidity can pique a weary appetite. Try an unctuous, honeyed wine with paté or *foie gras* at the start of a meal, and the sumptuous play of textures and flavors will announce a special occasion like no dry wine could. You can even serve sweet wines with the cheese course and forgo dessert.

With lots of acidity behind all that sugar, sweet wines can surprise, add flair, and bring a little hedonistic edge to any meal. And all you need to achieve that little extra something is a corkscrew.

Okay, and a little money to buy them. As you may have noticed, sweet wines can get pretty expensive, but when you find out the work and risk that go into making them, you'll understand why. And you don't have to spend a lot: some terrific sweet wines are affordable, too. In this chapter, as I walk you through all the most popular possibilities, from light, bubbly white to rich, jammy reds, I hope you'll become a fan of sweet wines, too.

Let It Hang: Waiting for Sugar

How do sweet wines get sweet? Vintners can't just add sugar to make a good sweet wine. They must wait, leaving the grapes on the vines long into the autumn until they are super sweet, and hope that rain, wind, snow, sleet, hail, animals, and rot don't get to the grapes first.

Off the Vine

Many places in Europe outlaw *chaptalization,* the addition of sugar to wines, to protect the quality of the region's sweet wines. That's because sugar can only add sweetness, not flavor. A good dessert-wine grape holds everything it needs in its sweet fruit: sugar as well as acid to balance the sweetness and all the flavors inherent in the grape.

Some of these factors will destroy some of the grapes every time, and the fruits often tend to shrivel a bit, too, as they dehydrate, and so the harvest for sweet wine will always be smaller than the regular harvest that preceded it and dearer for the sticky work that goes into it. Some dessert wines are even picked when the grapes have frozen on the vines—imagine the fun of that freezing cold harvest. So dessert wines are necessarily more expensive than still wines. But no one would bother to make or buy them if they weren't worth the effort.

Holding On to Sugar

If dry wine is made by yeasts that eat up all the sugar in grape juice, what stops the yeasts from eating it all up in sweet wines? There are a couple different answers.

Gluttonous Yeast

In the most straightforward sweet wines, the yeasts simply eat themselves to death before they finish all the sugar, leaving some residual sugar, or RS in winespeak, in the wine.

Noble Rot

Another way to retain sweetness is to use grapes that have been infected with a mold called *botrytis cinerea*. Often referred to as noble rot, botrytis both concentrates the sugars in a grape and adds a haunting, smoky, honeyed note to the wines. It also knocks the yeasts out early, so the wines from botrytised grapes can have lots of sweetness and low alcohol.

Alcohol Overdose

Yet another way to make a sweet wine is to kill the yeasts with an overdose of alcohol. The vintner literally adds alcohol, usually a neutral spirit made from grapes, to the wine, which kills the yeasts before they finish eating the sugar. The resulting wines are called fortified wines, and they usually weigh in at about 16 to 20 percent alcohol—significantly higher than your average table wine at 9 to 13 percent (see Chapter 20).

These different winemaking methods are just one variable in a sweet wine's final flavor. Made all over the world from any number of grapes, sweet wines come in a huge variety of styles. Let's look at some of the best, from light to heavy.

Light, Fizzy Sweet Wines

Bubbly sweet wines are some of the most fun and most versatile dessert wines around. Terrific on hot days when something heavier would feel cloying, they are the perfect answer when you want something sweet but feel you'd burst with a full-on dessert. The sweetness also ups the festivity of the bubbles, making them excellent pours for birthday parties and wedding cake.

Most sweet sparkling wines are also very affordable, especially Italy's; a light, refreshing, peach-scented Moscato d'Asti starts at $9. This means you can have one in the fridge to pull out whenever the urge strikes—no need to wait for a special occasion. But where do you find good sweet sparkling wines?

Italy's Vini *Frizzanti*

When it comes to sweet wines, Italy excels. Not only does the country offer several different styles, but most of them also tend to be ridiculously affordable. Its sweet sparklers are no exception. There are three major types:

- **Moscato d'Asti:** a light, slightly *frizzante* white wine made from Muscat grapes grown in the Asti region of Piedmont, Moscato d'Asti is one of the most refreshing dessert wines on the planet and is far finer than its lesser sibling, the foamy, sweet Asti Spumante. A favorite summer dessert, in fact, is chilled Moscato d'Asti poured over ripe, fresh peaches. Good examples (Chiarlo, Palladino, Vietti) run $9 to $16 for a 375-ml bottle.

- **Brachetto d'Acqui:** the pale red Brachetto grape grown in Piedmont makes for a lightly sweet, strawberry-scented bubbly red that makes a fun companion to chocolate cake or chocolate-dipped fruit. Most run less than $20. Banfi, Coppo, and Marenco are trustworthy.

- **Lambrusco:** frothy purple Lambrusco from Emilia-Romagna has a bad rap, but good Lambrusco *amabile* (slightly sweet) can have deep, soft, plummy flavors lifted by bubbles and refreshing acidity, good antidotes to a heavy winter meal. Most good examples run $15 to $25; try Lini, Medici Ermete, and Vittorio Graziano for starters.

Winespeak

In Italian wines, **frizzante** indicates a wine that is less bubbly than a **spumante**, or sparkling, wine. **Amabile** means lovable in Italian and indicates a sweet wine, sweeter than one marked *abbocato*.

France's Sweet Sparklers

Not surprising for the country that claims the most famous sparkling wine in the world, France offers an array of excellent sweet bubbly. They are typically denoted by the terms *demi-sec* (half-dry), and *moelleux* (marrow, as in soft and rich as warm bone marrow). The most famous examples are these two:

Winespeak

Moelleux means marrow in French and is used to indicate a softly sweet wine. **Pétillant** denotes a lightly sparkling wine.

- **Demi-sec Champagne:** while some extra dry Champagne has a sweet edge, demi-sec Champagne is fully in the sweet realm. Depending on quality, it can be a sweet, silly sparkler that foams like shaving cream or a delicate, softly sweet white with teensy, tickling bubbles. The price usually indicates the type of demi-sec in the bottle; if it's $25 or less, expect birthday party bubbly.

♦ **Moelleux Loire whites:** the term *moelleux* can be used anywhere, but some of the best moelleux wines are from the Loire, where Chenin Blanc's honeyed flavors and high acidity combine for particularly sumptuous dessert wines. Some are sparkling, labeled *pétillant*. Examples start at $14; some exalted bottles run up to $60.

Sweet, Still Wines

The most straightforward sweet wines are called simply late-harvest, which is exactly what they are: made from grapes that were harvested far into the fall when their sugar levels rose to sweet heights.

Any grape can be harvested late, and the later it's harvested, the more concentrated the wine it will make, so there's a wide range of styles and prices from which to choose. Some of the best late-harvest wines come from Riesling and Gewürztraminer. Examples are made all over the world, but some of the best come from Germany, marked *Spätlese* (late harvest in German). Not all Spätlese tastes sweet, though, so ask before buying.

Quick Sips

Some of the best late-harvested wines come from grapes with naturally high acidity, like Riesling and Chenin Blanc, though Gewürztraminer and Viognier also make some lovely lush examples.

Alsace vintners also excel at late-harvested wines from Riesling and Gewürztraminer as well as Pinot Gris and Muscat. They label their late-harvest wines Vendange Tardive or VT. These are always sweet and often richer than their German counterparts.

Chenin Blanc also has plenty of acidity, and its naturally honeyed flavors and rich, almost unctuous texture make for wines that feel sumptuous. Examples are made from California to South Africa, but, as with the dry versions, they reach their apex in France's Loire, particularly in the appellations Coteaux du Layon, Montlouis, Quarts du Chaume, and Vouvray.

Viognier is often low in acidity, but if treated carefully, it gives fat, soft wines heady with floral, peachy flavor. The greatest sweet Viognier comes from Condrieu in France's Rhône Valley, but you can find excellent late-harvest examples from California and Australia and often at lower prices than the $60 or so most sweet Condrieu asks.

Late-harvest wines can also come from red grapes, some of the darkest, richest, and most intense of which come from California's Zinfandel. These dark, jammy, berried reds are excellent after dinner with sharp cheddar or tangy blue cheese and are one of the few sweet wines that can stand up to chocolate desserts.

Shriveled Grapes

Some vintners take their late-harvested wines a step further and dry the grapes before pressing them. That way, the little bit of juice that comes out is super-concentrated. It also tends to taste more like dried fruit and can pick up flavors that recall spice or gingerbread. The most common examples are from Italy, such as:

- **Vinsanto:** a specialty of Tuscany, these spicy, nutty, golden wines are just the thing for biscotti-dunking.

- **Moscato di Pantelleria:** grown on the warm island of Pantelleria off the coast of Sicily, super-ripe Muscat grapes are dried for a month and pressed to eke out the teeny bit of juice left. The result is like a liquid version of golden raisins wrapped in light, spiced caramel. Pellegrino is the best-known in the United States.

> **Off the Vine**
>
> The island of Santorini in Greece also claims a wine called *vinsanto*, also made from dried grapes. In fact, some claim the wine originated here and the name is a corruption of *Vin Santorini*.

- **Recioto:** this indicates a wine made from dried grapes; it's a specialty of the Veneto in northern Italy. The most popular example is the sweet red Recioto della Valpolicella, although you can sometimes locate tawny, nut- and hay-scented white Recioto made from the same grape responsible for Soave (see Chapter 16).

Sweet dried grapes are also responsible for the nutty, spicy dessert wines of Samos, a Greek isle. France calls its dried grape wines *vin de paille*, *paille* meaning straw, a reference to the mats on which the grapes are dried. Examples are rare but can be found in the northern Rhône as well as in the Jura, a region far to France's eastern border with Switzerland.

Frozen Grapes

If you visit Germany's wine regions in late November and December, you can feel the tension in the air. Grapes golden with ripeness are still hanging on the vines as they wither in the waning sun and cool air; winemakers sit, praying it won't rain, the grapes won't rot, and too many birds won't pirate the harvest before the temperature drops below freezing. As soon as it does—and it's usually midnight or so—it's all hands on deck to pick the grapes and get them to the winery before they defrost.

What's the idea behind such madness? Sugar syrup can't freeze at 32°F, but water does, so when frozen grapes are pressed, all that comes out is pure, concentrated sugar syrup and the water is left behind as ice. The resulting *Eiswein* (icewine), as it's called in German, is intensely sweet and full of the pure flavor of super-ripe grapes frozen in time.

As you might imagine, Eiswein is delicious stuff, and it's mighty expensive, too—upward of $75 or even $200, for a small bottle—since the work is excruciating and the yield small. Yet other places in the world have followed Germany's cue, most notably Washington State and Ontario, Canada, two wine regions where the temperature actually dips below freezing with some regularity.

Off the Vine

While grapes have to freeze naturally on the vine in order to legally take the name ice wine, nothing stops vintners from making wines from grapes they've stored in a freezer. While the grapes don't have the advantage of picking up extra flavors from hanging on the vines so long, wines like Pacific Rim's *Vin de Glaciére* (wine of the freezer box) demonstrate that this method can make hedonistically sweet wines at a fraction of the cost of the traditional method.

Noble Rot—No Kidding

You've already learned the bizarre fact that some of the greatest dessert wines on the planet are made from rotting grapes. These are special rotting grapes, though, infected with *botrytis cinerea*, a.k.a. noble rot. The fungus dehydrates the grapes, concentrating the juice inside. The resulting thick, golden wine takes on an intense sweetness made complex with a smoky, honey-like flavor.

Sauternes is the most famous example, with Alsace's Selection de Grains Nobles and Germany's sweet Beerenauslese and Trockenbeerenauslese wines right behind, but the rot is courted all over the world. In no place is botrytis a sure thing; in fact, winemakers have developed painstaking methods to cultivate it, such as inoculating the grape bunches and wrapping them in plastic. But there are places botrytis strikes more often than others. Here's where to look if you want to taste the magic for yourself.

But before you go, take your checkbook, as these wines are expensive. Courting botrytis is risky business, as all sorts of less pleasurable molds can attack, too, ruining grapes or whole harvests.

Sauternes

Sauternes is one of the few places in the world that concentrates nearly 100 percent on sweet wines. It's what the region seems designed to do. There, in the warmer south of Bordeaux where the Garonne and a small tributary, the Ciron, meet up, Sauvignon Blanc and Semillon grow lush under blankets of fog that create a terrific environment for botrytis.

> **Off the Vine**
>
> If you like Sauternes but can't afford it, look for wines from Barsac, Loupiac, or Cadillac. Barsac is technically part of Sauternes; the other two villages are nearby.

The mold attacks slowly, and the best wines are picked a grape at a time—a task that can take weeks and hundreds of passes through the same rows of vines. That's why a bottle of a recent vintage of Château d'Yquem, the most revered of them all, goes for around $200.

For that price, you get a wine that's as sweet as honey, only brighter, fresher, livelier, and more complex all at once. Preserved by high sugar and high acidity, great Sauternes can live many decades, picking up pleasant notes of caramel and spice with time.

Alsace's Selected Grapes

Alsace is famous for the wines it makes from botrytised grapes, labeled SGN, or *Sélection de Grains Nobles.* The most common SGNs are spicy, heady examples made from Gewurztraminer or unctuously rich ones from Pinot Gris, though the few bright, peachy Riesling and floral Muscat beauties are worth searching out.

Germany's Nobly Rotted Treasures

In Germany, vintners classify their wines according to how sweet the grapes were when they were picked. Most wines are dry QbA or Kabinett wines (see Chapter 6); Spätlese wines can be dry to off-dry. To get to the rarer, richer, and botrytised stuff, look for wines marked Auslese (*ows*-lays-zuh), Beerenauslese (BA, or beer-en-*ows*-lays-zuh), and Trockenbeeren-auslese (TBA, or *troack*-ken-*beer*-en-*ows*-lays-zuh).

Auslese wines sometimes ride the line between dry and sweet, making wines that can play off rich foods, like duck or cheese, as well as they can accompany dessert. Many have little hint of botrytis. BAs and TBAs, on the other hand, are definitively sweet, botrytised, rare, and expensive; most start at $25 for a 375-ml bottle and climb well over $100.

Quick Sips

Austria uses a system similar to Germany's for classifying its sweet wines, although in Austria's warmer climate, its BAs and TBAs tend to taste richer and heavier.

Riesling's delicate flavors and naturally high acidity make it an excellent vehicle for sweetness, so it provides the bulk of Germany's sweet wines, but growers may use Scheurebe, Gewürztraminer, or any number of other grapes, too.

Sweet Legacies of the Austro-Hungarian Empire

In addition to coffeehouse culture and intricate, delicate pastries, the Austro-Hungarian Empire also gives us two sweet, botrytised wines: Ausbruch (*auws*-brook) from Austria and Tokaji (toe-*kai*) from Hungary. Once famed and now nearly forgotten, these wines can be fabulous bargains: at $30 to $80, they aren't cheap, but many will age as long as or longer than Sauternes, taking on equally fascinating flavors of honey, caramel, spice, and truffles.

The wines are made by an unusual method whereby botrytised grapes are combined with a base wine made with grapes unaffected by botrytis and left to macerate. The sweetness of the wine depends on the ratio of botrytised grapes to base wine. Tokaji wines list the sweetness on the label in terms of puttonyos, (somewhere between 3—fairly common and medium sweet—and 6—rare and thickly sweet). Essencia, the highest and rarest form of Tokaji, is made purely from the juice that oozes out of botrytised grapes due to the weight of the grapes alone. It's so high in sugar that it takes years to ferment. Even with such prodigious sweetness, the high acidity of the local grapes used (typically Furmint) keeps these wines lively rather than cloying.

All these sweet wines are only a fraction of what's out there; every winemaking country has a version or several of its own. Explore the dessert wine section of your local wine store to find other sweet elixirs. If you happen upon a bottle that's too sweet or cloying, use it to poach fruit, like peaches, apricots, or pears. Just keep trying: you have lots to explore.

The Least You Need to Know

◆ Dessert wines don't need to be reserved for dessert but can be good with rich foods like paté and *foie gras* at the beginning of a meal, too.

◆ Most sweet wines, especially ice wines and botrytised wines, are expensive due to the labor and risk involved.

◆ The typical 375-ml bottle most dessert wines come in might not look like much for the price, but a little dessert wine goes a long way.

◆ For sweet, sparkling white wines, look to Italy for Moscato d'Asti or France for Demi-Sec Champagne or Vouvray marked *moelleux* and *petillant*.

◆ Sweet red wines like sparkling Brachetto d'Acqui or late-harvest California Zinfandel are some of the few wines in the world that can match well with chocolate desserts.

◆ To find wines made from botrytised grapes, look for BA and TBA in Germany, Ausbruch in Austria, SGN in Alsace, and Tokaji from Hungary with a statement of puttonyos on the label.

Chapter 20

Port and Other Fortified Wines

In This Chapter

- ◆ Portugal's famous Port wines and its overlooked relative, Setúbal
- ◆ The delights of Sherry and Madeira, from dry to sweet
- ◆ The range of France's fortified *vin doux naturel*
- ◆ Australia's delicious, disappearing liqueur Muscats

The term *fortified wines* doesn't even begin to describe the pleasure hidden in these bottles, and I'm not talking about alcohol. Fortified wines do have more alcohol in them than most other wines, but that's not their point. The additional alcohol stops fermentation in its tracks, leaving unfermented sugar in the wine—and that sweetness magnifies flavor. The result can be a wine with flavors as intensely sweet and fresh as just-cooked jam or as sweetly complex as a dried fruit tart in a nut crust drizzled with cinnamon, caramel, and chocolate. Dry fortified wines also make fine aperitifs.

Most fortified wines are native to warm places that have been making wine for ages, where alcohol was originally added as a preservative. Many areas have set up unique appellations to showcase them, such as Porto, Maury, and Sherry. Some fortified wines can be made in a vast array of wine styles—some nearly dry, others extremely sweet. So don't stop reading yet; this is the last frontier of wine styles to explore in this book, and it's a broad, immensely enjoyable one.

Portugal's Port

Few wines are as warming as a glass of thick purple Port, its dense, smooth flavors a comforting blanket for the tongue. Made from grapes grown along the hot, precipitously steep slopes of the Douro Valley in Portugal, Port is like bottled sun: sweet, warm, and condensed into an impenetrably purple juice.

Sour Grapes

Only Port wines from the Douro in Portugal are true Port wines; any others are Port-*style* wines. While Port-style wines are often very good, know that they are not the real thing.

That's probably why the British took such a liking to it. You see, Port could very well have remained a local wine if it hadn't been for the British, who discovered it in the 1600s and began shipping it home from Oporto, the port city at the mouth of the Douro. The strong wine became such a hit that British companies set up shipping houses in Portugal and began blending Port themselves. Today, many of these houses are still British-owned, as is obvious from names like Cockburn (pronounced *co*-burn, by the way), Graham, Sandeman, and Taylor.

Port Styles

There are many styles of Port, from fresh and grapey to tawny as a walnut and just as nutty. The outcome depends partly on the mix of grapes (more than 40 are permitted), the district within the Douro (there are three, each with its own personality), and, most importantly, the intended style: White, Ruby, or Tawny.

White Port

White Port is a sweet wine made from white grapes. It's rarely found outside of Portugal, but if you do find it, drink it as the locals do: chilled with a splash of soda and lemon twist to cut its sweet white grape flavors. It typically runs $10 to $20.

Ruby Port

Ruby Ports are just what they sound like: vibrantly ruby-hued in color and flavor. They come in five different styles, which I've listed in ascending order of depth and complexity:

- Ruby
- Premium Ruby/Vintage Character
- Late-Bottled Vintage (LBV)
- Single Quinta
- Vintage

Quick Sips

Roy Hersch, a Port wine expert, downloads his extensive knowledge of the region and its wines at the aptly named www.fortheloveofport.com website. And www.ivdp.pt is the home of the *Instituto dos Vinhos do Douro e Porto*, with extensive information on all wines from Portugal's Douro.

Straight Ruby Port is the simplest, most affordable Port, made by blending a range of one- to three-year-old wines to achieve a vibrantly fresh, plummy, easy-drinking sweet red. Most run $10 to $20.

Premium Ruby Ports, sometimes called Vintage Character, are blended from a number of vintages to create a sort of Super Ruby, with deeper, more nuanced and concentrated flavors. They typically cost only a few dollars more than Rubys. Fonseca Bin 27, Graham's Six Grapes, and Sandeman's Founders Reserve are examples of this style.

Late-Bottled Vintage Ports, or LBVs in Port parlance, are Port wines from a single vintage that are left in casks for four to six years to mellow. While they aren't as powerful or complex as a Vintage Port, they offer the advantage of similar flavors without a decade-long wait—and typically, far lower prices; most don't go much above $30.

Single-Quinta Ports are Ports made from the grapes of a specific *quinta*, or farm, in this case used to denote a vineyard. Often, these Ports are made in years that aren't great enough to declare a vintage but are very good. More recently, single-quinta Ports have become more popular as interest in single-vineyard wines has increased. Many are as good as Vintage Ports, yet often cost less.

Winespeak

Quinta means "farm" in Portuguese and is often used to mean winery, estate, or vineyard, as well.

Vintage Ports are made from a single year's harvest, aged two years in wood, and then bottled to capture the wine's youthful, vivacious fruit flavors. Vintage Port wines are made only in exceptional years, and they are as concentrated, structured, and powerful as Port comes. They need to be aged for years in bottle to mellow out and show their best. Prices start at about $40 and can rise to $200; old Vintage Ports can demand considerably more, depending on age and vintage.

Quick Sips

Many Vintage Ports come with their corks sealed under a layer of hardened wax. How do you get it off? Wrap the neck of the bottle in a towel and, holding the towel shut, lightly but firmly bang on the wax with the back end of a corkscrew. It will shatter (eventually), and you can remove the shards in the towel.

Tawny Port

Tawny Ports are aged in wooden casks for at least six years before bottling so that they become tawny in color and taste. The longer the wine stays in a cask, the less fruity and more nutty it becomes. Straight tawnies are the simplest and most affordable examples, with sweet, caramel flavors. Better-quality tawnies state an age on the label, such as 10-year-old, which indicates the average age of the wines inside. The oldest age statement is 40; these rare, toffee-hued wines can ask over $100, as compared to 10-year-olds at $20 to $40.

Colheita Port

Colheita Port combines aspects of Vintage and Tawny Ports. They are Vintage Ports that have been aged in wooden casks for at least seven years, making them ready to drink upon purchase but also able to age for many more years. They are rare but worth looking up; Niepoort is the leader in this style.

Which Port When?

With all these different styles, how do you decide what to buy? Well, how much time do you have? If you can't wait a decade, leave the Vintage Port on the shelf. Then consider use. Do you want a fruity, sweet, fresh-tasting Port? Buy a Ruby style. Something less sweet, perhaps to match nutty or caramel-rich desserts? Then a Tawny style, or an old Colheita or Vintage Port, will do well.

Zinfandel "Port" and Aussie "Tawny"

California's Zinfandel grape can make a darn good approximation of a Ruby Port when it's left to get very ripe and the resulting wine is fortified. Examples abound and typically sell for less than $25 a 375-ml bottle. Peachy Canyon, Quady, and Renwood are three to look for.

Australia's Tawny Port can also be a great deal, with flavors that are similar if sweeter than the Portuguese original and prices that run $8 to $15 for basic bottlings. R. L. Buller, Hardy's, Seppelts, and Yalumba make terrific examples.

Setúbal, Portugal's Other Fortified Wine

Imagine a wine that tastes a little like a roasted apricot stuffed with butter brickle and wrapped in caramel. That's *Setúbul* (pronounced, in Portuguese fashion, with as closed a mouth as possible, like *schtoo*-bul), a fortified wine made south of Lisbon on a peninsula that juts out into the Atlantic. Here, superripe, super-sweet Moscatel grapes (as Muscat is called here) are made into a wine that's mellowed in wooden casks for 5 to 25 years or more. The longer the wine has aged (an age is stated on the label), the darker, nuttier, more complex, and less fruity it gets. José Maria da Fonseca sets the standard.

Sherry

Many people think Sherry is some sickly sweet wine sipped by grandmas. Good Sherry, however, can be one of the most complex, intriguing wines you'll ever taste.

Sherry can be bone-dry or caramel sweet, but it all comes from the same general place: the region surrounding the town of Jerez de la Frontera on the southwest coast of Spain. Sherry is an English corruption of Jerez.

Flor and Soleras, Sherry's Special Touches

What makes Sherry so unusual is not just the grapes—mostly the local Palomino—but also the method with which it's made. Once the grapes are superripe, which isn't so hard given that this is the hottest area in Spain, they are left in the sun to dry and concentrate their sugars.

When these near-raisins are pressed, the juice is traditionally put into wood casks to ferment, leaving some air between the wine and the top of the cask so that it will *oxidize*. Some Sherries will also develop a film of yeast, called *flor* (flower); the flor protects the wine from some amount of oxygen and contributes flavor to the wine. Wines that develop flor make Fino Sherries.

Winespeak

When oxygen comes into contact with something that reacts with it, the substance will **oxidize**. In wine, slow, controlled oxidation (as happens in oak barrels) can help mellow the wine and add extra flavors, such as nuts and caramel. Excess oxidation, however, can make for an oxidized wine (one that's lost its freshness and fruit flavors) or even vinegar.

After fermentation, the wine is put into a *solera*, a pyramid of casks with the oldest wine at the bottom. As wine is taken out of the bottom casks to be bottled, the casks are replenished with younger wine from the casks above, which are then topped off by the casks above them and so on up the pyramid.

The combination of different ages of wine and exposure to oxygen makes for wines with lots of complex, nutty, caramel-like flavors.

In the end, seven styles of Sherry are possible. From driest to sweetest, they are …

- **Fino:** dry, pale, lightly fortified wines with a salty, pungent tang from the flor.

- **Manzanilla:** Fino Sherries made closer to the sea in Sanlúcar de Barrameda, where the flor grows heavier and the wines get tangier and saltier.

- **Amontillado:** an old Sherry in which the flor has died, letting it turn darker in color and flavor. True Amontillados are dry, though some commercial versions are slightly sweetened.

Quick Sips

Amontillado means of the style of Montilla, a region not far to the east of Jerez that makes it own Sherry-like wines. More delicate, less known, and, therefore, often less expensive, it's worth looking for wines labeled Montilla-Moriles, the official name of the wine region.

- **Palo Cortado:** a rare Sherry that develops flor late in its life, turning out dry but dark with toasty, nutty flavors.

◆ **Oloroso:** Olorosos never develop flor, so they remain completely unprotected from oxygen, which turns them more caramel-hued in color and in flavor. Dry versions are marked *seco*; others tend toward light sweetness balanced with tangy, nutty acidity.

◆ **Cream Sherry:** Oloroso Sherry that's been sweetened.

◆ **PX:** Pedro Ximénez is the name of the grape as well as the outrageously sweet wine it makes, though it's typically referred to as simply PX. These wines are often aged for decades, even more than 100 years, before they are released, making for molasses-dark wines that are so thick they are best applied to the tongue with an eyedropper.

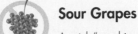 **Sour Grapes**

Avoid "cooking sherry" at all costs (even for cooking); made from cheap wine with salt added, it has nothing to do with real Sherry from Jerez.

You can get terrific Fino Sherries for less than $20 (Hidalgo La Gitana, for example); some rare or old bottles cost triple that. Alvear, Domecq, and Lustau are also good names to look for.

When to Pour Which Sherry

As you can see, most Sherry is dry—bone-dry, actually. These Sherries are terrific sipped cold with salty snacks like olives, cured ham, hard cheese, and fried fish. For dessert, try a sweet Oloroso with nut tarts or a thick drizzle of PX over vanilla ice cream.

Madeira

Madeira is another overlooked, oxidized wine from a very hot place. The place—also called Madeira—is a Portuguese island closer to Morocco than Portugal that's actually a defunct volcano; the wines are made by leaving the casks in the sun (or putting them in an oven) to roast, the object being to imitate the taste of a wine that has roasted in the hold of a ship that's slowly crossed the equator.

This all may sound bizarre, but the result is delicious. Made from grapes with tenacious acidity yet prodigious ripeness, Madeiras take on rich flavors of roasted fruit, burnt oranges, espresso coffee, and sugar-roasted nuts.

Most Madeira is blended from many different grapes from different vintages and will simply list an average age on the label, such as 5 Year Old. There are four varietal Madeiras as well, each sweeter than the last:

- Sercial

- Verdelho

- Bual

- Malmsey

All these wines can age for many decades, whereupon they might lose color but they will gain in spice and earthy, mushroomy flavor, all the while retaining acidity that makes them feel vibrantly young and energized.

Notice Rainwater Madeira isn't on this list: Rainwater is typically cheap Madeira best suited for cooking. Expect to pay at least $15 for a decent Madeira; very old Madeira can cost significantly more.

Turtle Soup to Trifle

Madeira is often ignored—who on Earth knows what to do with it? Use dry Madeiras like dry Sherries, as appetite inducers with salty snacks. Try them also with first courses, and slip a tablespoon into the mushroom or seafood soup.

Bual and Malmsey Madeira make excellent, even refreshing, dessert wines on their own or with desserts that would be too rich for most other wines, like pecan pie.

While good Madeira can be expensive, one of its great advantages is that it's already been fortified with extra alcohol and exposed to so much heat and oxygen that it's hard to hurt it. Keep the bottle corked and refrigerated and it will last for months.

Vin Doux Naturel

Vin Doux Naturel isn't exactly natural; it's a catchall name for fortified French wines. VDNs, as they're called in wine shorthand, are made all over the country, but particularly in the warm south, in appellations such as …

- Muscat de Beaumes de Venise
- Muscat de Frontignan
- Rivesaltes
- Rasteau
- Banyuls
- Maury

Basically, we can break these wines into two categories: those made with Muscat (the first three) and those made with Grenache (the rest).

Most of these wines are also made in *rancio* versions, meaning that they have been purposely left out to get hot or exposed to air. This gives the wines prematurely aged, oxidized flavors of roasted fruit and toasted nuts—not nearly as unpleasant as *rancio* sounds.

Winespeak _____

Rancio on a wine label indicates the wine has purposely been exposed to air, which causes it to give up some of its fresh color and flavor in exchange for a softer, warmer, nuttier taste. Some wine tasters will also describe a wine as having *rancio* notes, meaning that it's a little oxidized in a pleasant way.

Muscat VDNs

Muscat can make some of the most delicate VDNs as well as some of the heartiest. Since the grape grows all over the country, it depends on the particular region to define the style.

Muscat de Beaumes de Venise is one of the lightest fortified Muscat wines, a delicate, honeyed, orange-scented wine from the southern Rhône. *Muscat de St-Jean-de-Minervois* is its biggest competitor in the pale, delicate fortified Muscat field.

Richer fortified Muscats come from Frontignan on the Languedoc coast, so ripe they can be bright orange or even brown. *Muscat de Rivesaltes* is even richer, grown farther south on a hot, sun-soaked crescent of the Roussillon coast. You can pick up a 375-ml bottle of any of these for $15 to $30. Cazes, Château de Jau, and Ey are trusted names.

Grenache Sweets

Grenache, that Spanish grape that makes the heady red wines of Priorat in Catalonia and then crosses the Pyrenees to France to make a huge range of wines, finds one of its best interpretations in the fortified wines of southern France.

Let Grenache get ripe in a nice warm area, such as Banyuls in the very southern tip of Roussillon, and it tastes like cherries on steroids, fat and impossibly sweet. Stop it from fermenting to dryness with some extra alcohol, and let it rest in oak barrels for a year or so, and you'll have a fabulously sweet, plump wine with a kick of alcohol that keeps it from feeling too thick. Put it in the cellar for a decade or two, and it will begin to taste more like dried cherries and nuts enrobed in caramel—not a bad thing, either. Clos de Paulilles and Mas Blanc make Banyuls in all of these styles.

Wines from Maury, a small area farther inland from Banyuls, are also made from Grenache, but they are even darker and sweeter—excellent with chocolate desserts. Mas Amiel sets the standard.

Farther east, in the Southern Rhône, the village of Rasteau makes similar fortified Grenache wines in both fresh, grapey styles and nuttier, more caramel-like examples labeled *rancio*. La Soumade and Trapadis make great versions.

All these Grenache wines tend to cost a little more than Muscat wines, from $20 to $50 per 750-ml bottle, but the flavors are so intense they go a long way.

Australia's Liqueur Muscat

Australia, like California, makes a wide range of dessert wines, from delicate, sweet Rieslings to dense, Port-style Shiraz. One style shines more than any other, though: liqueur Muscats and Muscadelles or tokays, as they call them, or, more commonly, stickies.

Off the Vine

In Australia, Tokay is commonly used as a synonym for Muscadelle, a grape unrelated to Muscat but used in small amounts in the sweet wines of Sauternes, France. Due to regulations protecting the wines of Tokaj in Hungary, the Australians have recently stopped using it, though you'll still see it on wines bottled prior to 2008.

If you've ever tasted sticky toffee pudding, that English dessert of sweet, soft, gingery cake that feels like it's been baked in buttery brown sugar syrup, you have an idea of what these sweet brown wines taste like—only good stickies have acidity and alcohol to cut any cloying sweetness and complexity that can hold your attention all evening long.

Once broadly loved, now revered by just a small, devoted fan club, liqueur Muscats and Muscadelles are a little tricky to find, but they are well worth the hunt, selling for as low as $15 per 375-ml bottle. Some sought-after examples, such as very old wines from Chambers Rosewood Vineyards in Rutherglen, cost as much as $300.

The Least You Need to Know

♦ Fortified wines, which get their name from an addition of alcohol, are typically 16 to 20 percent alcohol.

♦ Fortified wines include Portugal's Madeira, Port, and Setúbal, Spain's Sherry, France's Vin Doux Naturel, Australia's liqueur Muscats, and Port-style wines from around the world.

♦ Port comes only from Portugal; mimics are Port-style wines.

♦ Cooking Sherry has little to do with Sherry from Jerez and won't make a tasty substitute.

♦ Not all fortified wines are sweet; Madeira and Sherry come in high-acid, bone-dry styles perfect for sipping with salty snacks, cheese, and nuts.

Part 5

Shopping Time

If you've read this far, you have more than 50 grapes under your belt, and you're familiar with a huge range of wines that they can produce. That's a lot of wine, and there's more we haven't even touched on.

But enough: there's only so much you can learn from reading. It's time to go shopping. The more you taste, and the more different wines you taste, the more you'll learn. In this part, you find out why a bottle of wine costs what it does, how to savvily buy it, and why you might want to start a little wine stash for yourself.

Chapter 21

Why Wine Costs What It Does

In This Chapter

- Starting a winery
- The cost of making a wine
- Taxes and markups
- The power of perceived value
- Wine costs in restaurants

Why do some bottles of wine cost $5 and others cost $50? How much is too much, and is there such a thing as too little? How do you know you're not getting ripped off?

I have no hard-and-fast answers to any of these questions, but finding out what's behind the price does at least make it obvious that most vintners aren't getting rich from the sales. Making wine is hard work, and many costs are tacked on in the process. Chew on some of this information the next time you're at the store.

The Bare Necessities

Let's say you want to be a winemaker. So what do you need to make wine? Well, first you need …

Land

Just as you can't grow good peaches in the tropics, you can't grow good wine grapes just anywhere. Generally, you need a large patch of fertile-but-not-too-fertile soil that's well drained and close to a source of water. Preferably, you'd like a parcel on a slope that faces south (at least if you're in the Northern Hemisphere), so that the vineyard gets sun all day long. And you'd probably like to have it in a proven wine-growing area.

If you dream of making wine in California's Napa Valley, you better have a fat bank account, as unplanted land—which is a little tough to find these days given the competition between wineries and land preservation laws—runs up to $160,000 per acre.

Quick Sips

The cost of wine partly depends on where the vines are grown and what sort of vines they are. Some places and some varieties pull in far higher prices than others.

You could save a little money by going to Chianti; prime land in the Chianti Classico region is going for just $50,000 an acre. And either place, you could save half or more by buying land in lesser areas. Of course, you might end up with lesser wine. Or you'll end up with excellent wine that doesn't command the same prices that wines from the known regions do.

So you buy your land. Now you need to plant it.

Plants

What are you going to plant? In Napa Valley, probably Cabernet Sauvignon. For good clones, you'll pay $2.50 to $3 per plant. At 1,000 plants per acre (relatively wide spacing by modern standards), that's $2,000 to $3,000 for a single acre. And you have to get them into the ground. So you must clear some trees or brush, till the land, level it, put in end-posts, stakes and trellises, potentially dig a well (good luck), run an irrigation system, erect a fence to keep out the deer and wild pigs, install access roads, dig little holes and plant the seedlings in them, and then wrap the fragile plants in some sort of protective barrier (usually plastic tubing) to keep animals from nibbling at them. Estimate about $25,000 per acre in labor alone to get all this done and another $10,000 an acre in materials.

Now that you've spent about $195,000 on one acre of vineyard, guess what? You get to sit and wait as it'll be a few years before those plants produce grapes worth making wine out of, and a few more years again before the grapes are really good. All along, you'll have to prune the vines, pound stakes into the ground, run trellising, and replant the vines that die, as some will, regardless of how well you care for them.

Perhaps you're impatient and can't afford to sit on your investment for so long. So you could just buy some grapes and make wine from them while you wait. Good idea. But first you need someplace to make the wine.

Winery

Let's assume you're not going to engage Frank Gehry to design your winery; that cost Vincor in Ontario, Canada, several million dollars. No, let's settle on a more modest goal: a shed someplace near the vineyard, so that you don't have to haul your grapes long distances in trucks where they might bake and begin to fester along the way.

But in that little shed, you need equipment.

Equipment

The first thing you need is a crusher-destemmer (for a small used one, figure about $9,000). Then you need something to ferment the wine in (let's say a bare-bones 1,500 gallon stainless-steel fermenter and the stand it sits on, for $4,000 or so) and some yeast ($30 per pound) with which to make it ferment. (You could hope for ambient yeasts to work their magic, and save that cash.) And you'll also need to cool your fermentation, as fermentation involves heat, so you'll have to scrounge some sort of used refrigeration system, which will set you back a few thousand.

After the wine has finished fermenting, you'll have to get it out of that tank (one hose and pump, plus hose adaptors, clamps, and gaskets, about $16,000) and into some barrels.

Barrels = Big Money

Barrels are big money, but they aren't strictly necessary, of course. If you want a simple, fruity, drink-now wine, you can skip the barrels and stick with stainless steel, which should last 20 years or more with good maintenance. But if you're aiming for a fine Cabernet Sauvignon, you'll likely want oak barrels for the fine smoothness they lend a wine, the hints of flavor that add complexity, and the bit of wood tannins they can add to the wine's structure.

The kind of oak you choose will greatly affect the cost. For an average-size barrel (60 gallons), the highly sought-after French barrels run about $900. Eastern European barrels (mostly Hungarian) run about $500. American oak can cost as little as $400, but better-quality barrels can cost as much as the French.

If you make just one tank of wine, you'll need 25 barrels. That's a minimum of $10,000 on barrels. And unlike stainless-steel tanks, barrels wear out. Every year you'll have to buy some new ones to take the place of the old if you want your wines to taste similar year to year.

So you can already see how the costs of making a fine wine stack up. You want the best vineyards, the best plants, the best machinery, and the best barrels, and you'll pay much more than you would were you to grow some Concord grapes, ferment them in stainless steel, and bottle without them ever seeing the inside of an oak barrel.

But we've only begun. Once you have the basic equipment (and remember that we haven't included things like rakes and shovels to rake out the tanks, trucks to transport grapes, equipment, people, and such), you need grapes.

Getting Good Grapes

While you're waiting for your vineyards to come on line, as they say in the wine world, and produce good wine grapes, you can buy grapes from someone else. If you want Cabernet Sauvignon grapes of the quality you hope to grow, you're going to pay through the nose. In 2006, the average price for a ton of Napa Valley grapes was $3,042.71. One ton of grapes makes about 750 bottles of wine, so you'll need a few tons at least. Sonoma grapes were comparatively affordable, at only $1,990.74, but if you're really on a budget, you'll have to settle for some Mission grown on the hot, dusty flats around Modesto for about $181 a ton.

So already, the price of the wine is being determined, and we haven't even started paying the staff yet.

Labor

Running a winery isn't a one-man job. You might be able to make it a part-time job, though talk to anybody who's done that and he'll tell you it's nuts. Why? Well, let's start in the vineyard. After you get all those vines planted, you need to tend them, pruning them and training them to trellis. Most of the year it's pretty quiet, so you can do that on your own if you're fast with pruning shears or a sickle and good at pulling trellises. Figure in some time and money for laying compost to enrich the soils and office work for recordkeeping.

Come harvest time, though, speed is everything. You must get those grapes into the winery when they're at their peak—not a little early, like peaches being shipped to the store; not a little late or they'll lack vibrancy and freshness. Just right. If it's threatening to rain (as it tends to come autumn), you'll have extra pressure to get the grapes in for fear that the rain will dilute their precious, long-awaited juices.

So you assemble a team and send them into the vineyards. (You picked quality land, remember, on the side of a hill too steep for machines, and you want the higher quality that selective picking can give, so you go with humans instead of machines.) If you're really into it, you'll hire an experienced, trained staff, who will earn higher prices for their expertise. They'll work longer hours, too, as they'll need to make many passes through the vineyards over many days to pick only what's ripe. The California rule of thumb says to expect to pay a minimum of $2,500 per acre for manpower; add an extra $1,000 for very skilled labor.

Those pickers will need plastic crates to put the grapes in ($2 each), and you'll need a truck to get the grapes to the winery where another team will be waiting. If you're really quality conscious, you'll have a sorting table ($22,000 for a rolling conveyor-belt type) so that a team can comb through the grapes and remove any bad berries, leaves, bugs, and other unwanted items.

You'll need people to dump the grapes into the crusher-destemmer, pump the juice into tanks, and keep everything clean, as cleanliness really is next to godliness in the winery. Typically, something will go wrong during harvest, so be prepared for someone to drive a forklift into one of your $4,000 tanks, for a hose to spring a leak and spray your $3,042.71/ton juice around the room, or for some other completely unforeseeable, expensive disaster. It comes with the territory.

Quick Sips

The price of a wine also depends on how much time and work is put into it—the more skilled the workers, the higher the price; the more involved the winemaking process, such as time spent in barrels, the higher the price yet again. Normally, these factors intersect with higher quality, too.

If you're nice, and you want your workers working at top function, you'll feed them, too. And what's the cost of feeding 12 overworked, underslept manual laborers? Depends on how flush you're feeling, but tuna sandwiches won't do.

Once all the wines are in tanks, they'll need to be inoculated and tended regularly until it's time to put them into barrels.

Aging, or Taking Up Space

If the juice is really good, deep, concentrated stuff, then it'll benefit from some extended time in barrels. If you have room to keep the barrels (preferably some cool, humid, out-of-the-way space), great. It'll cost you only what you don't make while the wines age. If you don't have the space, you can buy some for only $18 to $25 per barrel per month. Sounds like a bargain, hmm? With two years in barrel, you've just added up to $600 to the cost of your Cabernet Sauvignon.

Bottling

At some point, the wine will have to be put into bottles. Chances are you haven't sprung for the fancy $400,000 bottling line yet or even a small-scale, hand-operated set-up, since it'll run you about $40,000, so you'll rent one that will cost about $2 per case. The bottle itself, a plain, Bordeaux-style bottle with high shoulders, runs about 48¢; a showier, I'm-big-and-baaaad bottle of thick, heavy glass and a deep *punt* (the dent in the bottom of the bottle) can run six times that. Good wine deserves good corks, so forgo the 10¢ ones for the 68¢ ones.

> **Winespeak**
>
> The **punt** is the indentation in the bottom of a wine bottle. It's mainly there for decoration, a vestige of early, hand-blown wine bottles, although the punt is essential for sparkling wines because it makes the bottles strong enough to withstand the internal pressure.

Then you'll need a label. A basic label, nothing fancy, no big-name-artist artwork, runs about 20¢ for the label itself, independent of the cost of designing it. Altogether, the bottle without the wine could potentially be worth $4—something to remember when you encounter those fancy bottles in wine stores.

Getting It to the Market

Now the wine's all bottled and ready to go. What's next? For easy and safe shipping, you'll need some cases to put it in (about $8 for a cardboard box fitted with a Styrofoam insert to keep the bottles from breaking). And you'll need to publicize it, a task you'd probably rather farm out to a public relations company than attempt to do yourself (after all, you have a winery to run), but either way, it will cost you money.

Even if the wine is going no farther than your tasting room, you have to pay taxes on it, especially because it's alcoholic and therefore a luxury (or taboo, depending on viewpoint) item.

Taxing Taxes

In the United States, there's federal tax, which is charged on a sliding scale depending on the size of your winery. Wineries making less than 150,000 gallons a year pay just 17¢ per gallon, as opposed to a larger winery's tariff of $1.07 for still wine, $3.40 for sparkling wine. If you made a whopper of a wine and it comes in at more than 14 percent alcohol, you'll pay an extra 50¢ per gallon.

State taxes differ, but let's say it's California; that will be 4¢ a bottle for still wines and double for sparkling.

That's all before we get to the sales tax, which can range up to 9 percent depending on state and county.

Now, that's only if the wine gets sold directly from the winery door or tasting room. Otherwise, it must pass through the three-tier system.

America's Three-Tier System

In the United States, every bottle of wine must go from the winery (or importer, in the case of imported wines) through a distributor to get to your local store because of our three-tier system, where the distributor is put in between the winery and the retailer to protect against corruption.

So now you need to sell that bottle, worth, say, $15 to you at the winery, to a distributor, who will then sell the bottle to the retailers in its area, adding a few more bucks to its price so he gets to take home some profit, too.

 Quick Sips

Want to know more about the cost of wine? Check out www.wine-economics.org, home of the American Association of Wine Economists, who publish a semi-annual journal, or wineeconomist.wordpress.com, a self-described cross between *Wine Spectator* and *The Economist.*

The retailer needs to make some money on it as well, so he adds some extra dollars to the price. Since no one has ever heard of your wine, there's a risk not much of it will sell, so the wholesaler and retailer will probably build in some protection for themselves by marking up the price a little more than they would for a well-known brand that's sure to fly off the shelves. So that $15 bottle of wine might be going for $30 or so now.

Price, Positioning, and Posturing

While it sounds unfair that a simple bottle of wine is subject to so many taxes and markups, it could be a good thing. Since it's hard to know everything about wine, price and perceived value are powerful marketing tools. This is a trick long known to wine managers at restaurants. If a wine is too cheap, people won't buy it. Mark it up, and it starts moving off the list. Some wineries have figured out that if they offer very little wine at a very high price, people will want it whether they've tasted it or not because they assume it's quite good.

This is risky business, of course, because if the product doesn't live up to the hype, the market will dry up, and you'll have a hard time getting back into business.

Off the Vine

Expensive wines really do taste better, according to a study done by researchers at the California Institute of Technology. The researchers had subjects taste five glasses of Cabernet Sauvignon, knowing only the price, and rate each one. Two of the wines were identical: a $90 wine also presented as a $10 example, and a $5 wine presented as a $45 bottle. Not only did the subjects consistently rate the more expensive wines higher, but brain scans showed increased activity in pleasure centers in their brains, indicating that they really did enjoy the wines more when they had higher price tags.

Retail vs. Restaurant Prices

Getting onto a restaurant wine list is a compliment and a boon to business. Think of what a compliment it is to be one of the 100 that made the cut to get on the list when there are thousands of wines from which to choose. So you're excited when your wine gets on that list. But now the price is double the wholesale price, and do you get any of that?

No. Restaurants make most of their money off of alcohol sales so they can keep the food prices reasonable. So when a restaurant buys a wine from a wholesaler, the wine typically gets marked up two or three times what the wine would sell for at retail.

Any more than three times, and the place had better be pretty special; any less than that, and you can be sure you're getting a great deal.

To Recap

So let's see: we've now spent something over $30,000 building a makeshift winery with the bare minimum of equipment and another $195,000 on the vineyards. You'll need to wait years until you can make wine from those newly-planted vines, but you'll have to pay staff to tend the vines in the meantime. When you do get to harvest the grapes and bottle your hard-earned juice, it'll cost at least $50,000 in labor and supplies, and that's a very rough estimate. Then there are federal, state, and sales taxes, and two tiers to go before the bottle gets into the consumer's hands.

Of course, you could cut corners here and there to make a perfectly decent but less impressive wine: a vineyard in a less desirable place or a less wanted grape; a less trained and less well-fed staff; less or no barrel time; less time aging; lesser-quality bottles and corks ... and you would have had a wine at half the price. But would it be the same wine? No. Would it be good enough? That's the essential question for wine-maker and wine buyer alike.

The Least You Need to Know

- ◆ Making wine costs *lots* of money.

- ◆ The cost of a wine is a reflection of what went into it, such as the quality of grapes, the experience of staff, the use of barrels and of what sort, and so on, all the way down to the price of the cork used to seal it.

- ◆ Every wine in the United States must go from the winery through a distributor before it gets to a store, accruing markups at each stop.

- ◆ If a wine is more talked about than seen and costs a fortune, approach with caution: the hype may be driving the price more than its intrinsic worth.

- ◆ Wine in restaurants will cost two to three times its retail price, due to the traditional pricing strategy of emphasizing profit off alcohol rather than food.

Chapter 22

Buying Wine and Starting a Stash

In This Chapter

◆ Navigating the wine aisles

◆ Finding the bargains

◆ Ins and outs of ordering wine by mail

◆ Starting a stash

I love shopping for wine. All those possibilities, all that potential deliciousness, available even on a $10-a-bottle budget! Every trip shows me how much I still don't know after years in the business and how much is left to explore.

But it wasn't always like that. I used to look at all those choices and run away empty-handed, preferring instead the anonymity of the beer aisle in the grocery store. I didn't know anything about beer, either, but nobody expected me to.

When I finally figured out that nobody knows everything about wine and the people who think they do are just jerks, shopping for wine took on a whole new feel. Now it's exciting. What will I find? How good can it get? How little can I spend? These questions keep me coming back again and again.

If you're not at this point, I hope I can help you get there. And if you are—hurrah! Let's go shopping and see what deals we can find.

Finding Your Dream Store

You walk into a wine store you've never been in before, and a wall-to-wall sea of wine lies before you. Signs dangle overhead suggesting organization; tags festooning the shelves scream for your attention, promising guidance in the midst of the jockeying shopping carts.

Or maybe it's one of those library-like stores, as impressive in the polished bottles on mahogany shelves as it is in its deafening quietness.

Perhaps it's as slick as The Gap, all clean lines, brightly lit, with pulsing music and a bubbly staff selling a slim but very thought-out collection. Or maybe the only place to buy wine in the neighborhood is the package shop, where a guy behind Plexiglas passes bottles through a metal gate.

Wine stores come in myriad styles. The key is to find the one that works for you. These tips will help you find that place.

Location, Location, Location

Regardless how good the store, if it's hard to get to, you're not going there very often. Find a store you can visit regularly so you can get to know it and the staff can get to know you.

Choice

If the closest store caters mostly to a paper-bag crowd, you may soon tire of the limited selection. It's better to go a little farther for a store that offers more choices than you can get through in, say, a month.

Size Isn't Everything

Size doesn't necessarily indicate a great selection. While some super-size wine shops have an incredibly wide wine selection, others have lots of the same mediocre stuff. Look for tip-offs to mass-market mentality, like mountains of wine from the same producer stacked on the floor or only big names like Kendall-Jackson and Sutter Home lining the shelves. It's not that K-J and Sutter Home don't make good wine; it's that there are just more wines worth your attention.

Advantages of Focus over Breadth

Some small stores are just small; others are carefully edited, with a selection honed to reflect the passions of its wine buyers. Some wine stores focus mostly on Italian wines; on Burgundy; on Germany, Australia, organic wines, old-fashioned wines— you name it, somebody loves it enough that they've started a collection. These places are a boon to the wine lover. Deep interest in certain wines or styles of wines often leads wine buyers to deep relationships with the makers of those wines, giving them entrée to wines and prices other stores might not have, as well as knowledge they typically love to pass on to anyone interested. It also makes for a selection that bears the mark of someone's taste, and after a few trips, you can figure out whether you share that taste in much the same way you might wind up liking wines chosen by a particular importer (see Chapter 20). If so, the chances of walking out with a bottle you like are high; if not, it's time to move on.

But focus isn't exclusive to small stores. At some large stores, like Sam's Wines & Spirits in Chicago, different people focus on different regions of the world, so the large store feels almost like a collection of small stores, each section run by someone with a clear view of what he likes and a deep knowledge of what's available.

Price Concerns

Few places go to the trouble of actually ripping you off, so don't worry about that. Think more about what you're getting for the price. Warehouse stores can get prices that no small store could afford simply because they can buy in quantity. Price margins are usually so slim that few amenities—like knowledgeable staff—can be afforded. That's fine when you know what you're looking for.

However, if you like to be introduced to new, tasty things, an extra buck on a bottle of wine here and there pays itself back if the wine-store staff is kind and helpful. A store could be stocked to the gills with well-priced, fabulous selections, but if no one is around to help you sift through the choices, how can you take advantage of them? You could end up paying for wines you don't really like and miss out on the ones you would have loved.

> **Sour Grapes** _____
>
> The wine store can be a strangely uncomfortable place for women, even though we buy far more wine than men do. I've been directed to more bottles of sweet pink wine than I care to think about, though nothing beats the clerk who answered all of my questions to the guy standing beside me. In cases like these, there's little to do but leave, tell all your friends about the awful service, and spend your money somewhere else.

Ordering In

Stopping into a wine store every Saturday sounds like a really nice idea to me, but I live in a big city; it's easy, even at 11 P.M. What about those of you who live in the boondocks or work a 12-hour day and have family demands?

Order in. Many wine stores will deliver wine, even for free if you live close enough. It's harder to strike up a personal relationship via the telephone, but it can happen over time.

Mail-Order Complications

Even if you can get to the wine store frequently, you might want to check out mail-order options. Not every wine available in the United States is available in every state, so mail-ordering wine can greatly enhance your wine-drinking options. It's the only way to get some wines without driving to the winery.

> **Winespeak** _____
>
> A **reciprocal state** is one that allows the shipment of wine over state borders. Most states are nonreciprocal, so check with your local alcohol board before mail-ordering wine from out of state.

Ordering wine on the Web can also save money, as virtual retailers save on overhead. However, and this is a big however, mail-order wine shopping is only an option for those who live in a _reciprocal state_, one that allows the shipment of wine over state borders.

The rise of Internet wine sales has made wine shipping across state borders a hot issue. Most wineries and retail stores would like to be able to sell wines to whomever wants them, regardless what state of the union they live in; most buyers would like to be able to buy wine from whomever they choose, just as they do any other product. However, some people, distributors in particular, staunchly oppose interstate shipping. The legal battles being waged mean that the rules are frequently changing. So while many retail sites will let you know right up front which states they cannot ship to, to be on the safe side, check with your local alcohol control board or go to www.freethegrapes.com to check the current shipping laws in your state. You can also keep up on the drama at www. shipcompliantblog.com/blog.

> **Off the Vine** _____
>
> Even if you can't order wine from out of state, the Web is an excellent tool for wine lovers. Visit retail sites to find out what's available; check out winery sites to find out more about the people and land that produce the wines you like. You can even keep wine notes and compare them with other wine lovers through social networking sites such as www.snooth.com, www.vinorati.com, and www.winefetch.com.
>
> The Web is also terrific for checking out the going price for any given wine. It's particularly easy with www.wine-searcher.com. Just plug in the wine and its search engine rifles though the inventory of thousands of stores, wineries, and auction houses, with direct links to the places that carry the wine you ask for.

If you live in a nonreciprocal state, ask your local wine merchant if he can get the wine you want; he may well find a way.

Finding Wine You Like

So you've found a store that makes you feel welcome. Now how do you find what you want?

You ask. Yes, you must open your mouth and admit you need help. You are not alone; not a person in the world knows every wine. The only stupid people are those who think they do.

Besides, part of what you're paying for every time you buy wine from a store is the staff. Get your money's worth, and use them to your advantage.

Asking Without Embarrassment

Get the most out of your interaction with the staff by giving them information they can use to figure out what might best fit your needs. It will help if you tell them:

1. How much you want to spend. Don't be embarrassed: you wouldn't go to buy a car and act demure about what you can afford, would you? Just say it.

2. Why you are buying the wine. For dinner tonight or a gift? Is it for sipping while you cook or for drinking with steak?

3. What sorts of wines you like. Any sort of information you can give the salesperson will be helpful. It can be as simple as "I like red wines" or as specific as "I really like that red you sold me last Saturday." You could talk about a wine you had recently—anything to give the clerk a point of reference.

Off the Vine

Even savvy wine lovers ask questions in wine stores, knowing that the staff may know of a great buy they've overlooked or might propose something wonderful they didn't think about.

If the wine is a gift for someone and you're not sure about her wine preferences, tell the clerk as much as you can about the person. She has expensive tastes, she is conservative, she likes to cook—whatever might help him guess what sort of wine this stranger might like.

4. What wines you're interested in learning more about. Have you always wanted to visit Tuscany? Maybe you'd like to taste the region's wines. Have you tried something in a restaurant you'd like to try more of?

Armed with this information, the two of you should be able to find a few good bets. It may take a couple of tries; one person's lightly earthy is another person's disgustingly funky, but if you come back and tell the clerk what you thought about his selection, a good salesperson will eventually be able to divine your tastes and lead you to some terrific wines.

Navigating on Your Own

At some point, you'll end up in a store where there's not a soul around to help—or at least not one you'd want to help you. How are you going to find the good buys then?

First, ask yourself all the questions a clerk would have asked you, so you have an idea of how much you want to spend and what sort of wine you're looking for. Then think like the clerk: subtract a few dollars from the price (because a good clerk knows how thrilled people are when he pulls out something that's even cheaper than they'd expected), and start looking around in places bargains often lurk.

Sale Savvy

As you look around, do you see anything on sale that looks good? Wines go on sale for different reasons. Some wines seem to be on sale always and everywhere; basically, the sale has been built into their marketing plan, like the 25 percent more in the toothpaste tube. You're not really getting a better price; you're paying normal cost.

Then we have The Big Dump. There are different reasons for dumping wines on the market, the worst of which is that the wine is so bad nobody bought it and they just want to move it without losing their shirts. If the wine seems unusually old (like a $5.99 Chardonnay from 1996), leaky (it's been baking in some cellar), or too cheap ($2.99?!?!), it's probably better to avoid.

The best reason for dumping is that the distributor or retailer needs to clear out inventory to make space for new stuff and has put a few last bottles of great wine out at deep discount. If you've never heard of the wine, haven't seen it advertised any-where else, and think it looks in good shape, check it out.

Bargain Hot Spots

You've checked out the sales. Now for the rest. First, scope out the store for any par-ticular slants. A wine buyer's wine loves often show in the selection on the shelves, and those areas can hold good deals. For instance, a store I go to doesn't look like much on the surface, but upon closer look, I found it has a terrific array of Portuguese wines. That's unusual, so I asked the reason. It turns out the owners are Portuguese and are proud of their country's wines, so they sell them for very reasonable prices.

Next, think about where bargains often hide. You'll have better luck finding a bargain Cabernet Sauvignon in the Chile section than in the Napa Valley section, for instance.

Super Seconds

Second labels offer another good bet for good values. Second labels are the lesser wines from a winery, wines made from grapes or barrels of wine that didn't make the cut for the house's hallmark wine but were too good to sell off as bulk wine. These second-label wines sell for less and tend to be a bit simpler but can be great buys.

The only issue is figuring out which wines are second labels. If the name of the parent winery isn't prominently featured on the label, read the fine print across the bottom of the label: it names the responsible party. These examples should get you started.

Second Label	Primary Winery
Bishop's Peak	Talley, California
Carruades de Lafite	Château Lafite-Rothschild
Coudelet de Beaucastel	Château de Beaucastel, Rhône Valley, France
Decoy	Duckhorn, California
Echelon	Chalone, California
Hawk Crest	Stag's Leap Wine Cellars, California
Les Fiefs de Lagrange	Château Lagrange
Les Forts de Latour	Latour
Pastiche	Joseph Phelps, California
Reds	Laurel Glen, California
Saison des Vins	Copain

Often it pays to buy in bulk. Many stores offer case discounts of 5 to 10 percent; that could be the equivalent of a free bottle. Only be careful: once you start buying wine by the case, you may decide it's time to start a little stash for rainy days and aging.

Quick Sips _____

A few undersung, high-performing wine-producing areas:
- Argentina (Malbec)
- Chile (Sauvignon Blanc, Carmenère)
- Germany (Riesling)
- Languedoc-Roussillon, France (village whites and reds)
- Loire Valley, France (Anjou, Touraine, Chinon)
- New York State (Riesling, Cabernet Franc)
- Southern Italy (Apulia, Campania, Sicily, Sardinia)
- Spain (Jerez, Jumilla, Rueda, Rioja)

Starting a Stash

At some point in most wine lovers' lives, dreams of a little wine cellar begin to crop up. I mean, wouldn't it be nice to have a little store of great wines, so you always have something good to drink on hand? Wouldn't it be nice to have a place to put all the bottles that have been proliferating around the kitchen and under the bed? And think of the savings: you can buy wines young and let them age into beauties that would then cost too much to afford were you to purchase them at that age.

Then worries about where it would go, how much it would cost, and how it would all work begin to eat away at the dream. Listen, I've got news for you: it doesn't take much to start a decent collection or to add an iota of control to one that accidentally blossomed. Read on.

The Advantages of Getting Older

The majority of the wines in the world are meant to be drunk immediately upon purchase. They are simple, affordable wines, not meant to be stashed.

Some wines, though, have enough tannin, acidity, and concentration that they taste better after some years in the cellar. Over that time, good white wines will take on a deeper color and richer flavors, often like roasted fruit, caramel, and nuts. Red wines will lose some of their tannic bite as well as some color, while the fruit flavors will become more ethereal and layered with spice, nuts, earth, and mineral notes. These flavors can't be achieved without time, and it's hard to find older wines for sale.

That's because it's hard for a winery to age a wine until it's at its peak because everyone's definition of peak flavor is different. Besides, it costs money and space for the winery to hold the bottles in its cellar, so most sell the wines as soon as possible to get them out of the way and to keep up cash flow.

Most stores don't age bottles, either: it takes too much space, record keeping, and expensive insurance. So they sell the wines to you, the buyer, whether they are ready or not.

Over the years, these wines become more rare as the supply gets bought and drunk. This means that $12 Chinon you bought 10 years ago becomes essentially priceless, as it's impossible to find it for sale. Lucky you if you saved it.

What Wines Age Well

No hard-and-fast rules tell how well a wine will age and how long it will take to get to the moment it will taste the best to you. There are, however, a few basic requirements for a wine to age well:

◆ Tannin (for red wines)

◆ Acidity

◆ Concentration

Without tannin or acidity, the most obvious structural components of a wine, the wine will turn flabby and dull. Alternatively, without concentration of flavor, a wine could end up tasting of nothing but puckering acidity or hard tannin, or it might just seem washed out.

Some wines have a long history of aging well, like upper-level bottlings of …

◆ Australian Shiraz.

◆ Barolo (Italy).

◆ Barbaresco (Italy).

◆ Bordeaux reds (France).

◆ Burgundy whites and reds (France).

◆ Cahors (France).

◆ California Cabernet Sauvignon.

◆ Chianti Classico (Italy).

◆ Riesling (Alsace, Austria, Germany).

◆ Port (Portugal).

◆ Rhône whites and reds (France).

◆ Rioja (Spain).

◆ Madiran (France).

◆ Savennières (France).

◆ Sauternes (France).

But you don't have to stick to wines in these categories. You can cellar anything that feels like it might benefit from a few years. If a wine bites back with tannin, put some bottles of it in the cellar; if it feels big-boned but strangely bland, as if the flavors haven't grown into the structure yet, tuck the rest of the bottles away. Sometimes a year or two will make even a $9 Côtes du Rhône or Zinfandel taste a little more interesting. Simple curiosity is reason enough to cellar a wine, especially if it wasn't too expensive to begin with.

How to Catch a Wine at Its Peak

Now here comes the hard part. You've stored all these wines away, but how do you know when to take them out? No one can know for certain; even a winemaker will admit that he can only give it his best guess. Tips from people who have had experience with a particular winery's wines or at least wines from that region, can often offer valuable insight; many wine journals, in fact, include loose predictions of when the wine will be "drinking best."

Off the Vine

Some wines are so sought after that people actually buy them as investments on which to trade and sell, rather than to drink. Red Bordeaux, Port, and Napa Valley Cabernet Sauvignon make up the bulk of the wine investment world, though others bring in big bucks on resale, too.

It takes time, though, to see good returns on wines. Expect to wait at least 5 years and more likely 10 to 15. If you're interested in wine investment, contact a store that specializes in high-end wines; many have investment consultants or can suggest an investment consultant to guide you. Also check out www.investdrinks.org, which will give you a vivid idea of the possible pluses and pitfalls.

Nothing takes the place of experience, though. The best way to catch a wine at its peak is to taste it every year to see where it's at in maturity. When you find a wine you think will age well, buy a case and put it away. Try a second bottle in a year, just to check in and see how it's progressing. If it seems to be aging slowly, maybe skip the next year, and taste it again in two years. At some point, the wine will taste so good you can't believe your good luck, and you'll know it's time to drink the rest.

Sometimes you'll miss the golden moment, or the wine will never have one, in which case regular tasting will allow you to cut your losses sooner rather than later and fill those spaces with something else more promising.

Auction Advantages

Auctions can be tremendously helpful in stocking your wine collection if you've the time and stomach for them. Most wines sold at auction are older wines, so they are one of the few ways to regularly get your hands on aged wines.

An auction house basically acts as an agent for people or estates that want or need to sell their wines. A good auction house will look over the wines before it sells them, to ensure as much as possible that the wines are still in good shape. If the soundness or provenance of the wine is at all in question, the auction house may refuse to sell the lot or do so with a warning to the buyer.

Quick Sips

Some of the major bricks-and-mortar wine auction houses in the United States are Chicago Wine Co., Edward Robert International, and Hart Davis Hart in Chicago; and Acker Merrall & Condit, Christie's, Morrell & Company, Sotheby's, and Zachys in New York City. There are also numerous online auction houses such as www.cellarexchange.com or www.winebid.com.

Anyone can attend an auction and bid on wines. First get the catalogue (often available to download free; print versions typically run $15–$35). It lists the contents of the lots, the shape they are in, and the estimated bid prices.

Often a wine tasting is held before the auction, for which there is a charge (about $40–$100, depending on the wines and the house). This is an opportunity to check out some of the wines for sale at the auction and determine whether you like them enough to want to bid on them. It can also be a great way to simply taste a lot of old, great wines (and some old, dead wines) and meet some wine collectors, many of whom are excellent sources of information on old wines.

If you can't make it to the tasting in person, many auctions allow call-in and online bids. There are also online wine auctions that can hold terrific deals, but, as you can't even see, let alone taste, the wine, it's buyer beware.

Where to Put It All

Oh, right. Where do you put all these wines you're acquiring? You can spend a large fortune on a cellar, and if you spend time in it or like to show it off, you might want to. But you certainly don't have to. A closet, a cellar, a garage, an unused bathtub— whatever you have you can make do, as long as you keep a few things in mind.

What Wine Needs

Once wine is in the bottle, it's pretty safe from the elements: the glass, cork, and capsule keep it safe from air, and the shaded glass keeps out the light.

However, even given such protective housing, wine needs a little care. You need to keep it away from ...

♦ Direct light: fades wines.

♦ Heat above 80 degrees: cooks wines.

♦ Freezing temperatures: freezes the wine, which makes it expand, pushing the cork out or even breaking the bottle.

♦ Wild fluctuations in temperature: tires the wine out, making it taste prematurely aged.

Quick Sips _____

Simply have no space for wine? Call your local wine store to ask about wine storage. Many stores rent space or know of rental storage spaces specifically designed for wine.

♦ Humidity: not usually a big deal, but if it's excessively dry and the wine is stored for a very long time, the cork might shrink a little, letting air in.

♦ Lots of movement: riles up the sediment in old bottles. Accent here is on lots, as in the tremors caused by a closely passing subway.

Beyond these few concerns, you have little to worry about; many people think it's not even necessary to keep wines lying on their sides—though it does usually save space. Use what you have. Just remember to keep track of the collection somehow, or it'll be hard to access your treasures.

Taking Notes

Whatever you do, if you start a wine collection, keep a log book so you can keep track of how it's progressing. Otherwise, you may end up with a cellar full of great wine and no idea why you chose it or when you're supposed to drink it. And part of the fun of a cellar is watching your wines grow up. Don't think of it as a chore. Instead, think of what great luck it is to have all these wines and the time to drink and enjoy them.

The Least You Need to Know

♦ Find a store with a helpful staff, and you're golden.

♦ Ordering wines via the web can get you some good prices and a wider selection available in your state, but check on your state's alcohol shipping laws before ordering.

♦ Even if you can't order wine from out of state, use the Web to find out what's out there and what it typically costs.

◆ Auctions are one of the few ways to regularly find old wines for sale, and anyone can attend and bid.

◆ Aging wines yourself is a lot cheaper than buying them old, and all it takes to start a stash is a cool, dark space and an adventurous spirit.

Part 6

Now You Have the Wine List ...

Now that you've put in all this study, your friends have no doubt begun to peg you as the wine "expert" among them. Don't deny it. Enjoy your knowledge and the status it gives you at the dinner table. Grab that list and pluck out a winner. It's not that hard.

In this part, you learn how to spot the deals, how to handle the tasting ceremony with aplomb, how to pick wines that complement the meal, and yet how not to look like a snob. You just like wine, and you know how to pick it—no big deal.

You'll also find advice on how to keep learning about wine, whether through wine tastings at home or through courses, classes, clubs, festivals, and more.

WHAT KIND OF WINE GOES BEST WITH FISH?

BARR

Chapter 23

Navigating the Wine List

In This Chapter

- ◆ Ordering wine without becoming a wine bore
- ◆ Handling the wine list in business company
- ◆ Getting the most out of the sommelier
- ◆ Approaching the wine list on your own

There's something inherently strange about getting just one wine list for a table of four at a restaurant. It immediately suggests a hierarchy—that one person will take the responsibility for the tastes of everyone around the table or that there's only one expert.

It also limits conversation. Unlike the quiet that descends on a table as everyone pores over the menu, which is typically broken with exclamations of what sounds good and questions about what others will have, the wine list tends to draw one person into a quiet vortex from which some of them (like me) need to be rescued.

There's nothing social about that isolation; in fact, it's downright rude. But a wine list is often big, unwieldy, and filled with confusing or endlessly fascinating choices. How does one handle it gracefully? I'm still practicing, but I'll tell you what I've figured out.

Basic Etiquette

Typically, when you're out with friends, they want to talk to you, not watch you stare trancelike into a wine list. So rather than hogging the wine list for yourself, ask for lists all around. If the list is some big, leather-bound novel, the restaurant probably won't have enough for more than one per table, but small, cheaper-to-produce lists are often in good supply.

Some friends will ignore the proffered list, but insist they take it. I've found that even when they declare they don't have anything to say about the wine, faced with the list, they'll find something to say or ask, and you won't be alone in your wine gazing.

If joint custody of the wine list doesn't spark debates about what to drink, work a little harder to involve the table. Ask people what they like and dislike. Throw out some suggestions. Whatever you do, don't be a rude wine geek and lose yourself in the list.

Business Dinner Etiquette

Business dinners are a little trickier, as there isn't the level of familiarity and casual social air of dinner with friends. Still, do not disappear into the wine list and leave your business companions outside.

If you're the host, you have control of the list, but show your guests some respect and take interest in their likes, dislikes, and interests. If someone else at the table is very interested in wine, you might hand the list over to him.

If you're the guest at a business dinner and some twist of fate lands the list in your hands, don't abuse that honor. Show your hosts the same qualities they'd want to see in you as a business partner: social grace, financial responsibility, and thoughtfulness. That can be a tall order in the already charged setting of a business dinner, where you've undoubtedly got bigger things to worry about, but these few tips will make it easy:

- If you can at all divine where you're going to dinner—or even narrow it down to a few pretty sure choices—call ahead and ask each restaurant to fax or e-mail you the wine list. Then you won't have to spend time fumbling through it trying to figure out how to deal with it.

- If you have to choose the wine on the fly, order the wine after everyone has decided what they are going to eat. (If you're with food lovers, this will probably be expected, but lots of people think it's important to order the drinks right away.) Ordering food first makes it easier to figure out what the vibe is and what the price point is—and it buys you time.

◆ Show interest in your hosts; ask about their wine likes and dislikes. Test the waters by throwing a few suggestions out, too.

◆ Even if your hosts go for the most expensive items on the menu, err on the affordable side of the wine list. Stay away from the extremes; look instead for wines that fall in the middle of that range or slightly under.

If you follow these tips, you're likely to come across as impressively confident, smooth, and thoughtful. You've got a jump start on sealing the deal whether they like the wine or not, but it's always better, for business and pleasure, when the wine impresses everyone as much in taste as in idea. How can you figure out which bottle will satisfy everyone? You can never know for sure, but you can make some pretty good guesses, especially if you start with the sommelier.

What's a Sommelier?

A *sommelier* (som-mel-yay), or wine manager, beverage manager, or wine gal or dude, is the person responsible for buying and serving the wine. The sommelier may not serve every bottle in the restaurant (there's often only one or two sommeliers as compared to a team of servers), but he (or she—women are sommeliers, too) trains the staff about wine and is often in the house to answer your questions.

> **Winespeak**
>
> A **sommelier** is the person responsible for buying the wine and setting up the wine list. A **tastevin** is a cup for tasting wine that sommeliers used to wear on chains around their necks.

The sommelier position used to be the exclusive domain of older gentlemen who dressed in tuxes and wore a silver cup around their neck on a heavy chain. They'd use this *tastevin* to taste the wine before serving to make sure it was okay, and they'd use their attitude to make certain you didn't argue with their pronouncement.

Few old-school sommeliers remain. More likely than not these days, the sommelier looks like everyone else on the floor, only maybe more excited. And why is that? Well, who takes a job that involves hauling 45-pound cases of wine down stairs; keeping inventory of fragile bottles filled with expensive, irreplaceable liquid stuffed into cramped spaces; and memorizing every bottle on the list? Only someone with a deep love of wine, right? You can bet that the sommelier these days really wants to talk to you. So take advantage, and don't be shy.

Take Advantage of the Sommelier

Repeat after me: the sommelier is your friend. He's there to help, and in fact, he'll be really sad if you don't ask him for help, because no matter how much you know about wine, he knows both the wine list and the menu better than anyone else. He knows where the treasures lie, and he knows how the chef's preparation of certain dishes makes them tricky with some wines and perfect with others. Take advantage of this knowledge. Invite him over to talk with you.

The sommelier will probably have questions for you, but to help get the conversation moving, these tips should help him understand what you want.

Talk About Yourself

Tell the sommelier what you like. You don't have to be exact or even eloquent; a simple "light whites" or "fruity reds" helps. However, the more details you can give, the easier it will be to choose a wine that pleases you. If you have a favorite wine, grape, or region, let the sommelier know, and as best you can, tell him why. Is it the fruitiness of the wine or its density? Whatever clues you can give will help him find a wine with the qualities most important to you.

Talk About Food

Choose your food first; then tell the sommelier what you're eating. Chances are, he's discovered some knockout combinations in the course of his career. Even a wine you doubt you'll like will taste great when it's placed with the right dish. And if you do know a thing or two about wine, ask for pairing advice anyway. He may know something about the dish you don't, which could lead to an even better match.

He'll also have some ideas about what to do in seemingly impossible situations, like when one person is having fish and another the T-bone. He might know of some wines that could make that stretch, or he might have a special bottle of red opened behind the bar that he could pour by the glass for the steak. Some half-bottle hidden in the list might fit.

Point Out Price

Show him how much you want to spend. You don't have to be blatant about it: literally point to a wine that costs about what you want to spend, and run your finger over to the price. Savvy sommeliers will pick up on your sly hint and propose wines in that range without saying a word.

Do-It-Yourself Sommelier-ing

What do you do if no one on the floor has a clue—the sommelier's out sick, or the restaurant didn't bother to hire one? Delve into the list. Everything you need to know is in there. It's just a matter of knowing where to look.

The first thing you do is figure out how it's set up.

Deciphering the List

Wine lists come in all shapes and sizes, from a laser-printed piece of paper to an oversize leather portfolio. The look of the list won't tell you much more than the level of pretension.

Size Isn't Everything

There are three major ways to design a wine list: throw money at it, stocking the cellar with all the wines you can afford; hand it over to your wine distributor, who will fill it with wines he'll make good money on; or pick and choose a manageable amount of wines carefully tailored to the style of the restaurant's cuisine, prices, and vibe.

All three methods can lead to good lists, and all have the possibility of ending badly, so give the list a hard look. In a big list, check out how they've filled the space. Does it read like the catalogue for a wine store, with lots of everything and nothing that stands out, or is the list a treasure trove of older vintages, hard-to-find wines, and verticals, different vintages of the same winery's wines? Does it have a slant that suggests the list is so big because the sommelier can't contain himself when it comes to his favorite country's wines?

In a small list, does it offer some interesting options beyond the usual Chardonnay, Merlot, and Cabernet Sauvignon? Do the prices feel reasonable compared to those for the food?

Arrangement Offers Hints

How's the list arranged? There are no rules here. The traditional method, modeled after wine lists in Old World countries like France where wines are typically labeled by the region in which they grew, is to group wines by country and within country by region.

That works well if you know about a country's wines, but it can leave the rest of us out. Therefore, a lot of restaurants in the United States have taken to arranging wines by grape variety.

The downfall here, as you know by now, is that not all Merlots, for instance, are created equal, and the range of styles can make choosing by variety a bit of a minefield.

Many restaurants compromise by arranging the wines by style. The divisions might be as straightforward as light, medium, and heavy, but usually they are also whimsical, like light and flirty and big and brooding, or librarian types and hussies.

Picking Out the Best Buys

Once you've figured out how the wine list is laid out, use these tricks for divining which wines might be the best buys.

Look Past the Familiar

The typical American cuisine restaurant carries more California Chardonnay, Merlot, and Cabernet than anything else because those wines sell without effort. That leaves less room for other categories, and those other wines take more effort to sell—so the sommelier has to be pickier, especially when it comes to price/quality ratio.

Aim for the Heart

Is there a bizarrely grandiose Austrian wine selection? An out-of-proportion array of Australians? Is the Burgundy section bursting at the seams? You can bet these areas are where the wine manager's heart lies, where he can't control himself—thus the eye-catching length and perhaps a lower markup.

Avoid the Extremes

The least expensive wine may be good or simply be on the list to hit a price point. The most expensive wine, on the other hand, often bestows status more than any-thing. Typically, most people buy wines that fall in the middle price range of the list or just above. The sweet spot, however, is usually right under the median price. These are the wines the sommelier works harder to sell since people don't gravitate there naturally, and, therefore, they have to be good.

Search for the quirks. A Slovakian wine is not going to fly out the door, so someone must have chosen it because he or she liked it.

Be Price Sensitive

Scan the list for familiar names, and check whether the prices are higher than normal (on average, a restaurant bottle sells for about twice its retail price). If so, there may be no bargains here, and so it's safer to play toward the bottom of the list.

Know When to Cut Your Losses

If the list just offers White Zinfandel and big-name, bargain-priced reds and whites, order a margarita and save your wine drinking for another list. Life is just too short for bad wine, and bad wine is an insult to good food. Eventually, the restaurant might ask itself why everyone is drinking margaritas instead of Riesling and change their ways. But you'll be gone by then, and that's too bad for them.

Sour Grapes

Steer clear of cult wines, those big-name, hard-to-find wines with prices inflated by high scores from wine critics. Unless you're dining with a label hound, there's always a better buy for the money.

The Least You Need to Know

- The sommelier is your friend, has more knowledge about the wine and the food than anyone else in the restaurant, and would love to share it with you.
- Don't get so absorbed in the wine list that you become anti-social; use it instead to spark conversation.

♦ Ask for wine lists for everyone at the table whenever possible, as each deserves a look and a say in the question of what he'll be drinking.

♦ Decide first what you're eating: it's easier to pick wine to go with food than pick food to go with wine; plus, it will allow you extra time to consider the wine list.

♦ Avoid the obvious and the price extremes on any wine list, and you'll raise your chances of getting a better bottle right off the bat.

Chapter 24

The Tasting Ceremony

In This Chapter

- What to do with that cork
- Sending wine back gracefully
- The pros and cons of decanting
- The rules on bringing your own
- Tipping for wine service

You've ordered the wine. Whew! One big step out of the way. But here comes the guy with the bottle, a corkscrew, and a little plate. What's all the rigmarole about? Why doesn't he just pour the wine and let you get on with it?

In many restaurants, that is all that happens, and though it's less embarrassing, it's not with your best interests in mind. There is a possibility that the wine will be bad, and the tasting ceremony is your chance to find out and correct the situation.

Some parts of the tasting ceremony are more for show than for use, though, so here's a primer in What to Do with That Cork and other ways to handle the tasting ceremony coolly.

What to Expect

You might feel uncomfortable when all eyes at the table train on you as the waiter presents you with the wine, but be glad you have that chance. The waiter brings the wine to you so you can ...

Quick Sips

Sometimes it pays to smell the glasses before the wine is even poured. Soap or damp rag smells can add unpleasant notes to a perfectly good wine.

♦ Make sure it's the one you ordered.

♦ Make sure it tastes like it should.

If it's not the bottle you ordered or it is but doesn't taste like it should, this is your chance to reject it and request it be replaced with the correct bottle in good shape. Think about it: the embarrassment the tasting ceremony might cause is nothing compared to what would happen were a bad bottle poured all around.

This moment, however, is not a chance to decide you don't like what you've chosen. Let's go through the steps so you'll know exactly what to expect and how to handle it.

Check the Label

The waiter should give you time to check the name, vintage, and any other identifying information on the label to make sure it's what you ordered. (If he's really good, he'll point out all the salient information for you, as it's sometimes hard to find the details quickly in a dark restaurant.)

Once you've determined that it is indeed the wine you ordered, he'll step back and open the wine. When he's uncorked it, he'll put the cork on the table.

What to Do with the Cork

What do you do with the cork? Nothing. The cork used to be presented so you could check the name printed on it and ensure the wine in the bottle was the same as the label promised, not a bottle of plonk upon which some fraud slapped a fake label.

That situation used to happen with enough regularity that people felt it necessary to check the cork, but frauds come in slicker styles than label swaps these days, and IDing the cork probably won't help.

As the Cork Crumbles

What if the cork is broken or crumbly? A broken cork could have more to do with the person who opened it than with the cork itself; the biggest problem there will be theirs as it's tough to extract it once it breaks.

If it does break and a few crumbs of cork fall into the wine, it won't hurt anything. A quick splash into a glass should get rid of most of the offending pieces, and no off flavors will be transmitted.

If the cork is very wet and crumbly and the wine isn't decades old, there may be a problem, as that could be a sign that the fit wasn't tight and so air may have seeped in. But you can't know if it adversely affected the wine by looking at or smelling the cork. You have to smell and taste the wine.

The Tasting Pour

Now the waiter will pour a small amount into your glass and stand back, waiting for your response. What will you do? Exactly what you do whenever you taste wine.

- ◆ Swirl
- ◆ Smell
- ◆ Sip

If the wine tastes fine, then nod for the waiter to continue pouring. He'll move on to the next person and fill the glass a little less than half full, so there's room to swirl the wine, and continue like so around the table before coming back to finish filling your glass.

What happens, though, if the wine tastes bad? It all depends on the definition of bad.

> **Off the Vine**
>
> You pay for a glass of wine, but what you get is a glass that's less than half full. What's the deal? The waiter isn't trying to rip you off; he's giving you the room you need to be able to swirl the wine and fully appreciate its scent as well as its taste. In fact, when the wine is poured to the rim, that's the time to get miffed.

The Rules of Rejection

You can't send a wine back simply because you don't like it. If you order it without asking for help, you assume full responsibility for your choice, just as you would for food. If the selection is a recommendation from the wine waiter and you're not happy with it, he may offer to find you something else, but he's not obligated to—just as a waiter wouldn't be expected to replace your entrée with another one if it's something he suggested.

In other instances, it's perfectly acceptable to send the wine back, and it should be taken back without any argument.

Critical Timing

If you order a wine at the same time you order your food, you have a reasonable right to expect the wine to arrive to the table before the food. If that's the case and the wine shows up in the middle of the course, you can decline the bottle on the spot *before* it's opened.

When Good Wine Tastes Bad

It's always a sinking feeling when you smell the splash of wine the waiter's poured for your tasting and find the wine has spoiled. It might be corked (infected with TCA), or it might have turned to vinegar. It might have been stored above the stove or it might be refermenting. These things mean it's ruined, and you have the right to send it back. How do you recognize these faults? Like this:

◆ **Corked wine:** Sometimes it's difficult to tell a corked wine from one that's innocently musty, but often one whiff is all it takes. A corked wine smells like it's been held in a cardboard box rather than in glass or like an old, moldy attic. Nothing will repair this, and it won't fade away.

◆ **Vinegar:** No wine should, by definition, smell like vinegar, so if a wine smells more appropriate for salad dressing than for sipping, send it back.

◆ **Maderized/oxidized:** Heat saps the life out of a wine, flattening its flavors and giving it a caramel-like note; too much oxygen is similarly destructive, turning wines brownish and taking away the fresh flavor. If the wine tastes as if it's been stored over the stove or it's been open too long, say something.

♦ **Refermenting:** Very occasionally, a wine will begin to referment in the bottle. This is an easy one to catch, as it looks fizzy or at least bubbles strangely on the tongue.

Sometimes a wine will have a vegetal or sulfurous stink to it; if it's really bad (like it makes you cringe and pull back violently from the glass), that's also grounds for refusal. But if it's less disturbing than that, don't worry—those scents will probably dissipate as the wine sits in the glass.

If you're not sure whether the wine is sound, that is, free of cork taint or any other problems, ask the wine waiter. He should be able to smell the wine and tell you. He wants you to enjoy your wine, so you might order more and come back to his restaurant another time.

Besides, restaurants can get a credit for the bad bottle from the distributor, so there's no reason why the sommelier would want you to drink a bad wine—and no reason you should feel guilty for sending it back.

> **Sour Grapes**
>
> It's heartbreaking for a wine manager to clear a half-empty glass from a table at the end of the night and discover from a quick whiff that the wine was corked. There went an unhappy customer, no doubt, one whose wine troubles could have been avoided if only the wine guy had known. So speak up when you think the wine in your glass is faulty; it may well be, and you can have it replaced.

The Invisible Tasting Ceremony

In some restaurants, the staff doesn't want to take the risk of having a customer drink a corked or flawed wine, so they do the tasting themselves. In this situation, expect the wine waiter to show you the bottle before it's opened and then take it away after you okay it. Then, at a station specifically set up for tasting wines, with a spittoon for the sommelier so he doesn't get a buzz on over the course of an evening, the sommelier will open and taste your wine. If it's bad, he'll get another bottle. If it's sound, he'll bring it back and pour it around. Seldom do sommeliers of this caliber call a wine wrong, but if you happen to get a bottle that has a major flaw he missed (it happens to the best of us), do mention it.

Decanting

Why do some people get to drink their wine out of beautiful glass decanters while the rest of us get it poured straight out of the bottle?

Most wine doesn't need decanting; pouring it straight from the bottle is fine. Some wines, however, have a thick layer of gritty sediment at the bottom of the bottle that you'd rather not end up in your glass.

Some people, too, think that some wines benefit from extra air contact, and pouring them into a wide-bodied container will do just that. (So will shaking a glass up and down vigorously with your hand cupped over the top, but that's a little messy and doesn't look so good.)

Which Wines?

Wines that typically benefit from decanting are those that have been bound up in their glass bottles the longest. These wines are likely to have thrown some sediment—that is, to have a layer of tannins, pigments, and other compounds that have fallen out of the solution to the bottom of the bottle. Decanting helps keep the sediment out of your glass.

Old wines can also seem to have very little aroma at all right after opening, after they've been hidden away from oxygen for so many decades. Putting an old wine in a decanter lets it breathe a bit or literally sit in the presence of oxygen so its aromas and flavors slowly unfold. In a wine with very mature flavors, though, the amount of oxygen it comes into contact with while going into the decanter can blur the line between old wine and vinegar.

Some people like to decant almost all wines, except for sparkling (the bubbles would dissipate), the very old (they tend to disintegrate), and the very young and simple. For a fit, still wine, extra oxygen helps bring out aromas and flavors.

It's hard to prove, but everyday experience gives the theory some strong support. Ever notice how some wines change in the glass? They start out with almost no aroma and little taste, and then, 15 minutes or an hour later, startle with seductive scents and luscious flavor. Or have you noticed how the leftovers in a bottle taste better the day after it was opened?

The opposite happens, too. A wine tastes great for the first 15 minutes, but as it sits in the glass, it begins to taste duller, more acetic, less pleasant, as if it's falling apart by the minute, or the leftovers taste awful the following day.

The change in a wine from bottle to decanter won't be as drastic as from one day to the next, but it can be significant. The thing is, you can't know for sure how a wine will react. If the wine is simple and juicy, aeration probably won't improve it; if it's tannic, acidic, and very dense with concentrated fruit, it well might. At home, you can experiment. At a restaurant, follow the opinion of the wine steward, who should have an opinion about these things.

How to Decant

In the simplest situations—a young wine that you want to decant just for the benefit of some air or a pretty container—just dump the wine from bottle into decanter.

An older wine requires more care. If the wine is a special one you ordered earlier in the day, the sommelier will have stood the bottle up in a quiet place for the sediment to fall to the bottom.

If you order it that night, he'll just carefully take it from the cellar and move it into a decanting rack, if he has one, which keeps the bottle at an angle, or stand it up, endeavoring not to rile it up.

Then comes the entertaining part: out comes a candle along with the decanter. Over the candle, he'll slowly pour the wine into the decanter. The light the candle throws helps him see the sediment as it flows toward the neck, so he can stop pouring before it comes out.

Often this will leave an inch of wine in the bottle, which might seem like a waste, but it's better than a mouthful of grit.

BYOB

What if you want to bring your own bottle? Well, first, call ahead to see if it's even possible. Some places do not allow it; others discourage it with a hefty *corkage fee*, a charge (typically around $15, though it ranges wildly) for bringing your own instead of ordering off the restaurant's wine list.

Winespeak

A **corkage fee** is an extra charge sometimes levied by restaurants when diners bring their own wine.

That corkage fee makes business sense. After all, a restaurant makes a hefty portion of its profit (not to mention covers glassware and service costs) on alcohol sales so it can keep food costs in line. If diners bring their own wine, they are cheating that system.

Also, in a good restaurant, the wine list is a carefully considered part of the whole dining experience, and the diner who brings his own bottle is missing out on that part of the experience. The restaurateur who's proud of his wine list wants to share his finds with you; bringing a bottle takes away that opportunity.

If you do have a special bottle or bottles you'd like to bring, let the restaurant know what they are; if the wines are special enough, they may give you a deal on the corkage fee. (For example, say you wanted to open up an array of Romanée-Conti Burgundies from 1945 and have some of the chef's fine food to accompany it. That might be justification for some leniency.) Either way, remember to tip as if you had purchased full bottles of wine. Your bill may not be as high, but the staff worked just as hard.

To Tip or Not to Tip

The range of sommeliers is so wide in talent and experience and the array of pay scales restaurants use are so huge that there's no clear answer to the question of whether to tip the sommelier. Generally, if the sommelier went out of his way to accommodate you (like found some special bottle of wine for someone's birthday or decanted old wines you brought in from home), then do offer a tip.

If you brought wines, add the cost of the bottles to the final bill and tip on that total; each bottle added work for dining room staff and dishwashers alike.

Otherwise, it's up to you, but my advice (and I've worked in restaurants) is not to feel obliged to tip the sommelier separately from the staff unless he's gone out of his way for you. A nice alternative gesture, when you bring or order a special bottle, is to save a glass for the sommelier or the kitchen. It's not like most restaurant workers can afford to open such bottles that often for themselves.

The Least You Need to Know

- When the wine comes, check the label to make sure it's the wine you ordered.

- You don't have to do anything with the cork the sommelier leaves on the table.

- You can send a wine back if it's fatally flawed but not simply because you don't like it.

- Call ahead if you want to bring your own wines; some places don't allow it, whereas others charge a corkage fee.

- In general, it's not necessary to tip the sommelier; do, however, leave a tip that includes the cost of wine (even if you bring your own bottle) on the final bill.

Chapter 25

Pairing Wine and Food

In This Chapter

- All you already know
- What grows together goes together
- Classic combinations
- A few basic mechanics

Now that you're familiar with more than 50 grapes from California to Greece, have a stocked cellar, and know how to parse a wine list like a pro, it's time to eat—because what is wine without food?

There are no rights and wrongs when it comes to pairing wine with food—just matches you like or don't like. But it's worth learning the basics of wine pairing because when you hit on a great match, the whole is greater than its parts. In the best instances, wine enhances food, like a splash of lemon, a pinch of salt, or a tangy sauce that draws out more and different flavors in a dish. Wine can be more exciting and interesting than any condiment because it brings its own delicious set of flavors and sensations to the table. And that means more deliciousness, which is the whole point of all this study, right?

Common Sense Counts

If choosing wine to go with a meal makes you nervous, relax: you know more about pairing food and wine than you think you do. You know, for instance, that a big glass of dense, dark red wine isn't going to feel very refreshing on a 95°F day. In fact, you'll probably want to reach for a beer. So on hot days, think light, crisp whites, like unoaked Chardonnays and Sauvignon Blancs. No doubt you've already chosen light foods.

And the same thing goes for wintertime. If you're starting dinner with a white wine, look toward richer whites, like toasty oaked Chardonnay or lush Rhônes.

> **Off the Vine** _____
>
> An easy way to think about what wines fit the climate is to think of what people drink in similar climates. Summertime whites? Think of the Mediterranean. Wintertime reds? Think of northern Italy and central and northern France. It's not infallible, but it's a good trigger when you're feeling lost.

Guided by Vibe

This is a bit of a no-brainer: match the wine to the vibe of the occasion. For instance, burgers and Grand Cru Bordeaux can be a wonderful match, especially if the burgers are served on bone china at a clothed table. But at a backyard barbecue, fancy Bordeaux might look pretentious and be a bit of a waste since the spread won't feel like an occasion to pay much attention to the wine. A good $12 Zinfandel might be a better pick.

Weigh the Choices

You can answer many wine-pairing questions simply by asking yourself how weighty is the dish. Take a nice filet of sole with a butter sauce, for instance. How about a big, juicy Shiraz with that? I didn't think so. The wine is going to knock that fish right out of the sea, not because it's a red wine with white fish but because the wine's flavors are simply bigger, louder, more aggressive. How about a big, oaky Chardonnay? Better, but that's still going to clobber the delicate sole. Well, then, a wine as delicate and plain as the fish itself, like a crisp, unoaked Chardonnay or Sauvignon Blanc? Now we're talking.

Pairing Wine and Food: Quick Reference

There are exceptions to every food and wine in these lists, but this quick reference can get you started. Feel free to add your own favorite combinations.

Type of Wine	Goes With ...
Light, Crisp Whites Chardonnay (unoaked), Fino Sherry, Grüner Veltliner (basic), Italian whites (most), Muscadet, Muscat (dry), Pinot Grigio, Riesling (basic), Rueda whites, Santorini, Sauvignon Blanc, Sparkling wines, Vinho Verde, White Rioja	Raw seafood, including sushi; poached/steamed fish, chicken; deep-fried fish, chicken, veggies; green vegetables; green salads; salty snacks; spicy foods; fresh or salted cheese (feta)

Rich Whites
Chardonnay (oaked),
Chenin Blanc (Loire),
Graves white,
Grüner Veltliner (Smaragd level),
Pinot Gris, Rhône-style blends,
Riesling (Spätlese or Smaragd),
Scheurebe, Semillon Soave,
Viognier
	Grilled or roast fish, chicken, pork;
	rich seafood (crab, lobster, salmon,
	  scallops, tuna),
	cream-sauced fish, vegetables, pasta,
	  white meat;
	sweetbreads; root vegetables; pâté;
	creamy, fruity/milky/nutty cheeses
	  (Brie, Camembert, Compte)

Light, high-acid reds & rosés Bardolino, Beaujolais, Burgundy reds (basic), Cabernet Franc (Loire), Chianti (basic), Dolcetto (basic), Gamay, Nebbiolo (Langhe), Pinot Noir, Rosés, Tempranillo (Crianza), Valpolicella (basic)	Rich, meaty fish (salmon, tuna); grilled chicken, pork, duck, game, tofu; pork belly; mushrooms; truffles; root vegetables; tomato sauce; cold cuts; spicy meat and cheese dishes; creamy, earthy cheese, such as Morbier

continues

continued

Type of Wine	Goes With ...
Rich, tannic reds	
Aglianico, Amarone di Valpolicella, Bordeaux reds, Cabernet Franc (US), Cabernet Sauvignon, Greek reds, Languedoc red blends, Malbec, Merlot, Mourvèdre, Nebbiolo (Barolo, Barbaresco), Portuguese reds, Primitivo, Priorat reds, Rhône reds, Syrah, Tempranillo blends (reserve), Zinfandel	Beef; lamb; organ meats; braised or roast pork, beef, duck, goose; cheese-rich dishes; portobello mushrooms; olives; hard, strong cheeses (Parmesan, extra sharp Cheddar, aged Gouda)
Sweet white wines	
Icewine, late-harvest white wines, Muscat, Sauternes, Tokaji, Vinsanto	Cake (vanilla, spice, fruit); cookies (not chocolate); apple and stone fruit desserts; foie gras; blue cheese
Sweet, dark wines	
Banyuls, late-harvest Zinfandel, Madeira (sweet), Maury, Port, PX Sherry	Berries; cookies; caramel; chocolate; blue cheese; nuts

Feeling It Out

We tend to think of wines as simply wet, but when you get down to it, some are smooth as silk; others are heavier, more like velvet. Some are rough with sandpaper-like tannins; others use bubbles to more genteelly rough up the tongue.

Think of a food's texture when you're pairing it with wine, and ask yourself whether you'd like more of the same or some point-counterpoint. This isn't the sort of interaction that will ruin a pairing, but it might make it more interesting. For example, with a smooth, rich pâté, which would you rather have—a sweet wine as smooth and rich as the spread or a bubbly that will scrub it off? One isn't more correct than the other; they're just different pleasant effects.

Learn from the Locals

It sounds corny, but what grows together often goes together. It makes sense, too—the land in any particular place supports only so many crops, which in turn inspires the local cuisine. Chiles, for instance, don't tend to grow in winegrowing regions. That's not to say that wine doesn't go with chile-spiked food, but chiles often do pose a challenge to wine. Beer, on the other hand, has historically been made where chiles grow and is the no-brainer match.

What people eat in a particular place also affects what wines they make. The wines, in a sense, are preselected to go with the cuisine. For instance, Galicia's fish-based cuisine seems perfectly suited to its light, fresh white wines, and even the few red wines Galicia claims are so light they are almost white. Sure, climate has something to do with it, but you have to think the vintners also made some good choices. Wine is made to drink with food, and light white wines are what they wanted to drink.

> **Off the Vine**
>
> Asparagus gets a bad rap for being difficult to pair with wine. I avoided it until I arrived in Austria's wine country one spring. Asparagus appeared everywhere—in the markets, at roadside stands, and on every plate in every restaurant. Did the Austrians fret? No. They drank Grüner Veltliner or Riesling, two high-acid whites. And it was good.

Tuscany is another good example—heavy pasta, tangy, high-acid tomato sauce: this isn't food that needs a big, fat red wine. It needs something medium-bodied with good acidity, with flavors that will bridge the whiteness of pasta and the redness of tomato sauce. Hey, that describes Chianti, Tuscany's starring wine!

Classic Pairings

You can learn much from tried-and-true wine-and-food pairings—even if it's just that the combination isn't for you. Some examples:

Champagne and caviar: Whether or not it's a great flavor match, this certainly says "celebration" like little else. You could also make an argument for texture, as good caviar bursts like little Champagne bubbles on the tongue.

Muscadet and oysters: Light, crisp, and mineral-tinged, a cool glass of Muscadet matches the bracing oceanic flavor of the oysters that come from the nearby Atlantic oyster beds.

Chablis and oysters: Chablis might be far removed from the ocean but not as far as it looks on the map. The land used to be an ocean bed, and the soil is still filled with ancient oyster shells. Its wines seem to pick up a bit of chalky, oyster-shell flavor, too, which makes them great pairings with oysters themselves.

Chianti and red-sauced pasta: Traditional Chianti has the acid to compete with the acidity of tomatoes.

Gewürztraminer and choucroute: Gewürztraminer's flamboyant spice and fruit stands up well to Alsace's famous sauerkraut-and-sausage dish without overwhelming it.

Fino Sherry and olives, chips, and other salty snacks: Sherry's super-high acidity cuts through the richness of tapas, those little plates of salty and often fried snacks.

Port and Stilton: Some people actually make a hole in a wheel of Stilton and pour the Port right in. It's volume that counts most of all here: both have very big, mouth-filling flavors and rich, palate-coating textures. Sweetness counts, too, to play off the cheese's tang.

All these combinations illustrate some basic tenets of pairing wine and food. You only have to recall them to get the gist, but if you want to delve deeper into what exactly those machinations are, keep reading.

Underlying Mechanics 101

Now you see you already know a lot about pairing wine and food, and it didn't take much more than common sense. But if you really want to be able to figure out what to do when, say, a mango-crusted catfish with strawberry coulis comes your way (besides run), then you need to delve deeper into the very basics of taste.

First Choose Your Food

So you order that mango-crusted catfish after all, and it comes with french fries and a side of coleslaw. How are you going to find a wine that matches every component on the plate?

You aren't. You won't even if you order something as straight-up as steak, mashed potatoes, and creamed spinach. Instead, you need to generalize; ask yourself, what's the main event here? Is it rich or light? Acidic or sweet? What you're looking to describe is the overall feel of the dish, not individual flavors. That would drive you nuts.

Besides, what really matters in pairing wine and food is how a few dynamic elements of flavor balance. Pay attention to …

- Fat (richness).
- Salt (like chips or cured ham).
- Piquant spice (like chiles).
- Acid (like vinegar, lemons).
- Sweetness (like fruit salsas, brown sugar glazes).

Quick Sips

When in doubt, order roast chicken: it goes with nearly any wine, from sparkling through Zinfandel.

Each of these elements plays a dynamic role in flavor—it enhances, magnifies, or suppresses it—and in how food and wine feel in the mouth—smooth, rough, hot, or sticky. Wine can emphasize some characteristics and downplay others; the trick is to decide what tastes best to you. Knowing a bit about how they combine will help you make choices that work more often than not.

Fat

As any cook will tell you, fat is flavor. Fat comes in many guises, as blatant as the sizzling, juicy fat edging a steak, or more hidden, as in the dry crispiness of a french fry. Wherever it appears, it adds richness (not to mention deliciousness).

But fat can put up a barrier to wine, as it coats the taste buds, making it hard to perceive delicate flavors. Rich, fatty foods need wines with enough acidity to cut through the fat and announce themselves. A wine with good acidity can cut through fat like a squeeze of lemon on fried fish, making it feel less rich and heavy.

When the wine doesn't have enough acidity, the combination collapses under its own weight.

What works: fatty foods and high-acid wines

What to avoid: fatty foods and low-acid wines

Salt

Salt magnifies flavor until there's too much of it, at which point everything just tastes like salt. Likewise, salty food can enhance the flavor of a wine, a good thing unless the elements don't need exaggeration. Tannin in particular gets more unpleasant in the presence of salty things. This makes sense, right, since both of them are dehydrating? Also, salt accentuates oak flavors, something most wines don't need.

Salt also tends to come with fatty foods—think cocktail nuts, potato chips, french fries, caviar—so look to high-acid whites for the most addictive, refreshing pairings.

What works: salty foods and high-acid whites

What to avoid: salty foods and tannic or oaky wines

Piquant Spice

A hot pepper adds a bright, lively accent to foods and creates a warming sensation that can spread from the tongue to the belly. To keep that heat in check, we often pair heat with sweet: sweet and spicy Szechuan chicken, for instance, or sweet-hot barbecue sauce. Wine can work with spice in the same way: sweeter wines tamp down a pepper's fire.

When you don't want sweetness, go light and crisp. Big wines tend to have lots of alcohol, which fuels fire. And tannic wines fan the fire by drying out your tongue when it's looking for something to quench the fire.

What works: heat and sweet, or cold and crisp

What to avoid: heat and alcohol, tannin

Sweetness

Sugar enhances flavors, magnifying them and making them feel softer and gentler (think of black versus sugared coffee). Sugar is tricky when it comes to matching wines, though—if the wine is too sweet, the combination can be cloying; if it's too dry, the dessert will seem sweeter and the wine drier; neither item wins.

What's the answer? With desserts, look for wines that have plenty of acidity as well as sweetness; the acidity will help keep the overall sweetness in balance.

With savory dishes that have a sweet edge, like barbecued brisket with sweet sauce, that sweetness wants a wine that's similarly balanced between sweet and savory— something soft and ripe, like an affordable California Zinfandel or Aussie Shiraz. Here, heavy tannin would only feel violent and miserly next to such sweetness.

What works: sweet matched with sweet

What to avoid: sweet foods and low acid or heavy tannin

Acidity

Acid is tough on wine; after all, its most frequent appearance in food is in salad, as vinegar, wine's mortal enemy. Generally, it's best to avoid highly acidic foods when you want to drink wine, but if you're going to do it, and we all are, then fight acidity with acidity, and find a wine with the acidity to match.

Otherwise, the acidity in the dish will slay a soft wine, making it feel flabby in comparison.

What works: acidity with acidity

What to avoid: acidic foods and low-acid wines

Or Start with Wine

Sometimes it's easier to think about what the wine will do for the dish, rather than what the dish needs in a wine. For wine, you have just four basic things to worry about: tannin, alcohol, acidity, and oak.

Tannin

Tannin can feel pleasant, a light grip that keeps the wine's flavors lingering, or it can be like super-strength Velcro, leaving the tongue feeling dry and fuzzy. You can use tannin's power to your advantage with food, but it can also do some damage.

Tannin loves protein; it literally binds to it. If you drink a tannic wine without any food, the tannin has nothing to bind to but the protein in your saliva—and thus the unpleasant drying feeling.

However, give that wine a steak to sink its tannin into, and the tannin will leave your tongue alone. They work almost like tenderizers on the steak, making it go down more easily.

Quick Sips

When you're at a loss for a pairing, go to www.matchingfoodandwine.com, a site from UK-based food-and-wine writer Fiona Beckett that covers the basics free of charge and offers extras such as individual advice with membership. When it comes to cheese, check in with cheese guru Max McCalman; he offers wine recommendations for hundreds of cheeses at www.artisanalcheese.com/searchprodfilter.asp.

Since tannic wines usually have lots of flavor, they typically have the oomph to cut through super-rich dishes like blue-cheese burgers or cheesy, meaty lasagna. Sic those tannins on a popcorn shrimp, though, and they'll destroy the little guy by sheer overwhelming power. Think of tannin as a wine's muscles, and be careful with what it flexes them on.

The shrimp's briny notes won't do it any favors, either. Just as salt enhances flavors, it accentuates tannin, too. If you don't want a wine to taste any more tannic than it already is, go easy on the salty foods.

What works: tannin with protein (think steak or cheese) and big flavors

What to avoid: tannin with delicate foods and salt

Alcohol

Alcohol falls only on the wine side of the food-and-wine equation, but it's important to know how food can affect it. Alcohol stokes a fire in a wine, one that's usually kept under wraps by the wine's own sweet, ripe fruit flavors. Toss a hot pepper into a dish, though, and when the wine and pepper meet, a bonfire might start on your tongue, so keep some bread handy or, better yet, avoid fiery foods and wines with high alcohol. Opt for something lightly sweet and low-alcohol instead, like a German Riesling or a white Zinfandel.

Alcohol can also ignite a fight with salt, which will bring out the heat of a wine in a white pepper–like burn. In most foods, mitigating elements keep this from being a problem, but if the dish of the evening is Chinese salt-and-pepper squid, a 15 percent alcohol Viognier is not a good bet.

High-alcohol wines are usually high in flavor, too, and often have a slightly thicker texture. This is excellent when the match in mind is something as rich as salmon with a cream sauce, but delicate dishes can get lost under that thick blanket of flavor.

What works: high-alcohol wines with fatty, flavorful food

What to avoid: high-alcohol wines and delicate, salty, or spicy-hot dishes

Acidity

Acidity is the lemon squeeze of the wine world. It magnifies flavors; it brightens; it lightens; it cuts through fat like a knife. Think of that lemon squeeze over a fish fry; replace the lemon with a bright, crisp white wine, and the effect is very similar. It makes the heavy flavors feel livelier, and more importantly, it scrapes the film of fat off the taste buds so they won't get fatigued.

What works: high-acid wines with high-acid or fatty foods

What to avoid: nothing, really; high-acid wines are a food lover's friends

Oak

Heavy oak flavor—overt vanilla, coconut, toast, or butterscotch—add weight and sweetness to wines, and thus need rich dishes to stand up to them: think lush, vanilla-coated Shiraz with barbecued brisket with sweet sauce.

If you don't wish to accentuate the oak, beware of salt. It emphasizes oak's flavor and tannin.

What works: oaky wines with sweet or smoky dishes

What to avoid: oaky wines and salty or delicate food

Knowing a bit about the dynamics of food-and-wine pairing can help you make sure the dynamic you hit on is a good one. Still, sometimes you'll hit it and sometimes you won't; not even sommeliers get it right every time. Worse things could happen. After all, it's just dinner and a glass of wine.

The Least You Need to Know

- Match the weight of the dish's flavors to that of the wine.
- Pay attention to texture.
- What grows together often goes together.

- Take tips from classic pairings like Port and Stilton cheese.

- If you remember that tannin loves protein, acidity needs acidity, alcohol starts fires around chile heat, and oak likes smoke and sweetness, you'll be golden.

- The only correct pairing is the one that tastes good to you.

Chapter 26

Company's Coming

In This Chapter

- ◆ Wining and dining guests in your own home
- ◆ Planning what wines to buy
- ◆ Ways to gauge amounts
- ◆ Bringing wine to someone else's party

Here's your chance to show off or at least put your knowledge to the test. Invite some friends over, put on a wine-tasting party, or have a dinner with courses paired to the wines.

That might sound high-falutin', but really, who doesn't like good food and good wine? And why not take a little extra time to show off what you've slaved over in the kitchen to best effect? Or what you've ordered in from the Chinese takeout place uptown …

Planning Ahead

Inviting friends over for some grub and vino doesn't have to be a big deal. Caught off-guard, I've had plenty of spontaneous dinner parties, which consisted of a bunch of cheese and wine drunk out of coffee cups, for that's all I had. A little tacky, maybe, and not the best way to show off the wine, but fun—and that's what counts most.

Still, you can prepare a little better than I did on those occasions. It takes just a few accoutrements and a little advance planning. This will keep the panic down and the flow smooth.

Stocking the Pantry

My mom always had enough quick food in the house to be able to whip up dinner for 250 in the unlikely event that it would be needed without warning. I haven't gotten that good, yet, but she did teach me the value of summer sausages, cheese, and crackers. And I've added my own list of wines.

With a little stash of good, everyday wines and the most basic of foods, there's a party ready to happen whenever the chance occurs—even if it's 11 P.M. after a movie and everyone's a little hungry.

My basic *batterie du vin* tends to consist of ...

Quick Sips

To chill a bottle quickly, put it into a container (or a plugged sink) filled partly with ice; fill it the rest of the way with cold water. This will chill the bottle far faster than straight ice or the freezer.

- Two bottles cheap sparkling wine, like good Cava and Prosecco.

- Two bottles light, crisp white wine (Riesling, Sauvignon Blanc, white Bordeaux, Vinho Verde, Santorini, and the like).

- Two bottles juicy, ready-to-go red (like Zinfandel, Shiraz, southern Italian or French blends).

- One bottle sweet white wine (an affordable late-harvest something or a Moscato d'Asti).

- One bottle sweet red wine (an LVB Port or Port-style Zinfandel or a Maury when I'm feeling flush).

This way, no matter what the situation, I've always something to pull out for guests. Somebody got some good news? A toast is in order, and the bubbly's already in the fridge. It's been a rough day? Bubbly can fix just about anything. Guests stopped in at dinner time? Have a glass of white while we fix another plate. One of these other whites or reds will do fine with the main. Out with friends at a show and there's no place to go afterward? Invite them back for cheese or dessert: you've got some lovely sweet wines you've been waiting for an excuse to open.

Spur-of-the-moment entertaining like a pro is as simple as having a few bottles tucked away—and something to pour them into, perhaps.

Glasses

I've served good wine out of coffee cups, so don't look to me for any lectures about how each wine deserves the perfect glass. Whatever you have on hand will do in a pinch. The only place I put my foot down is with Styrofoam cups: not only are they terrible for the environment, but their chemical smell and funny texture ruin whatever's put in them.

Beyond that, it's a matter of getting as close to the ideal as you can and having enough of them to go around. The ideal is a thin-lipped glass with a pear-shaped bowl (to make it easier to swirl without spilling, and to capture aroma) and a stem (so that you don't get fingerprints all over the bowl or warm the wine if it's been chilled). Those trendy stemless wineglasses look cool and are fine for casual drinking, but if you want to get the most out of your glass, opt for stemware. And make sure the glass is large enough—at least 10 ounces—to get a good swirl going when it has few ounces of wine in it.

> **Off the Vine**
>
> White wine glass, red wine glass? Forget it. Traditionally, white wine is served in a smaller glass than red, but that tradition harks back to the advent of glassware, when the number of glasses on the table indicated status. White wine deserves as big a glass as red; the bigger the bowl, the bigger the swirl, and the more scent you can get out of it.

If you frequently drink sparkling wine, invest in some flutes. These tall, thin glasses are designed to channel the bubbles through the wine in a thin, steady stream—which is both beautiful and allows the bubbles to last longer.

If you can spring for glasses, do so: nothing beats glass in feel and neutrality of scent and taste. Buy more than you think you can possibly use. That way, when one breaks—which it will—you'll have another just like it to replace it and not have to worry about that style being discontinued.

With wine and glasses in stock, you're ready for anything.

Casual Affairs

The more casual the party, the more you'll enjoy it, and the more likely you are to have another, and that's a good thing. So let's say you'd like to have some friends over to enjoy some wine with you, but you have no time to prepare a five-course meal. No problem.

Order In

Get some pies from the local pizzeria, or order takeout Chinese or Thai. Make the food the theme of the wine tasting. With pizza, buy an array of simple Chianti wines; with Chinese, make it Riesling. Put all the wines out in numbered paper bags, so no one can see the labels, and have your guests vote on their favorite. That way, you'll not only eat and drink well, but you'll casually have done some good wine study, too.

Keep It Simple

A food-and-wine party doesn't need to be fancy. It can be as simple as some wine and some cheese or dry sausages and bread. Give it extra interest by creating a theme—buy an array of American farmhouse cheeses, for example, and a selection of American wines to match. Or make it Spanish wine and Spanish cheese, or Italian cold cuts and red wines. Not only will it narrow the choices, making it easier to make your selections, but pairing wine with the foods that it grew up around also greatly ups the chances that the two will go together well.

Go Potluck

Pick a theme, any theme, and a price range, like $1 to $10, and ask everyone to bring a bottle. The theme could be the starring dish: say, a deep pan of lasagna. Or it could be a variety, like Merlot. Or make it the movie you're going to watch that night—anything from sultry wines with which to match a showing of *Casablanca* to wines that would pair well with buttered popcorn. (Hint: Chardonnay.)

In order to keep competition down, you might want to paper-bag these wines, too. One bottle always goes faster than the others.

This is also a terrific way to learn about lots of wines at once: with 10 different Merlots, you are bound to have some clunkers. The few great ones you can add to your shopping list; the rest you never have to wonder about again.

Ambitious Affairs

The wonderful aspect of having a fine dinner matched with wines at home is that you have ultimate control. You're not limited by a set menu nor by an overpriced or underwhelming wine list. You don't have to consider the needs of three other people who ordered very different dishes nor that your appetite for different tastes might break the bank. You're in control: the menu and wine selection are in your hands.

The challenge, of course, is that you're cook, sommelier, and host all wrapped into one, so you'd better plan ahead.

Wine First?

Sometimes, the inspiration for a dinner party is to share a special wine. Designing a dinner around wine is often easier than deciding on food first and then wine. You know from Chapter 25 what you need to watch out for to show them at their best and what general combinations make them happiest.

If you want to focus on a single wine, put it in the starring role, with the entrée, even if it's a white wine. Build out from there, adding lighter wines to begin. If a meal isn't a meal without a red wine, add it at the end, with cheese or dessert. Some people think it's fine to go from red wine to white wine, but it doesn't work for me.

If you have an array of great wines to share, order them by weight and match the courses to their weight. That way, you won't lose people as they fill up on richer dishes first, and every wine and dish will get its chance to shine without being over-whelmed by the previous course.

Food First?

The whole world is open to you if you're starting from food, so make it easier on yourself and focus. Get inspired by the season, and design a menu around what's in the farmers' market, or choose a cuisine—from American to Zimbabwean—it doesn't have to be that of a wine-producing country.

Decide how many courses you want, and arrange them by richness; for example, start with a light salad, move on to a fish course, and end with beef. Then pick the wines, keeping the basics we covered in Chapter 25 in mind. Not every dish has to have its own wine, of course; some can share or go without. Which leads us to the question, how much is enough?

Judging Amounts

How much wine you need for a party depends entirely on what sort of party it is and whom you're inviting. If there are two pregnant women at the table, you can scale the amounts down; same goes for marathon runners with a race the next day. Use common sense to decide how enthusiastic your guests will get over the wine.

The kind of event also helps determine how much. If it's a casual dinner, with just one main event (a pizza party or a simple roast chicken dinner), you can figure two to three 4- to 6-ounce glasses per person. If there are up to three courses with different wines, the same applies, only you'll need fewer bottles of each wine.

If you're going all-out, though, for a 12-course wine-matched meal, you'll need far less of everything, unless you want your guests to be under the table by dessert. Plan on just 2 to 3 ounces of each wine; it sounds like a little, but it will feel like plenty by course four.

Off the Vine _____

Unabashed wine geeks like me who love to put people through extensive multi-course meals matched with wines often put out a large container of some sort into which people can dump their glasses, so they don't feel compelled to finish each glass to get on to the next wine. The thing about wine appreciation, you see, is that you have to be sober to do it.

Etiquette

Whatever you do, make your guests feel comfortable. Always offer water, whether they ask for it or not, and have some nonalcoholic options on hand. If someone doesn't want to drink, don't make a big deal about it. Offer him something else, and give it to him in a wine glass, so he doesn't have to stand around feeling like the odd man out. I do this with children, too: it makes everyone part of the party.

Always have a receptacle into which guests can dump their leftovers—or even spit, if they prefer. It's not gross; it's respectable. It's much better than their getting sick on your carpet, right?

Since you've volunteered for the care, feeding, and wining of your guests this evening, make sure they can get home safely, too. If they have to drive, don't let them get drunk unless you're ready to have them stay over. Saying no can be really tough, but it's better than risking the chance of a much worse outcome. Besides, who wants to hang around with a drunk?

When You're the Guest

Since I write about wine for a living, hardly anybody ever brings me wine. But I wish they did. There's something wonderful about having someone else choose a wine.

Often, people choose a personal favorite, which makes it feel like a very personal gift since they are willing to share it. It also may be something I never saw or thought to pick up, so it's a chance to get acquainted with another wonderful wine.

Of course, we all have a few bottles received as gifts that we wish never appeared, and we've all probably given a wine like that, too. How can you make sure you're not ever again one of those people? Asking a few questions before you get there is a good place to start.

What to Ask

Always ask before you go to someone's house whether you can bring anything—wine, perchance? It might be that they've planned an elaborate dinner paired with wines, in which case you're better off bringing flowers. A gift of a bottle of wine often makes people feel obligated to open it, and that might create some discomfort if the wine is already planned.

> **Off the Vine**
>
> A host isn't ever obligated to open the wine a guest brings, so if you have a special bottle you really want to taste, leave it at home. Don't be offended if your hosts choose not to open the wine that evening. You've given them a gift, and it's not yours to dictate how they use it.

If, though, the answer is yes, find out what's for dinner, so you can choose a wine that might go well with it. Try to gauge the style of the dinner party, too. If this is a backyard barbecue, an $8 bottle of red will go over much better than it might at a white-tablecloth sit-down dinner. If the host is going all-out for a nice dinner, do the same with the wine. Unless you know a wine to be better than its price would suggest, spend at least $15 on a bottle, more if it's a wine from an expensive place like Bordeaux or Burgundy.

What to Bring

If you've no idea what sort of scene you're going to walk into, opt either for a pricey favorite that you'd be happy to drink, should they want to open it, or that you can be pretty sure they'll be happy to have. Don't ever assume that because your hosts don't know much about wine, or, in your opinion, don't have very good taste in wines, that this is an excuse to palm off plonk. If you give them a nice bottle, they just might start liking better wines.

Another good ploy is to bring something sparkling to start the evening. That way, the wine won't interfere with dinner plans, and it won't matter if there are nibbles to start or not—sparkling wine goes with just about everything (including nothing). Or bring something sweet. A lot of people don't think about dessert wines, though most everyone enjoys them when they are poured.

In the end, whether host or guest, aim to please. You don't have to spend a lot, but spend enough in thought and money that your guests or hosts can tell you care.

The Least You Need to Know

- ◆ Keep a couple each of sparkling wines, white and red wines, and dessert wines, one white and one red, and you'll always be prepared for spontaneous get-togethers and drop-in guests.

- ◆ If there are more wines than people, provide guests with a place to dump out wine they don't want to finish.

- ◆ Have water for everyone and nonalcoholic drinks for those who don't want to drink wine.

- ◆ When bringing wine to someone's home, never underestimate your host's appreciation for good wine, and bring him the best you can afford.

Chapter 27

Basics Down—Now What?

In This Chapter

- ◆ Places to look for more opportunities to learn
- ◆ The value of flights
- ◆ Restaurant options
- ◆ Classes and clubs

Congratulations: now you know a lot about wine! But you're just beginning an excellent adventure because no matter how much you know about wine, there's always more to know.

The More You Know, the More You Don't Know

You may have already figured out that the more you know about wine, the more you realize you don't know. It only gets worse from here. The only thing you can ever be sure of is that you have more to learn.

The wine world is getting harder to keep up with, too. Advances in knowledge and technology are making it possible to grow better wine in more places or even grow it where it never grew before. And whereas it was once unlikely that you'd find wine outside of the region it grew in, let alone the country or continent, today wine is shipped all over the place—and typically gets there in good shape. Add the sheer number of wines to the simple fact that each vintage brings something different to a wine, and the possibilities really are endless.

The upside of this realization is that it means the possibilities of excitement, discovery, and new and delicious sensations will outlast your ability to get through them all. You'll never, ever be bored.

Keep On Learning

If you keep drinking wine, and thinking about it every time you taste it, you can't help but continue to learn. Things will go a little faster, though, if you keep actively working at it—and you might create an encouraging network of wine-loving friends, too. That's fun, and it'll help you through those times when it seems there's so much to know and so many bad bottles.

Free Wine

Since learning about wine is all about drinking it, the learning can be pretty hard on your bank account. However, unless you live in a dry county, you might find more free wine-tasting opportunities around than you'd think. In particular, check out:

Wine Stores: Where it's legal, wine stores often have wine tastings, where they open up half a dozen bottles and pour you a taste of one or all. These casual tastings are almost always free, and the pressure is nothing; you can come in, taste, and leave without so much as buying a bottle. The store's hope is that you'll love one of the wines enough to buy something, but even if you don't, the tasting gives the store a chance to educate their consumers, and a savvy consumer is the best kind.

Wine Classes: Running a wine class takes a lot of glasses—and those glasses need to be set out, filled, and then washed. If you don't mind getting a little wine-stained and washing dishes, you might volunteer as a pourer. You'll be a little too busy to take as many notes as the students, and you might not even get to sit down, but you do get to taste the wines when you've done your duties and listen to the lecture as you work. Look for wine classes at culinary schools and in adult community education programs, or ask your local wine merchant where to look for classes in your area.

Wineries: Take a trip to wine country—now that wine is made in every state, a winery may not be very far away from you. Most wineries offer tastes of at least some of their wines for a nominal fee if not for free. They hope you'll buy something, but you're under no obligation.

Lots of Tastes, Little Cost

Scour your local restaurant and wine bar scene to find places that offer lots of wine by the glass. Many times, these places also offer wine by the half- or quarter-glass. That way you can get enough of a taste of a wine to get to know it, but you don't have to commit to a whole glass.

Wine-oriented bars and restaurants might also offer "flights" of wine, a taste of a few different wines grouped under a theme. These flights often offer a good chance to compare and contrast a group of similar wines, an exercise that really helps you get to know a variety or a style of wine.

The only time you might not want to take advantage of these programs is when no one around you seems to be drinking wine. That might mean that the turnover of the wines isn't very high, and many of the bottles may have been sitting there open, turning bad. Some places install a Cruvinet or similar system that pumps inert gas (like nitrogen) into the bottles, displacing the offending oxygen and keeping the wine fresh for days. But these systems are expensive, so many restaurants go without.

Off the Vine

One of the best ways to save leftover wine is to spray an inert gas into the bottle, thereby displacing the oxygen that would destroy it. Some restaurants can afford Cruvinets, large storage systems with a system for dispensing nitrogen into the bottles. You can also buy gas by the canister for home use, such as Private Preserve or Vintage Keeper. Gassed or not, open bottles will keep better in the fridge. The cooler temperature slows down chemical reactions, so the wine oxidizes more slowly. Just remember to pull your reds out a couple of hours before you drink them.

Charity Tastings

Charity tastings can be some of the best deals going. You donate money to the charity at the door, and in exchange they give you the chance to expand your knowledge. These tastings can be as few as 10 wines or as many as 100; it all depends on the event.

To find out about these tastings, watch the event listings in your newspaper's social pages and food pages, and look for fliers posted at your wine store.

If you are involved in a charity, you might try getting a wine tasting started yourself. Often wine stores, distributors, and importers are happy to donate or deeply discount wine for a good cause and the chance to have their wines exposed to a new group of potential buyers.

Restaurant Tastings

Restaurants that are really serious about wine often set aside some nights throughout the year for special wine tastings. These can be anything from a Monday night Bring Your Own party, where guests bring a nice bottle they can share with other guests, to a full-blown multi-course prix fixe dinner designed around the wines of a particular winery, with the winemaker in attendance.

Whatever shape it takes, restaurant wine events can be fabulous opportunities to taste great wine, and in context with food, which is another important aspect of learning about wine. Some restaurants hold wine events so often they have newsletters; sign up so you'll be notified regularly.

These dinners also tend to be chock-full of wine geeks, so you can learn from other diners. You might only learn the definition of wine bore, but put it in your book as a reminder of what not to become.

Courses and Classes

None of these methods will give you the same sort of intense, disciplined study as a formal class would. Classes come in all sorts of intensities, from fun one-offs to semester-length obligations. They may be worth a look.

One-Night Stands

Many cooking schools and evening education programs offer one-night wine classes. The themes run the gamut from serious inquiry into the wines of a certain place to classes on wines for Valentine's Day. Either way, you get to taste a handful of wines and have access to a wine-knowledgeable person whom you can grill with wine questions.

Going Steady

Fewer places offer longer-term classes, but it's worth a look if you're this devoted. A long-term class gives you the chance to taste more wines, as well as develop a rapport with the teacher, whom you should be able to rely on for knowledge.

If you think wine is something you might want to get into professionally, call the American Sommelier Society, the Court of Master Sommeliers, or the International Wine Center (NY) to see if they offer classes near you. These associations prepare professionals for a career in wine, as either a Certified Sommelier, a Master Sommelier (MS), or a Master of Wine (MW). They might give you more than you ever wanted to know, but they might be just what you're looking for.

> **Off the Vine** _____
>
> MS, MW, what's the difference besides one letter? To gain Master Sommelier certification, a person not only needs to know everything about wine, but he also needs to be able to serve it gracefully and correctly under pressure. The MW exam was created for retailers, and so the MW is tested more on the knowledge and communication of wine than service. Both require passing extremely challenging exams.

Tasting Clubs

If a class is too demanding, but you'd like a regular opportunity to taste and learn, look for wine-tasting clubs. Many cities have their own unique clubs; you can find out about these by asking at wine stores. Their frequency and level of professionalism depend on the people in charge.

Some nationwide groups have chapters across the United States that hold regular tastings. Some possibilities include:

- American Institute of Wine & Food (AIWF).

- Women for Winesense, a nonprofit group dedicated to encouraging women to become involved with wine.

- Slow Food, an organization dedicated to the return to chemical-free, unprocessed, real food—as opposed to fast food—holds occasional wine events.

Start Your Own Club

If none of these have what you're looking for, why not start your own club? Start by inviting good friends. Decide on a theme, and have everyone bring a bottle. (You might want to set a price limit, too, so people don't feel obligated to spend a lot.) Provide paper, pens, water, glasses, plastic cups for people to spit into, some crackers or bread, and a corkscrew; anything else would be icing on the cake.

Once you iron out any kinks, you might want to open it up to more people. Or have the club move from house to house every week, so that no one person is burdened with hosting it every time. A local restaurant might provide a space for your group, too, as long as you order food.

Besides having fun together, you'll learn a lot from each other even if none of you knows much about wine. After all, communicating about wine is half the battle, and this will force you to put wine into words. That's no small accomplishment.

Use the Web

The web is a boon to wine lovers. Want to know more about a particular bottle? You can ...

- Find the winery on the web and read what they have to say about it; send them an e-mail if you have questions.

- Explore the area from which the wine comes, from climate to cuisine and more.

- Comparison shop to see who has the best prices, using a simple search or using a search engine specific to wine, such as wine-searcher.com.

- See what other people have to say about it (and add your opinion).

- Instigate a conversation about it on any number of wine-focused message boards and wine-focused social networking sites, such as Cork'd, Snooth, and Vinorati.

- Buy, sell, or trade bottles (where legal).

Some wine stores now offer kiosks to look up the wines they have for sale online, enabling you to retrieve extensive information on wines even when the staff is too overwhelmed to attend to you personally. A few restaurants have even gone digital with their wine lists. At Aureole in Las Vegas and New York, diners are handed a tablet that holds a digital wine list; they can sort it in whatever way they please or search for particular wines, types of wines, price categories, bottle sizes, and so on.

The Internet is a powerful and highly seductive tool for wine lovers; in fact, the danger (besides spilling wine on your keyboard) is that you may forget that wine is best enjoyed among friends—real, live, flesh-and-blood friends. Remember to unplug sometimes.

Wine Festivals

If you live in wine country, you know that every summer and fall brings a rash of wine festivals. Wine festivals aren't exclusive to wine-country settings, though—many nonwine places will put on wine festivals to bring a sunny bit of wine country to an otherwise empty weekend. Food and wine magazines are a popular source of these several-day wine events; so are museums, which often use them to raise funds.

Many of the nonwine-country events are expensive, as it takes money to get wines and winemakers there, and the money is always going to a cause, whether charity or business. However, festivals can be as informative as they are fun if you focus amid all the socializing. With winemakers on hand, there are plenty of people to whom you can ask wine questions, and the higher tariff to get in promises some pretty special bottles.

Quick Sips _____

A slim array of some great wine festivals around the United States:

- ◆ Austin, Texas: Texas Hill Country Wine & Food Festival
- ◆ Boston, Massachusetts: Boston Wine Expo
- ◆ Hawaii: Kapalua Wine & Food Festival
- ◆ Kansas City, Kansas: Kansas City Festival of Wines
- ◆ McMinnville, Oregon: International Pinot Noir Celebration
- ◆ Miami, Florida: South Beach Wine & Food Festival
- ◆ Orlando, Florida: Epcot International Food & Wine Festival
- ◆ Paso Robles, California: Hospice du Rhône
- ◆ San Francisco, California: Annual Rhône Rangers Festival
- ◆ Santa Fe, New Mexico: Santa Fe Wine & Chile Festival
- ◆ Telluride, Colorado: Telluride Wine Festival

And look for more at www.localwineevents.com

Wine festivals in wine country tend to be as much for the locals as they are for visitors, and so they can be much lower key. They offer an advantage in that they put you right in wine country, where you can see, smell, and sometimes even taste the grapes that go into the wines. Which brings me to the next topic ….

Travel, Armchair and Otherwise

There's no better way to get to know a wine than to go to its source. Standing in a vineyard, somehow the look of the land, the feel of the air, the quality of the sun, the smell in the air—everything—can make wine make more sense.

You'll also be able to eat like the natives, which means drinking the wine with the food it grew up around, a deliciously enlightening experience. And you'll be able to taste all sorts of wines that never leave the regions, either because they are so dear to the locals or there just aren't enough of them to go around.

Many companies specialize in wine-and-food tours. These tours can be wonderful introductions to a place, as knowledgeable guides can offer extra insight into a region and its wines, and, often, entré to places you wouldn't be able to visit on your own. You can just as well take a tour on your own, though.

When travel isn't in the budget, read. Read everything about wine you can get your hands on. Read wine novels, like Kermit Lynch's *Adventures on a Wine Route* or Burton Anderson's *Treasures of the Italian Table*, where you can get a feel for not just the mechanics of the wine, but for the people who make it, the hue of the country-side, and the taste of the food. Primers like the one you're holding are only jump-off points; now it's time to take the wine and appreciate it in the way it was meant to be used: with friends and with food. Enjoy.

The Least You Need to Know

- You'll never know everything about wine, but there are plenty of fun ways to try, which don't have to cost a fortune.

- Look for free tastings in wine stores where it's legal.

- Charity wine tastings can be a good way to learn about wine and feel good about it.

- Take advantage of restaurants that serve wines by the glass or in even smaller portions, so you can taste more for less.

- Drink, read, drink more, read more, and keep on enjoying wine; the learning will come naturally.

Appendix A

Glossary

abboccato A lightly sweet wine in Italian.

acetic Like vinegar.

acetone An unfortunate smell sometimes found in wines, caused by ethyl acetate.

acidity The tangy element in wine that makes it feel bright, crisp, and lively.

alcoholic content The alcoholic strength of a wine, typically described in percentage by volume. Most wines fall between 7 and 15 percent.

Alte Reben Old vines, in German.

amabile Loveable, in Italian, used to indicate a sweet wine, sweeter than one marked *abboccato*.

Amarone Wine made from semi-dried grapes; a specialty of Valpolicella, Italy.

anthocyanins Pigments that give grapes their red–blue color.

AOC Appellation d'Origine Contrôlée, a French system of defining areas and the wines made within them. Not an assurance of quality.

appellation An officially delimited area of wine production, modeled after France's AOC system. Different countries have different appellation systems.

astringent   Drying, tannic.

Ausbruch   Austrian term for sweet wines made with botrytised grapes.

Auslese   A German designation of ripeness, typically, but not always, indicating a sweet wine.

austere   Not fruity; lean, hard.

AVA   American Viticultural Area, an official designation of a delimited geographical winegrowing area.

balance   When no part of a wine's flavor stands out too much.

barnyard   A funky, earthy scent, typically found in red wines. It can be a positive or a negative, depending on its intensity and your taste.

barrel-aged   Aged in wooden barrels.

barrel-fermented   Wine fermented in oak barrels instead of stainless steel or cement, so as to give the wine a richer flavor.

barrique   French for barrel and used to indicate a traditional, 225-liter oak barrel.

batonage   French for the act of stirring the lees to extract more flavor from them.

bead   A poetic metaphor for the bubbles in a sparkling wine.

Beerenauslese   Second-highest designation of ripeness in the German Prädikat scheme, indicating sweet wines made from botrytised grapes.

big   Very flavorful, mouth-filling.

biodynamic   a holistic method of farming that stems from the "Agriculture" lectures (c. 1924) of Rudolph Steiner, in which the forces of the entire cosmos are considered in every agricultural activity undertaken.

Blanc de Blancs   White of whites, meaning a white wine made from white grapes. Most often used in sparkling wines.

Blanc de Noirs   White of blacks, meaning a white wine made from red grapes. Most often used in sparkling wines.

blind tasting   To taste wines without knowing their identity.

Bocksbeutel   A squat, round bottle traditionally used by vintners in the regions of Franken and northern Baden in Germany.

bodega   Spanish for winery.

body   How light or heavy a wine feels in the mouth.

botrytis cinerea   Noble rot, a rot courted in sweet wines for the help it gives in concentrating the wine's flavors and adding a smoky, honeyed note.

bouquet   Winespeak for the complex aromas developed in an older wine, and frequently misused in place of aroma in a young wine.

Bourgogne Rouge   French for red Burgundy, a Pinot Noir wine; Bourgogne Blanc means white Burgundy, a wine made from Chardonnay.

brett   Short for Brettanomyces.

Brettanomyces   A yeast that sometimes infects wine, giving it a smell often described as sweaty saddle.

Brix   Unit of measure of soluble solids (sugar) in grapes; typically 20 to 25 at harvest.

brut   Indicates a dry sparkling wine.

chaptalization   The addition of sugar to a wine, not legal everywhere.

château   French for estate.

clone   A strain of a particular grape variety.

clos   A walled vineyard.

complex   Having many different flavors and facets.

cork dork   A person devoted to the study of wine.

corkage fee   An extra charge sometimes levied by restaurants when diners bring their own wine.

corked   Infected with TCA, a bacteria which makes wine smell like wet cardboard.

Crémant   French term indicating sparkling wine made by the traditional method used in Champagne, but made outside Champagne's boundaries.

crisp   High acid.

cru   Means growth in the sense of vineyard. A Grand Cru wine, for instance, comes from a "great growth," or, a vineyard recognized as producing great wines.

cuvée   A blend.

decant   To transfer a wine into a larger container, usually for the purpose of separating the wine from the sediment in the bottom of the bottle or to aerate the wine.

deep   Having lots of flavors that seem to last a long time and keep changing in the mouth.

disgorge   To take out, typically used to refer to the process of removing the sediment from the neck of a Champagne bottle.

DO   Denominación de Origen, the Spanish appellation system.

DOC   Denominación de Origen, Calificada, Denominacão de Origem Controlada, Denominazione de Origine Controllata; the Spanish, Portuguese, and Italian (in that order) appellation systems.

dosage   The small amount of wine and sugar added to a sparkling wine after it has been disgorged and before it is corked for the last time. The sweetness of the dosage affects the sweetness of the final wine.

dumb   Not expressing much scent or flavor.

Edelzwicker   A term used in Alsace to identify a wine made from a blend of two or more of Gewürztraminer, Muscat, Pinot Blanc, Pinot Gris, Pinot Noir, and Sylvaner.

Eiswein   German for wines made from grapes that have frozen on the vine.

en primeur   To buy wine en primeur is to purchase it before it is bottled. Bordeaux was the first market to sell many of its wines en primeur, but the practice has been adopted by some wineries in other places today.

Erstes Gewächs   First Growth in German, a designation sometimes used in the Rheingau meant to signify the very best vineyards of the region.

exposition   The position of a vineyard, with respect to its interception of sun during the course of the day.

fat   A wine with lots of fruity flavor and not so much tannin or acidity.

filtration   The mechanical removal of small particles from wine to make it clearer, brighter, and, in some cases, free of any potentially harmful microbes.

fine, to   The addition of a clarifying or softening agent such as egg whites or skim milk to a wine.

finish   Winespeak for how long a wine's flavor lasts in the mouth, e.g., "The wine has a long finish."

flabby   Lacking in acidity.

flor The yeast that grows on the surface of certain wines in the barrel in and around Jerez, Spain. Flor is essential to most Sherries.

flute A tall, thin glass designed for sparkling wines.

fortified wine Wine to which extra alcohol has been added, such as Port, Sherry, and Vin Doux Naturel.

frizzante Lightly bubbly, in Italian. Frizzante wines are less bubbly than spumante wines.

fruit-forward A pretentious way to say fruity.

galets The large, smooth, rounded stones that cover many vineyards in Châteauneuf-du-Pape.

garrigue A French term used to describe the mix of fragrant wild herbs and brush common to the Mediterranean countryside, which sometimes turns up in the scent of wines from southern France.

Gewürz Spice in German; it's also shorthand for Gewürztraminer, the grape.

grafting The act of attaching one plant to another so that the two will grow into one. *Vitis vinifera* vines, for example, are often grafted onto rootstock from American vines that are resistant to phylloxera, an aphid that damages *Vitis vinifera* roots.

Grand Cru Great growth in French, applied to vineyards that have proven over time to produce exceptional wines.

green harvest To remove grapes before harvest in the hopes of concentrating flavor in those that remain.

halbtrocken German for half-dry.

hang-time The length of time grapes remain on the vines before harvest.

histamines Naturally-occurring, nitrogen-based compounds found in wine that are the likely culprit behind most wine headaches.

horizontal tasting To taste an array of wines made from the same grape or the same place.

hybrid A cross between two species, such as a *Vitis vinifera* vine with a *Vitis labrusca* vine.

IGT Indicazione Geografica Tipica, an Italian category in between *vino da tavola* and DOC wines that defines where a wine is grown, but not what grapes must go into it.

internationally styled   A wine made in the current popular style, with very ripe grapes and lots of oak, that tastes as if it could come from anywhere. It's the opposite of a *vin de terroir*, or a wine expressive of the place it grew.

Kabinett   The lowest level of Germany's ripeness designations, indicating a dry wine.

late harvest   Harvested late in the season, when the grapes are very ripe.

laying down   Putting a bottle away to age.

L.D.   *See* R.D.

lees   The sediment that precipitates out of a wine after it ferments, typically consisting of bits of grapes and dead yeast cells.

legs   A very un-P.C. term for the glycerol trail left on the side of a glass after swirling the wine. The longer the legs, the richer the wine.

length   How long a wine's flavor lasts in the mouth.

Liebfraumilch   Originally wines from a vineyard in Germany called Liebfrauen-kirche, the term has been corrupted to typically indicate a cheap, slightly sweet German wine.

lugs or lug boxes   Small plastic or wood crates used for transporting grapes from the field to a truck, winery, or warehouse.

maderised   A negative trait (unless the wine is actually Madeira) typified by the nutty, baked, caramel-like flavors of Madeira.

malo   Short for malolactic fermentation.

malolactic fermentation   A second fermentation in which hard malic acid is turned into softer lactic acid.

Meritage   An official term used in the United States to designate wines made from a blend of traditional Bordeaux varieties.

méthode champenoise   The technique used to make Champagne in Champagne, France. Also called *méthode traditionelle*.

méthode traditionelle   Made in the same way as Champagne.

mineral   Tasting of, or recalling, minerals.

moelleux   Marrow in French, used to indicate a medium-sweet wine.

mousseux   Bubbly wine, in French.

MS   Master Sommelier, a person who has passed a difficult exam on wine and wine service.

MW   Master of Wine, a person who has passed an exam that tests knowledge of wine and the business of wine.

must   The mashed-up grapes before and during fermentation.

New World   Typically refers to North and South America, Australia, New Zealand, and South Africa, wine regions that have a young wine industry compared to Old World regions like France that have been making wine on a large scale for centuries.

noble rot   *See* botrytis.

nose   In winespeak, used as both a verb meaning to sniff and a noun meaning scent.

oak   Typically the preferred wood for wine barrels.

oaky   To have many flavors of oak, like vanilla, spice, and wood.

oenologist   One who studies wine, also spelled enologist.

oenology   The study of wine, also spelled enology.

off-dry   A little bit sweet.

Old World   Refers to countries such as France, Italy, Spain, and others that have had a major wine industry for centuries.

organically-grown wines   Made with fruit that meets the farming requirements set forth by the government for organic farming but employs practices in winemaking (such as added sulfites) that do not qualify it for the overall organic label.

oxidized   Affected by exposure to oxygen, typically noted in a brownish tinge to the wine and scents of nuts and old, dried fruit. A little oxidation can add complexity and pleasant flavors; too much, however, leads to an oxidized wine or one that has lost its freshness.

passito   Italian term to indicate wine made from dried grapes.

peppery   Can mean many things, from a pleasant, fresh-crushed black pepper–like spice to the green note of a jalapeño. Often, however, it's a polite way of saying the wine's alcohol burns like too much white pepper does in a dish.

pétillant   Lightly sparkling, in French.

phenolics   Compounds responsible for color and texture, such as tannin.

phylloxera   A vine aphid that sucks the life out of grapevines through their roots.

Prädikat   Means distinction, a designation of ripeness of grapes at harvest in German wines. Includes, in ascending order of ripeness, Kabinett, Spätlese, Auslese, Beerenauslese, and Trockenbeerenauslese.

punt   The indentation in the bottom of a wine bottle.

quinta   Portuguese for farm or estate.

rack   To transfer wine from one container to another to separate the clear liquid from any sediment.

rancio   Indicates a wine purposely exposed to the elements, giving it the nutty flavors of oxidation.

R.D.   Recently disgorged, used in sparkling wines to indicate a wine left on the lees for an extended time to pick up extra flavor and complexity. Also called, confusingly, L.D., or late disgorged.

recioto   A style of wine typical to Italy's Veneto region, whereby grapes are dried before pressing.

reciprocal state   One that allows the shipment of wine over state borders.

reserva   Spanish for reserve, and used to indicate a wine with more aging than non-reserva wines.

reserve   Term typically used to indicate a wine of higher quality than nonreserve wines, although the term has no legal meaning in the United States.

residual sugar (r.s.)   Any sugar left in a wine after fermentation.

Retsina   A wine to which pine resin has been added, giving it a distinctly piney flavor. Traditional to the Mediterranean; still found in Greece.

riddling   To turn a Champagne bottle incrementally so that the residue will fall into the neck of the bottle, where it can be more easily removed. Riddling used to be done by a human riddler, though now it's more common to use gyropalletes, mechanized crates that hold the bottles.

Ried   Vineyard in Austria.

ripasso   To repass, used to describe wines made by passing the wine a second time over the skins left over from pressing.

ripe When the color, scent, texture, sugar, acidity, and all other aspects of a grape (or other fruit) have reached their peak.

riserva Italian for reserve, riserva indicates a wine that has undergone more aging before release than a nonriserva wine.

rootstock The roots of a plant.

rosado Spanish for pink, as in pink wine.

rosé French for pink, and frequently used on its own worldwide to indicate pink wine.

saignée "To bleed" in French, a term used to describe rosé wines made from grape juice that has barely had time to take on the color of the grape skins.

screw cap A cap that screws off, which is becoming increasingly popular with wines as a replacement for cork.

sec Dry in French, though sec Champagne is a little sweet.

second-label wines Wines a winery makes under a different label than its flagship wines, typically of lesser yet good quality.

Sekt German sparkling wine.

Sélection de Grains Nobles French term used in Alsace to describe wines made from botrytised grapes.

sommelier A person responsible for wine service in a restaurant.

Spätburgunder Pinot Noir in German.

spumante Sparkling wine, in Italian, more bubbly than frizzante wines.

Steen South African name for Chenin Blanc.

still wine Not sparkling.

structured Having many tannins and acidity that give the wine a very firm feel.

sulfides Naturally-occurring sulfur compounds with hydrogen elements that can give wine a sulfurous smell, like bad eggs. Harmless if unpleasant and usually remedied by aeration.

sulfites The salts left over from sulfur dioxide (SO_2), a gas frequently used in winemaking to inhibit spoilage.

Super Tuscan   A term invented to describe Tuscan wines that, because they were made with untraditional grapes, had to take the lowly *vino da tavola* designation and yet fetched high praise and high prices in the marketplace.

sur lie   "On the lees," a phrase that indicates the wine stayed in contact with the lees for an extended period of time before bottling.

sustainably grown   Not legally defined, but generally means to farm with concern for and respect for the soil and the organisms that live in and around it.

table wine   Used in the United States to indicate dry wines and elsewhere to indicate dry wines of very basic quality.

tannins   Structural components in wine that affect color, help the wine to last long, and cause a drying sensation in the mouth, like oversteeped black tea.

tartrates   A by-product of tartaric acid that often leaves small, harmless crystals on the end of the cork or the bottom of the bottle.

tastevin   A small, shallow cup for viewing and tasting wine, traditionally worn around the neck of old-school sommeliers.

tears   A poetic reference to the drips of wine left on the side of a wine glass after it has been swirled.

tenuta   Winery in Italian.

terra rossa   The iron-rich red soils of Coonawarra, South Australia.

terroir   The sum total of a number of natural elements that lend a unique quality to the wines of a particular site.

texture   How a wine feels in the mouth.

tight   Not showing much flavor but having the feel of lots of tannins and acidity.

tinto   Red, in Spanish and Portuguese.

toasty   Tasting of toast or of toasted wood, usually a result of time spent in toasted oak barrels.

trocken   Dry, in German.

Trockenbeerenauslese   A wine that's reached the highest level of ripeness in the German designation scheme and made from grapes infected with botrytis.

ullage   The space between the wine and the cork in the bottle; a large ullage usually means some leakage or evaporation.

unfiltered A wine not run through any filters. Some people believe filtering removes flavor as well as particulate matter.

unfined A wine not treated with a fining agent, such as egg whites, charcoal, or bentonite, to remove tiny particles from the wine.

uva Grape, in Italian.

VA *See* volatile acidity.

varietal wine A wine made from one variety (or at least the legal minimum of one variety) and labeled by the name of the grape.

variety The kind of grape; Merlot is a grape variety.

VDN *See* Vin Doux Naturel.

Vendange Tardive Late harvest in French.

Vieilles vignes Old vines in French. Not a legally defined term but usually used to indicate wine made from vines 40, 50, or even 100 years old.

Vin Doux Naturel A catchall term used in France to indicate wines to which alcohol has been added to stop fermentation before all the sugars have been fermented, resulting in a sweet wine.

viniculture The study of winemaking.

vinify To make into wine.

vintage The year a wine was harvested.

vintner One who makes wine.

viticulture The study of vine growing.

Vitis vinifera The species of grape vine responsible for most of the great wines of the world.

volatile A way to say a wine smells a little vinegary.

volatile acidity (VA) All the acids in a wine that are volatile, like acetic acid.

Weingut Winery in German.

Wine Resources

Here are a variety of sources to aid your wine exploration.

Recommended Reading

General References

Allen, Max. *Red and White: Wine Made Simple.* San Francisco: Wine Appreciation Guild, 2001.

Broadbent, Michael. *Michael Broadbent's Wine Vintages.* New York: Mitchell Beazley, 2003.

Clarke, Oz. *Oz Clarke's New Wine Atlas.* New York: Harcourt, Inc., 2002.

Colman, Tyler. *Wine Politics.* University of California Press: Berkeley, 2008.

Goode, Jaime. *The Science of Wine from Grape to Glass.* Berkeley, Calif.: University of California Press, 2006.

Johnson, Hugh, and Jancis Robinson. *The World Atlas of Wine, Sixth Edition.* London: Mitchell Beazley, 2007.

Joly, Nicolas. *What Is Biodynamic Wine? London:* Clairview Books, 2007.

Kolpan, Steven, Brian H. Smith, and Michael A. Weiss. *Exploring Wine, Second Edition*. New York: Wiley, 2001.

Kramer, Matt. *Making Sense of Wine, Second Edition*. Philadelphia, Pa.: Running Press Books, 2003.

Maresca, Tom. *Mastering Wine*. New York: Grove Press, 1992.

Matthews, Patrick. *Real Wine: The Rediscovery of Natural Winemaking*. London: Mitchell Beazley, 2000.

McGovern, Patrick E. *Ancient Wine: The Search for the Origins of Viticulture*. Princeton, N.J.: Princeton University Press, 2003.

Peynaud, Emile. *Knowing and Making Wine*. New York: John Wiley & Sons, 1984.

Robinson, Jancis, Ed. *Oxford Companion to Wine, Third Ed*. Oxford, New York: Oxford University Press, 2006.

———. *How to Taste: A Guide to Enjoying Wine*. New York: Simon & Schuster, 2000.

Stevenson, Tom. *The New Sotheby's Wine Encyclopedia, Fourth Edition*. New York: DK Publishing, 2005.

———. *Wine Report 2008*. New York: DK Publishing, 2007.

Trubek, Amy. *The Taste of Place: A Cultural Journey into Terroir*. Berkeley, Calif.: University of California Press, 2008.

Waldin, Monty. *Biodynamic Wines*. London: Mitchell Beazley, 2004.

Wilson, James E. *Terroir: The Role of Geology, Climate, and Culture in the Making of French Wines*. Berkeley, Calif.: University of California Press, 1998.

Grapes

Clarke, Oz. *Oz Clarke's Encyclopedia of Grapes*. New York: Harcourt, 2001.

Robinson, Jancis. *Guide to Wine Grapes*. Oxford, England: Oxford University Press, 1996.

American Wines

Gregutt, Paul. *Washington Wines & Wineries: The Essential Guide*. Berkeley, Calif.: University of California Press, 2007.

Halliday, James. *Wine Atlas of California*. New York: Viking, 1993.

Lukacs, Paul. *American Vintage: The Rise of American Wine*. Boston, New York: Houghton Mifflin, 2000.

Perdue, Andy. *The Northwest Wine Guide: A Buyer's Handbook*. Seattle, Wash.: Sasquach Books, 2003.

Sullivan, Charles L. *Zinfandel: The History of a Grape and Its Wine*. Berkeley, Calif.: University of California Press, 2003.

———. *A Companion to California Wine*. Berkeley, Calif.: University of California Press, 1998.

Australian & New Zealand Wines

Allen, Max. *Crush: The New Australian Wine Book*. London: Mitchell Beazley, 2000.

Cooper, Michael, and John McDermott. *Wine Atlas of New Zealand*. Calif: Wine Appreciation Guild, 2002.

Halliday, James. *Wine Atlas of Australia*. Berkeley, Calif.: University of California Press, 2006.

———. *Wine Atlas of Australia & New Zealand*. New York: Harper Collins, 1998.

French Wines

Coates, Clive, M.W. *Côte d'Or: A Celebration of the Great Wines of Burgundy*. Berkeley, Calif.: University of California Press, 1997.

———. *An Encyclopedia of the Wines & Domaines of France*. Berkeley, Calif.: University of California Press, 2000.

Duijker, Hubrecht, and Michael Broadbent. *The Bordeaux Atlas and Encyclopaedia of Châteaux*. New York: St. Martin's Press, 1997.

Kramer, Matt. *Making Sense of Burgundy*. New York: William Morrow and Company, 1990.

Jefford, Andrew. *The New France: A Complete Guide to Contemporary French Wine*. London: Mitchell Beazley, 2002.

Livingstone-Learmonth, Jonathan. *The Wines of the Northern Rhône*. Berkeley, Calif.: University of California Press, 2005.

Parker, Robert M., Jr. *Wines of the Rhône Valley*. New York: Simon & Schuster, 1997.

Stevenson, Tom. *Tom Stevenson's Champagne & Sparkling Wine Guide, Fourth Edition*. San Francisco: Wine Appreciation Guild, 2002.

Strang, Paul. *Languedoc-Roussillon: The Wines & Winemakers*. London: Mitchell Beazley, 2002.

Greek Wines

Lazarakis, Konstantinos. *The Wines of Greece*. London: Mitchell Beazley, 2005.

Italian Wines

Anderson, Burton. *Wines of Italy*. London: Mitchell Beazley, 2004.

Bastianich, Joseph, and David Lynch. *Vino Italiano: The Regional Wines of Italy*. New York: Clarkson Potter, 2002.

Cernilli, Daniele, and Marco Sabellico. *The New Italy*. London: Mitchell Beazley, 2000.

Kramer, Matt. *Making Sense of Italian Wine*. Philadelphia, PA: Running Press, 2006.

Spanish Wines

Jeffs, Julian. *The Wines of Spain*. London: Mitchell Beazley, 2006.

Peñin, Jose. *Peñin Guide to Spanish Wine 2008*. Spain: Grupo Peñin, 2008.

Radford, John. *The New Spain*. London: Mitchell Beazley, 2004.

Pairing Wine & Food

Dornenburg, Andrew, Karen Page, and Michael Sofronski. *What to Drink with What You Eat*. New York: Bullfinch, 2006.

Goldstein, Evan. *Perfect Pairings: A Master Sommelier's Practical Advice for Partnering Wine with Food*. Berkeley, Calif.: University of California Press, 2006.

Rosengarten, David, and Joshua Wesson. *Red Wine with Fish: The New Art of Matching Wine with Food*. New York: Simon & Schuster, 1989.

Werlin, Laura, and Andy Ryan. *The All-American Wine and Cheese Book*. New York: Harry N. Abrams, 2003.

Literature

Asher, Gerald. *The Pleasures of Wine*. San Francisco: Chronicle Books, 2002.

———. *Vineyard Tales*. San Francisco: Chronicle Books, 1996.

Campbell, Christy. *The Botanist and the Vintner: How Wine Was Saved for the World*. Chapel Hill, N.C: Algonquin Books of Chapel Hill, 2004.

Feiring, Alice. *The Battle for Wine and Love or How I Saved the World from Parkerization*. Harcourt: Hew York, 2008

Lynch, Kermit. *Adventures on the Wine Route: A Wine Buyer's Tour of France*. North Point Press: New York, 1990.

Prial, Frank J. *Decantations: Reflections on Wine*. New York: St. Martin's Press, 2001.

Robinson, Jancis. *Tasting Pleasure: Confessions of a Wine Lover.* New York: Penguin, 1997.

Steadman, Ralph. *The Grapes of Ralph.* New York: Harcourt Brace & Co, 1992.

Taber, George. *To Cork or Not to Cork.* New York: Scribner, 2007.

Teague, Lettie. *Educating Peter.* New York: Scribner, 2007

Wine Websites

The Web changes so quickly that these may be out of date before this book even hits the presses, but as of moments before press time, these and the websites listed throughout this book were some of the most useful, interesting, and consistent wine websites on line. (For websites focusing on a specific grape variety/aspect of wine, please see individual chapters.)

ablegrape.com   A Google-like wine-specific search engine.

bullworks.net/virtual.htm   The Virtual Corkscrew Museum.

epicurious.com/tools/winedictionary   Free dictionary with more than 3,500 terms.

jancisrobinson.com   Friendly, well-written wine info, from news to recommendations and general wine information from one of the world's most respected wine writers. Subscribe for full access to the online *Oxford Companion to Wine* and the very active, interesting Member's Forum.

localwineevents.com   Free directory of wine events in cities across the world.

newenglandvine.com   Guide to New England's wines and wineries.

newyorkwines.org/index.asp   New York Wine & Grape Foundation.

oregonwine.org   Oregon wine info.

sonomagrapevine.org   Sonoma wine info.

tv.winelibrary.com   Genuinely amusing and informative wine videos from the inimitable Gary Vaynerchuk.

washingtonwine.org   Washington State Wine Commission's site.

wineanorak.com   Extensive array of articles and resources compiled by Jamie Goode.

wineinstitute.org   Stats and info on the California wine industry.

wineloverspage.com   Tasting notes, articles, and resources from a range of sources.

wine-pages.com   Articles from respected, established wine writers around the world compiled by Tom Cannavan.

wineorigins.com   Home of the Center for Wine Origins, describing why appellations matter.

Great Wine Blogs

Again, by the time you read this, these may have moved or changed, but as of press time, these were some of the most consistently good and thought-provoking wine blogs on the Web.

alicefeiring.com

basicjuice.blogs.com

chateaupetrogasm.com

datamantic.com/joedressner

drvino.com

fermentation.typepad.com

foodandwine.com/blogs/tasting-room

gourmet.com/winespiritsbeer

grapecrafter.com/grapecrafter

redwinehaiku.blogspot.com

spume.wordpress.com

thepour.blogs.nytimes.com

vinography.com

Wine Tasting Sheet

Tasting of: Date:			
Wine name, vintage, price:			
Appearance Free of debris? Cloudy/clear/bright? Color?			
Now swirl and sniff			
Aroma Light/medium/strong? Unpleasant/okay/great? Fruit? What sorts? Herbs? Spices? What else?			
Now swirl, sniff, and sip			
Flavor Yuck or yum? Fruit? What sorts? Herbs? Spices? What else? How long does the flavor last?			
Feel Light/medium/heavy? Acidic or flabby? Drying or juicy?			
Final impression I'd buy it again. Might go well with …			

Index